My Mother, the Bearded Lady

With special thanks to Joanna Barlow for her support

My Mother, the Bearded Lady

The Selected Letters of Miles Kington

Miles Kington
Edited by Caroline Kington

unbound

This edition first published in 2019

Unbound
6th Floor Mutual House, 70 Conduit Street, London W1S 2GF

www.unbound.com

Text Design by Ellipsis, Glasgow

A CIP record for this book is available from the British Library

ISBN 978-1-78352-650-5 (trade hardback)
ISBN 978-1-78352-652-9 (ebook)

Printed in Great Britain by CPI Group (UK) Ltd

1 3 5 7 9 8 6 4 2

This collection is dedicated to Megan Jones who,
after Miles died, freely gave hours and hours
of her time to help sort and file thousands of his letters,

and

To Miles's dear friend, Terry Jones.

Contents

INTRODUCTION

Miles on Miles

I was born in Northern Ireland in 1941, grew up in North Wales and was sent to school up in Scotland, which was very odd because I didn't have any Welsh, Irish or Scottish blood in me, being pretty much English.

From an early age, perhaps confused by my shifting geography, I knew I wanted to be a humorous writer and a jazz musician, and even at school I had already started my own jazz band and set up a humorous magazine in opposition to the official school magazine. When I went to Oxford University (1960–63, studying French and German) I spent most of the time playing the double bass in jazz groups and writing undergraduate humour. Thus when I left university I was almost entirely unfitted for life, and consequently went to London to try my luck as a freelance writer, where I nearly starved to death.

To begin with I wrote with Terry Jones, but it turned out he was just waiting for his friend Michael Palin to leave Oxford, so he could write with him. If I had known they were going to go on to *Monty Python's Flying Circus*, I might have tried to go with them, but as it was I got an invitation to join the staff of *Punch*, which I jumped at and where I stayed until 1980, writing, among other things the popular "Let's Parler Franglais!" column. During that time I also worked as the jazz critic of *The Times*, which kept me up very late at Ronnie Scott's once a week, and as bass player for Instant Sunshine. This was – is – a singing humorous cabaret group in which the other three were all full-time doctors, thus allowing me as the only non-doctor to pick up lots of priceless information about doctors though not so much about medicine.

I left *Punch* in 1980 to make a programme in the BBC's *Great Railway Journeys* series – *Three Miles High*, about the railway which goes up the Andes in Peru – and after I came back I was asked to do a daily humorous column in *The Times*. This I did until 1987, when I switched to *The Independent*, where I have been doing a daily column ever since, God help us. I have done other TV (*Call My Bluff*, *Great Journeys*, *Steam Days*, etc.) and lots of radio. I have a dozen books to my name, some collections of pieces, some original. In 1987 I moved from London to West Wiltshire, because the pace of life was so slow in London, whereas in Wiltshire you can get anywhere you want in half an hour, and then find a parking space.

When I came back from Burma [now Myanmar] in 1987, having made the BBC *Great Journeys* programme there, I was asked by a BBC producer if I wanted to do a new programme called *Around the World in Eighty Days*, but it sounded a mad idea to me, so I turned it down and they asked Michael Palin instead. They also asked me to replace Barry Norman when he left his *Film* programme, and I said no to that as well, so you can see I know how to pick my opportunities. I can't say I regret either decision, though nobody ever believes me.

While I was with Instant Sunshine, I was not allowed to sing, but was encouraged to introduce the songs as nobody else could think of jokes. This was a good way of learning to speak in public, and gradually my introductions to different songs got longer and longer, until some of them could be used as entire after-dinner speeches. Maybe that is why, when I resigned from the group after leaving London, they did not fight to change my decision, and why I now find myself doing after-dinner speeches without a double bass . . .

Miles Kington

Miles Kington

I

Punch

Miles wasted no time in trying to establish a career as a writer once he left Oxford. He wrote copious scripts for radio and TV, and he wrote reviews for jazz concerts, which he sent, unsolicited, to The Times *until they gave in and employed him as their jazz reviewer (although he was not allowed a byline), when he was twenty-four. In addition he sent numerous articles to* Punch, *which was edited at the time by Bernard Hollowood. They liked his material, and in 1968 he was taken on as an assistant literary editor, later becoming the literary editor.*

PUNCH

10 Bouverie Street London, E.C.4

Telegrams: Charivari Fleet London—Telephone: Fleet Street 9161

from the Editor

23rd July, 1965.

Dear Kington,

        I want you to know that we are anxious to see more of your work.

Yours sincerely,

Bernard Hollowood

Bernard Hollowood

Miles Kington, Esq.,
76 Kensington Park Road,
London W. 11.

Punch

10 BOUVERIE STREET LONDON EC4

Grams: Charivari Fleet London—Phone: 01-353 9161

IGTA/MW

13th February, 1968.

M. Kington Esq.,
76 Kensington Park Road,
London W.11.

Dear Mr. Kington,

I am writing to confirm your appointment as assistant
literary editor of Punch for a six months' trial period
commencing on 26th February 1968. Your salary will be at
the rate of £1,250 per annum, payable monthly with one month's
notice of termination on either side.

The office hours are from 9.30 a.m. to 5.30 p.m., Monday
to Friday with one hour for lunch. When you start on Monday
26th February, will you please bring with you your National
Insurance card and Income Tax P45 if you have one?

Kindly formally acknowledge your acceptance of the terms
set out in this letter.

Yours faithfully,

I.G.T. Anderson
Director.

PUNCH PUBLICATIONS LTD. Directors: A V Caudery N A Whinfrey I G T Anderson A B Hollowood D J Quick
ONE OF THE BRADBURY AGNEW GROUP OF COMPANIES

Hollowood *was succeeded by William Davis, who, in turn, was succeeded by Alan Coren.* Punch *was a weekly publication, with
additional issues marking the seasons and other special occasions.
As an assistant literary editor, Miles would read the material sent in
from writers who aspired, as he had, to have their material appear
in what was still the foremost humorous magazine of the day. A
lot, inevitably, got rejected, but Miles nurtured and encouraged
talent. He wrote copiously. Along with the other employees of*

the magazine, he would be credited with one article in each issue, and anything else was not attributed. As literary editor, he was responsible for commissioning the literary content of the magazine, and he went to great efforts to get the best writers of the day to regularly review current fiction, i.e. Claire Tomalin, Fay Weldon, Margaret Forster, Melvyn Bragg. In addition, he encouraged contributions from the less conventional, such as Quentin Crisp, Philip Larkin and Vincent Price, as well as one-off reviews from unlikely contributors such as Prince Charles and Ronnie Biggs.

———————

To ANDRÉ PREVIN[1]
December 2, 1971

Dear André Previn,

We are asking six or eight different writers to say very briefly in the last issue of the year what they want from 1972, and I'd be delighted if you would be one of them. It's only 400 words we need, the deadline is Dec 15 and the tone, we hope, would be self-indulgent. In fact, I'd specifically like you to say what ideally you would like to see in next year's music, as I've asked one or two other specialists to look ahead frivolously in their own fields – the editor of the *Good Food Guide*, for instance. It wouldn't be a question so much of hoping that musical barriers will fall or equally idealistic things as of praying (for example) for better dressed buskers or for Herb Alpert, Mantovani and Sacha Distel to be lost at sea in the same shipwreck. Hmm, that's a bit tasteless. But I don't need to spell it all out, just hope you'd like to do it.

The editor has suggested offering each contributor a case of 1 doz bottles of champagne as a fee, I think it's an excellent idea. I wish I could ask myself to contribute.

yours sincerely

To PHILIP LARKIN
September 8, 1972

Dear Mr Larkin,

Unbeknownst to you I have been enjoying your poetry and your ideas on jazz for years (your introduction to your collected jazz reviews was one of the best things ever written on jazz) and although I too have been reviewing jazz for some time, in *The Times*, this letter is actually written in my capacity as *Punch* assistant editor; the request I'm about to make concerns, curiously enough, your interests in poetry and jazz.

You may have heard that a lavish volume has just been issued of Cole Porter's lyrics, called simply *Cole*. Would you like to review it for us? I imagine that the reviews it will receive generally will be showbiz golden era stuff, or unenlightening eulogy. It would be fascinating to hear what a practising poet, and a person experienced in the use of these lyrics, made of the book.

I'm not particularly anxious to tie the review to publication date, so you have at least a month from now. Length would be 800–1,000 words and the fee £40. I would be highly delighted if you said yes. If you demur, please let me know how I can persuade you.

    yours sincerely

———————

To MARION IRELAND[2]
April 19, 1973

Dear Marion, if I may be so bold,

Thank you for your velvet-lined letter. You are one up on me, remembering the words from *Call My Bluff*. They have all escaped me. Even when I remember the definitions, I have no idea if they are true or false. Still, I'm in good company – I asked Robert Robinson if he had a terribly enriched vocabulary and he said, Not by one iota.

As you see, the only way I can get my photo in *Punch* is by posing with eighteen others, but I am still working on the problem. Every time Bill Davis gets his picture taken, I creep up and start grinning over his shoulder, hoping to get included. That's why you don't see his photo in *Punch* either. They're all away at the retouchers, having me taken out.

And now a piece on
BYRON'S CLUB FOOT
Chapter One
"Egad," grumbled Lord Byron, heart-throb of a thousand heiresses and fifty-five publishers, as he stamped his foot and fell over.

"You don't grumble 'Egad', Byron," said Thomas Moore. "You ejaculate it. Look, like this."

"Egad!" ejaculated Thomas Moore.

Chapter Two
"Great stuff, Byron," said John Murray, as he waded through a random page of "Childe Harold". "Can't understand a word. The public will love it. But you need a gimmick."

"What sort of gimmick?" said his Lordship, getting up and falling over.

"Nothing personal," said Murray untruthfully, "but why do you keep falling over?"

"Club foot," said Byron tersely. "Had a bad accident out waltzin', don't you know."

"Great!" said Murray. "There's your gimmick!"

Chapter Three
Of an afternoon, Lord Byron liked nothing better than to go five rounds with the famous Regency figures, first man to lose his wig the loser. They still talk about his third round knock-out of Georgette Heyer in places where they talk about that sort of thing. But when John Murray organised the first press conference for Fleet Street to meet Lord Byron's club foot, he had to give up boxing, and take up Greek politics instead.

Chapter Four
"Got the *Sun* on the phone," said Thomas Moore. "They want you to write a feature on having a happy love life despite a club foot."

"Tell them to get lost," said Byron, falling over.

"For £5,000."

"Give me the phone," said Byron from the floor.

Chapter Five

CENSORED

Chapter Six

"I see old Byron's snuffed it in Greece," said the Prince of Wales to Mrs Prince of Wales.

"Byron?" she said. "The man who wrote 'I Waltzed My Way To Stardom Despite A Club Foot And Rotten Dance Bands'?"

"No," he said. "Lord Byron the poet."

"Never knew he wrote poetry," she said.

THE END
(Next week: TALLEYRAND'S CLUB FOOT)?

yours

To VINCENT PRICE

October 8, 1973

Dear Mr Price,

I wrote to you in Malibu saying how pleased I was that you'd like to try the unusual cookery book review. I'm still pleased, but not so sure that I got your address out there right. So I'm writing to your London address as well to confirm that you will give me a ring when you get here, when we can fix up all the details and, hopefully, get you safely invited to our Wednesday Table Lunch.

I look forward to hearing from you. Sorry about the wasteful stretch of white below – the management has gone over to some strange metric size of paper, which must cost a few forests to produce. Perhaps you are a doodler. I donate this space to you.

yours sincerely

To HUGH McILVANNEY[3]
March 1, 1976

Dear Hugh McIlvanney,

March 1st, St David's Day, seems as good a day as any to write to you about your forthcoming Celtic contribution to *Punch*. (Better when I tell you that I grew up in Welsh Wrexham, whom by the way I confidently tip to beat Anderlecht on Wednesday and remember you read it here first.) Chris Oram told me that you would like to write about Scottish drinking habits and that suits me fine. One slight error; I said the deadline was Mar 20, which is actually a Saturday. I meant Friday Mar 19, or any day during that week, but it has to be that week.

I'm sure you'll have plenty of ideas but there are two things from a stint at the Edinburgh Festival yesteryear which I observed and may be of interest. One, the surprising emphasis in Scotland on canned rather than bottled beer, caused I suppose by the shorter hours and therefore the bigger take-away trade. Even the ads seem geared to this canned standby market; one I heard on commercial radio went roughly "Next time you find the pubs are shut . . . and you haven't got a drop handy . . . you'll wish you'd remembered to buy half a dozen cans of Tennent's" or something similarly unEnglish. Unless it's a subliminal attempt by the authorities to phase out bottles to prevent civil disturbances; you can't smash the top off a can and ram it in a friend's face.

Other thing; Edinburgh this year for the first time experimented with extended drinking hours during the Festival. Most pubs till eleven, but many till 11.30 and 12, even after. And the police reported at the end that there had been a definite drop in the level of drunken arrests. They singled out two factors; people didn't rush to get it down them by ten o'clock, and they didn't all come out of the pubs at the same time and form aggressive groups on opposite street corners prior to a punch-up, but went home at staggered, so to speak, intervals.

The earlier you can do the piece, the better the chance of getting it illustrated; but all yours from now on. Very nice to have you in the paper.

yours sincerely

To ROBERT LASSON[4]
May 26, 1976

Dear Mr Lasson,

As Mrs Grogono is in floods of tears after reading your unhappy letter, it has been left to me to answer you. There is a quite simple explanation for the two misprints. Carelessness. But as you will be hardly satisfied with a simple explanation, I should add that the word "sheaves'" has a particularly obscene secondary meaning in London and we felt obliged to change the word to a similar one which the authors might not spot. Unsuccessfully, I'm sorry to say. Emptations comes from the Latin word meaning "to buy" (of "caveat emptor") and an emptation is a special offer, a cheap bargain, offered to unwary purchasers in order to clear shoddy goods. Hence in your context "experience those very emptations which, successfully resisted, lead directly to the Elysian Fields . . ." It had been mistyped in your original as temptation.

I hope we see more of your stuff. Regards to Mr Eynon.

yours sincerely

———————

To RONALD BIGGS
June 4, 1976

Dear Mr Biggs,

Your letter explains a lot. It explains, for instance, why earlier this week four large gentlemen asked me outside and filled me full of small lead bullets then tossed me into the deep end of the Serpentine. I had a lot of explaining to do when I turned up late for work the next day with unsightly bandages all over me. To prevent that kind of thing happening again, kindly tell your friends that it was not I who got in touch with the Yard but Alan Coren. I'll spell that again, ALAN COREN. Left to myself I would have printed your verses and paid you a quarter of a million.

We have been printing filthy language for many years. It isn't generally known that the originals of the famous cartoons in *Punch* are much dirtier than the usually quoted versions e.g. "I keep think-ing it's fucking Thursday" and (The Curate's Egg) "Oh no, my Lord – parts of it are fucking marvellous".

Well, fifty quid may be peanuts but at least we paid you, which I gather is more than some papers do, and all at the expense of get-ting readers' letters objecting to using a man who knocks poor defenceless train drivers over the head. Since Waterloo commuters regularly attack their drivers with razor-sharp umbrellas and lead-filled brief cases, I find this disingenuous to say the least, whatever that means.

Seriously, folks, I can't imagine that the fuzz will come flying out Brazil just because we used your gems. When verse-writing is against the law, I'll come and join you.

I enclose half a million in used sterling to keep you quiet. That should work out at three hot meals, the way the pound is going.

Please tell your friends not to waste their bullets on me. I am very ticklish. Any more verse or articles always welcome. We pay for prose better than for verse. That's because it goes right to the margin and doesn't waste space like poetry.

all the best

———————

To KINGSLEY AMIS
May 12, 1977

Dear Kingsley Amis,
Alan Coren and I still feel that if you would like to do the Music 'n' Socialism piece, it wouldn't really hurt if you leant more on Mozart than on rock and roll. One way in would be to greet the Music For Socialism Festival as the great culmination of a constant people's struggle in music dating back for many years, so that you could then flashback and show how Mozart, Wagner, Jelly Roll Morton etc had been freedom-loving, egalitarian, workers' struggles champions as is evinced in every note of their elitist music . . .

However, I feel that here I may be batting on a sticky wicket, on the fifth day, with 400 runs to get.

A small alternative. For our summer number the editor proposed collecting in the books pages some thoughts from eminent people on the books they had never read but would willingly take away this summer to enjoy at last. As a feature on books which none of the writers had read seemed a bit tiresome to me, I would rather have the same approach but to books which you have read and enjoyed but remain unaccountably unknown and unread. Would you care to do 400–500 words on a small handful of books that you swear by and no-one else seems to know about?

For that we'd pay £60. For the socialism piece, rather more; I don't control the purse strings but it's minimum £100.

yours sincerely

PS It would be a big boon if you could let me know the answer(s) on Friday. I think I've got your postal district right this time.

————————

To DIANE PETRE[5]
October 5, 1977

Dear Miss Petre,

I fear the editor is unlikely to answer your letter, partly because he is in America, partly because he does not often answer letters of that kind, so being intrigued by it (I know that is not the correct use of intrigued but I'm damned if I can think of a better word) I thought I would write to recommend that you investigate one very fruitful source of lies, excuses and deceits: journalists who have failed to meet deadlines. I blush when I think of the number of times when I have said of an unstarted piece that it is being rewritten or isn't working or is almost finished or needs retouching . . . Claud Cockburn once told me of a newspaperman "who had got procrastination to such a fine art that he would ring his paper, tell them to send a boy round to pick up the piece, and then start it."

I once commissioned Hugh McIlvanney to do a piece for a Scots issue of *Punch*, on the subject of Scottish drinking habits. Deadlines came and went, he promised it every day and produced nothing, until on press day itself I phoned the *Observer* in desperation, only to be told that he had just gone on the grand tour.

Meaning what? I asked.

He's drinking his way up Fleet Street, they said.

I followed his progress from El Vino via pubs (everyone saying, oh yes, he was in here a while back) until at about 4 p.m. I tracked him down in the City Golf Club. He blithely waved a full glass of Scotch at me and cried: Still doing research for the article, Miles!

We used the piece but not till a month had passed after the Scottish issue.

A thought strikes me. Cartoons. Mike Heath recently did a very good if sad cartoon set in a sex shop, where on the shelf there is a large talking sex doll. And she is saying "Not tonight, I have a head-ache, not tonight, I have a . . ."

RGG Price (who is a fund of such information) has a lovely story about a previous editor of *Punch* who had the task of firing a staff man but couldn't bring himself to do it. So as a reward he took him on a world cruise, with the staff man not quite knowing why he was getting this special treatment. And as they were coming from the docks back home after the cruise the editor summed up his courage, said "Oh, by the way" and broke the news to him. Richard Price, care of this office, would tell you the names if you were interested.

Rereading the letter I have the feeling that everything I have said is either irrelevant or boring.

Sadly, as I write this letter, Vincent Mulchrone's funeral is taking place. There was a man who could have told you stories. One he told me was a gem. It was about a gardening correspondent on a now defunct paper who was called in by the editor one day and told to gear his column from now on to the idea of My Garden Week by Week describing what was actually happening in one man's patch.

What the editor didn't know was that the man had that very week split up from his wife, leaving her with the house and garden in Ashford and moving to a gardenless flat in London. So (he swore this was true) the gardening writer used to take a train down to Ashford once a week, late, and peer over the garden wall with a flashlight to see what was going on. The editor liked the column and started buying equipment for him – mowers, sacks of this, bags of that. The poor man had nowhere to stock them and after he departed several years later they gradually found the most amazing cache of garden tools and material hidden in the most unlikely places in the newspaper offices.

I suppose you have got the nicest excuse of all, Oscar Wilde's refusal of dinner invitations on the ground that he unfortunately had a subsequent engagement. But I would like to suggest a child's excuse, used by the son of an American friend of mine, whenever he was found fighting his brother: "Jimmy started it all when he hit me back."

I could go on rambling all day, when I should be milking the cows or cooking the dinner or something. I know I shall start thinking about this damned topic as soon as I have signed the letter so I will put an end to it now.

yours sincerely

PS Another idea, dammit. What people say, backstage, first night, to actors who've just starred in terrible plays. How to sound nice without lying. Wasn't it Noël Coward who recommended: "Darling – you should have been in the audience!"? Or "Only you could have played the part that way." Or even "Darling! . . ." (stops, obviously lost for words and embraces the star).

———————

To QUENTIN CRISP
February 24, 1978

Dear Mr Crisp,

This is to confirm that we would like you to write a piece for our Spring (March 22) issue and that we will need about 1,000 words by March 14 at the latest.

Well, that's got the business out of the way; now down to a few notions which might help you on your way.

I warm to your idea that you tend not to notice the passing of the seasons; I only hesitate because you may feel that by writing about indifference to spring, summer, autumn etc you are repeating your views on how you should bend the outside world to your view rather than the other way round. And I do know that people who have no seasons tend to miss them. I have an aunt who lived in the Bahamas for some years and told me she was driven to distraction by the failure of any one day to vary from the one before; blue skies, warmth, mild breeze – she ended up praying for damp, showers and overcast skies. I have a friend who maintains that the British custom of talking about the weather is, far from being commonplace, an intensely practical preoccupation with a radical change in the environment. Just as there are more definite changes in the English landscape per mile than anywhere else so there are with the weather; who would have dreamt, for instance, three frozen days ago, that today it would be mild and balmy, necessitating a whole other wardrobe? I sometimes think that the British dress correctly for the previous day, never being quite able to keep up with the changes. I also fancy that when we read that 5,000,000 years ago Britain was covered in an icepack, we are not told that the next day it dawned warm and melting, and that the sudden thaw brought panic to the resident mammoths. I hope this has been of some help.

yours

PS My aunt in the Bahamas also told me that, sated with mangoes, limes etc, she missed apples dreadfully.

––––––––––

To DENNIS POTTER
December 7, 1978

Dear Mr Potter,
As there are probably elements of exaggeration in the rumour

that *Times* and *Sunday Times* writers are being deluged with more offers of work than they can possibly take on, Alan Coren and I would like to ask you if you are free, and willing, to do some book reviewing for us. We have inherited an odd book space; we only devote one page each week to books, but that is filled by a longish piece by one writer – at the moment, we have a panel of four (Paul Johnson, Claire Tomalin, Richard Boston and Melvyn Bragg) reviewers who each do one review a month, in rotation.

Well, Melvyn has just revealed that he is descending into the maelstrom of writing a novel and would like to opt out of reviewing. He has done nobly, but it couldn't have come at a better time for the purpose of asking you to take over. He reviewed nothing but fiction; I'd be happy if you wanted to go on doing that, but if not I think Claire would willingly take it on, leaving you free to review books of any category. The reviews are in and around 1,000 words long and we pay £85.

I hasten to add that the humorous policy of the magazine does not overflow into the book page; there we only ask people to be themselves. Or rather, we ask people only to be themselves. Obviously I'd like to know your answer before Christmas in case it's No. I hope it's Yes.

yours sincerely

———————

To JONATHAN MILLER
February 1, 1979

Dear Jonathan Miller,

Good God, is it February already? Sometimes I try to convince myself that time can be slowed down by carrying on with January 32, January 33, etc, but it's never worked yet.

It was nice to meet you again not so long ago in the unlikely circumstances of a visit to *Superman*. (Apropos – I had to go to my daughter's school, Godolphin, yesterday, and spotted a sixth form notice on the board: "If you think Superman's hunky, wait till you see Jonathan Miller!" followed by details of membership of the fan

club, which I won't bore you with. I wanted to add, in an anonymous hand "Jonathan Miller couldn't wait to see *Superman*".) I
wonder if you remember at the time we nattered about a book that
my colleague in Instant Sunshine, David Barlow, has coming from
the OUP – *Sexually Transmitted Diseases – the Facts*? I happened to
mention our conversation to Alan Coren a few days later and he
said, in those enthusiastic tones which editors adopt when lamp
bulbs marked IDEA flash above their heads, "Why don't you ask
Jonathan to review it for us when the time comes?" And here I am
to ask you. It will be out in the spring – not sure of the exact date
yet. It's an interesting subject; Barlow has lectured me keenly on the
subject from time to time and plainly reserves for the subject all
the excitement that other people tend to lavish on rock music or
football.

Let me know at your leisure how you feel. I just hope you aren't
directing five different operas that month.

yours sincerely

PS Our books coverage, I hasten to add, is quite normal, not satirical or even laughable.

———————

To MARGARET FORSTER
October 25, 1979

Dear Margaret Forster,

I haven't written to you before now, as Claire Tomalin's fate, not
to mention that of the *Sunday Times*, was so much in the balance,
but now that it seems certain, that is say quite probable, that
Thomson papers will be back on the street, I can write to you and
say that we'd be delighted to have you as our regular fiction
reviewer if you would like to be ditto.

Claire, and Melvyn B before her, did a piece a month, about
1,000 words, and covered only one or two novels in that space. I
know and you know that isn't really enough, but what novel coverage is? Auberon Waugh writes weekly for the *Evening Standard*

and yet only does four a month. Some novelists seem to write four a month. On the other hand it does mean that you can pick and choose, omitting famous authors who have nothing new to say and whom you would otherwise have to cover through sheer duty, and sticking to people who are either significant or damned good writers or, with luck, both. If we could aim at two books in one monthly piece, I'd be happy.

Claire, at the moment, is being sent vast amounts of novels from publishers all over Bloomsbury as well as other parts of the civilised world, and I shall start diverting this to you, till you cry halt.

The fee for the piece will be £85, which is what the other reviewers are getting; Alan tells me that it will go up to £95 in January. We'd like the first piece middish November, though this is open to negotiation. Openish, anyway.

It would be smashing if you wanted to fill this prestigious though not onerous job. The hours are short and we have a sherry party for reviewers once a year; I'm afraid you'll have to buy your own uniform.

Could you give me a ring when you get back and we can talk? Perhaps even meet?

yours

———————

To CLAIRE TOMALIN
October 26, 1979

Dear Claire,

Alan and I were both very touched by the letters we got this morning. Me especially, as running things doesn't come naturally and it's nice to feel that someone thought I was doing all right. You won't believe it when I say that you were the best novel reviewer we've had for ages, but you were and I'm really sorry the *Sunday Times* is coming back: if you don't believe me, believe someone very different, the manic Mike Horowitz, whose letter – copy enclosed – I got yesterday.

I suppose, now that you are becoming a top Lit Ed in your own right, you ought to have the fruits of wisdom I've gathered in my years as a bottom Lit Ed. Difficult to sum up, really, but the basic ground rules are:-

1) Always quibble over one point in a review, no matter how good it is.
2) Occasionally review a book before publication date, otherwise Quentin Oates[6] won't notice you.
3) Allow for 50% of incoming books to vanish in the post room. Send them notes from time to time, asking why their reviews of the books they kept are late.
4) Never get depressed by the thought of all the books you can't review. Think, instead, of how many of them should never have been published in the first place.
5) Don't meditate on whether book reviews have any effect on book sales. (The answer, if you're interested, is yes, they do. They diminish them. Most book reviews are read as a substitute for reading the book.)
6) Always remember that the chief task of a Lit Ed is to arrange free lunches for him/herself and his/her reviewers. I have failed dreadfully in this respect. Up to you, now, I guess.
7) Never listen to other Lit Eds.

love

———————

To JOHN CLEESE
November 7, 1979

Dear John,

I dimly remember saying the other night at supper that whoever Andrew Boyle thought was the real Fourth Man, *Private Eye* are bound to print his name. Well, enclosed bears me out, much to my surprise. To add soya sauce to the whole thing, Auberon Waugh on another page disputes it and prints two other names. The fact that I've never heard of any of them detracts little from what is a very wonderful controversy.

As you don't like Sir James Ingrams, I know you won't be buying *Private Eye*, so I take the liberty of xeroxing it, and infiltrating it into your house.

Oh, by the way, there's something I've often meant to raise with you but never have. It will probably come as a surprise to you to learn that I was planted on *Punch* ten years ago by the Russians to subvert the nation and to recruit other subverters. If you'd be interested in joining the payroll, we'd love to have you. The Reds pay marvellously, the drink is lavish and the work is not arduous. In fact, it's exactly what we're all doing already – producing comedy for the public to enjoy when they should be making cars.

Ciao, comrade.

Sir Miles Kington
(Seventh Man)

To CRAIG BROWN
November 29, 1979

Dear Craig,

Alas and alas. I really quite liked the piece, but the rest of the panel didn't. Alan Coren thought it was a Basil Boothroyd piece written too early, Guy Pierce thought it seemed a bit self-centred and somebody else has tax problems of his own and hated it. But I think you could easily get it published in one of them glossier type mags with literary pretensions. *Cosmo*? *Tatler*? *Harpers*?

Offer to pay your tax in instalments. Send a nice letter saying, I enclose a cheque for the first instalment, Forget to enclose the cheque. When they write back to point this out, send it, but undated. When they send it back ... but I'm sure you get the point.

The trouble with the piece is that you're asking the reader to believe utterly in your situation or even your situation, and it comes over a little bleak and sad for that. Well written though. Cheer up old chap and write some rip-roaring cheerful yarn, like about the difficulty of getting hard drugs in Perthshire and experimenting with heather root instead. Scottish ginseng, forsooth.

I have a cousin who lives just by Blairgowrie. I'll give you his name if you promise not to embroil him in tax troubles.

yours

———————————

To FAY WELDON
January 11, 1980

Dear Fay Weldon,

You must have wondered why you haven't heard from me since our initial splurge of enthusiastic activity before Christmas. Well, the reasons/excuses are, in no particular order, i) Christmas ii) a small log jam of book reviews iii) seasonal sloth iv) the situation in Afghanistan v) a chance to let you welcome 1980 vi) a small dearth of novels in and around Hogmanay. However, I have now sent a letter to all the main publishers (copy enclosed) to let them know the good news – and it is good news that you would like to write for us, in fact I consider myself lucky – and I hope you will be drowned in novels in the near future. Many will be unreadable. More, even worse, will be sort-of-worth-reading-but-not-terribly, and to a large extent I think I ought to leave the initial sifting up to you.

Claire tended to have a policy of "Ah, Updike or Naipaul has brought out another one, we ought to look at it", which is fair enough, except that it meant ignoring a lot of new novels, by new writers. I can see that tackling unknown quantities and qualities is harder work than plumping for names one knows, and I think you would be quite justified in going mostly for the latter. The last thing I want you to do is get bogged down in a morass of duty reading, so can I leave it to your instinct plus knowledge of form as to what and how many we cover?

Anyway, I would like to get you started as soon as possible, so if we can have a piece by the end of January I would be delighted.

Have you had enough novels to make a piece? If not, let me know and a small lorry will be round in the morning.

This does mean, dammit, that we can't review *Puffball*. But rest assured there will be a large footnote when you appear in late Feb saying "Fay Weldon, author of new best-seller *Puffball*".

Liked your piece on *Grange Hill*.

yours sincerely

Working for Punch *was clearly more than just a means of earning a living. Many of his work colleagues became lifelong friends: Geoffrey Dickinson and Francis Smith (cartoonists), and David Taylor (who became* Punch's *penultimate editor in the 80s) and Basil Boothroyd among them. They worked and played together. The* Punch *lunch was a weekly occasion which the editorial staff were expected to attend along with some honoured guest or two. All were expected to join in the* Punch *outings, and the* Punch *cricket match was one of the highlights of the magazine's summer days.*

It was not all roses, but the Punch *years meant that Miles had the best training possible in meeting deadlines, in finding humour in the most unpromising of subjects and in earning a living doing what he loved above all else, writing, whether it was articles, scripts or books, and letters of which he left behind some 20,000.*

But after ten years at Punch, *Miles was getting restless. The media were increasingly interested in using him, and he was frequently approached by other publications to write for them. This placed a strain on his relationship with Alan Coren, exacerbated by a promise to make him* Punch's *deputy editor when Alan succeeded William Davis which was not honoured.*

To ALAN COREN
March 21, 1980

Dear Alan,

You probably won't be entirely surprised to get this letter, as it is partly written at your suggestion, as indeed are many of the things I've written over the years. It is, as you may have guessed, about your suggestion that I should think about going freelance. You obviously feel that freelance work is taking up more and more of my time, to the point where it now interferes with my office work, or at least enforces my absence at times when press day is in operation or staff is needed for page-reading etc. While very happy that I should go on writing for the magazine, you feel that my day-to-day duties might well devolve to someone younger and more omnipresent.

I guess, too, that this has been brought to the fore in your mind by the fact that I have been offered a (as yet unmaterialised) niche in the *Mirror* as a freelance columnist and been invited to go to Peru to make a TV film about the Andes railways. If I am to be away in Peru for six weeks, you said that you couldn't consider giving me a sabbatical for that time, which I regret, despite which I very much want to do the Peru job. Dear me, this letter is wooden; I hope it loosens up in a moment. I expect, too, that you feel that the *Mirror* job, being five times a week, might also start to interfere with office work and there again you could be right.

From my point of view, and after twelve years, I guess I can dwell on that for a little while, the suggested move has big pros, big cons. In favour of my going freelance is the fact that I do get offered more work than I can do, and I would on the whole prefer to be devoting x hours to writing rather than plodding through unsolicited manuscripts. I think a big move like this (being at *Punch* is, believe it or not, the only job I've ever had) would get my adrenalin going less sluggishly and lead me to doing things like writing the smash hit play of which I have spoken so much and written so little. It's also perfectly possible that you and I might get on better at a slight distance. We don't get on badly of course, and ever since you sent me your doomy letter a year or two back I think I can say that I have not been curmudgeonly in the office (he hasn't been in the office, they cried). What I mean is that our chemistries seem to work differently and they might combine better with the catalyst of distance.

Against my leaving are lots of little things, some big things. I would lose an office, a phone, a secretary, a space; I would lose the company and stimulus of the lads; I would lose security; I would lose over £5,000 a year. I would also have to face the fact that Sally and I probably can't both work at home together, so I may find myself going to the ridiculous and expensive lengths of hiring a small corner of an office somewhere.

What I suppose would be an ideal solution would be if I were to come to *Punch* on a part-time basis, and did my work in a few allotted days. You suggested, for instance, that even if I left I should still come to the Monday meeting and Wednesday lunch; it's possible, now that I think of it, that having done the travelling for those two days I could convert them into two full days. But there again, they are not the days on which you really need extra hands and eyes; Thursday is the important day there. And there again, the job I'm in needs constant attendance; you never know when titles/reading/cuts/confabs with artists/subbing are going to crop up. Even doing the book page couldn't really be a part-time thing, as you can't arrange for books and reviews to arrive, and authors to phone, on the very day you have arranged to be there.

So although it's tempting to suggest a part-time existence, I guess it isn't on. It's the old *Punch* story; easier to take a week off than a half-day.

I can no doubt make up the missing £5,000 (gosh, I am suddenly glad my salary is so small though it's going to be sweaty getting extra work just to come back to square one). And if the *Mirror* comes good, that will more than compensate. You can tell from the way I'm rehearsing these arguments out loud, and mumbling to myself, that I'm still not entirely sure that it's a good idea; what decides me finally, I suppose, apart from the Peruvian stumbling block, is the feeling that, yes, a change of air would get the system racing over, even if it involves penury, though the thought of clearing my office . . .

I would like to put one thing on record. Although I have an aura of absenteeism about me, this is due as much as anything to my chronic failure to cover my tracks. Most of the times when you have been cursing in the office, thinking that I have just walked off to do something blithely disregarding, I have in fact most often been engaged in something which I thought would end sooner and am desperately and prayerfully, urging the clock to stand still. It never did. All of us vanish from the office now and again (I thought ruefully about this on Wed and Thurs this week when you and Dave had vanished at 4.30 and I was plugging through with Alan Brien till 6) and I am not guiltier by such a margin as might be thought, simply less well-planned about it.

It is probably true, as you aver, that I have become somewhat less involved in the magazine. I think sometimes this is due to ten years of having battered my brains out against Bill David's in-tray (kicking his desk was to come later) and that some of the muscles involved have gone dead. I think it is also fair to say that on the literary side I am the only one here who is primarily a humorous writer, and that in conversation, suggestion, casual asides, meetings and general chat I have contributed fairly well and generously.

But there again, a bloke who finds himself with more outside commitments will also find himself with his mind outside more and more. It's what we doctors call the Boothroyd/Turner/Dickinson syndrome. Peter, of course.

Brass tacks, now.

We agreed that my three months' notice could be worked out over the time I shall be away in Peru. It looks now as if I shall be away for a fortnight at the end of April, start of May. I shall be away again from mid-June to mid-July. The first absence, you'll notice, has changed from May. So let's do as we said and date it from May 1st. I'll be here most of May, half of June, then off to Peru, then off. I'd like to write from Peru, if poss; they have in fact got elections in both the countries I'll be working in, Peru and Bolivia, and my producer promises that at least one will be accompanied by coups and interesting bloodshed. But we can talk about that.

This means that I'll be paid for May, June, July, though here for only half of it. After that I'll be just freelancing.

As by a foolish oversight I forgot to get a golden handshake clause written into my contract, I shall of course be rather dependent on *Punch* writing when I leave, and I hope that *Punch* will go on being dependent on me for the normal output, or even more now that I shall have extra time. So in lieu of a tax-free £1m, I think it's fair to ask that you should agree to go on using my writing for my first year off, at least to the value of the previous whole year. I would also, of course, like to be allowed to drift in like the ghost of Roger Woddis and use the odd typewriter as an article nears its end, even at the appalling risk of people saying that ever since Kington left he's been here more than usual.

Oh God, he's not going on to the fourth page, is he?

I certainly am. Just to say that if this parting of the ways goes through, amazing as it seems, I would like to say what a great time it's been. There's nowhere else like *Punch* to work, as everyone knows, and not so nice a bunch of people to work with. Anyone who leaves wants his head examining. I've had my head examined and the doctor says it's probably just incipient baldness. You, sir, have been particularly inspiring to work with. I hope, when I creep back in a year's time saying it's all been a ghastly error, you will remember this tribute.

One small but vital thing. I have to go to Manchester next Wednesday to see some BBC 2 film, all part of the Peru caper. And Thursday I have to my horror found myself involved in the Glenfiddich Wine and Food Judging Panel, which starts at 11.30. I hope this is not too injurious. I'll have all my stuff in before Wednesday, of course. I should be back Thursday p.m.

Finally, what about that TV comedy series we were going to write one day?

yours

———————

To ALAN COREN
November 8, 1981

Dear Al,

Thank you, dear lad. I agree to all the conditions you mention, especially the one about if I publish a book of pieces I have to come to lunch on Fridays. I am not quite sure how a book of mine could be construed as being against the best interest of *Punch* (unless you are thinking of my forthcoming volume *People I Have Seen Hopelessly Drunk at the Punch Lunch*), but I would never act against *Punch*'s interest except in the purely financial matter of trying to retain rights, and that is what it is all about anyway, isn't it, squire?

Right. I'll sign all those cheques now. Just got to find them first. You've no idea what my room is like. Well, maybe you have.

Smashing cover to *Punch* this week (parrot with hook). Some nice gags. Good piece. But you gotta doctor the rag pages. Trouble is, anything I say is going to sound like the twit across the water sounding off, but I can see so clearly from out here what's wrong with *Punch* rag pages. Let me come and bend your ear one day.

Working for *The Times* is weird. I have four or five masters, and they are all in conference. None too soon I have discovered that the secret is, as you might expect, to be in cahoots with the Court Page sub. It's like establishing relations with J Bale.[7]

The other night I heard on the radio an admiring profile of Lurie, the *Times* cartoonist, a man for whom I don't have very much admiration. They mentioned during the programme that he drew one cartoon recently of an articulated lorry which somehow was eating its own tail, and was labelled British Leyland. Ha ha. Except that was only in *The Times*; when it was syndicated abroad the lorry was labelled The Middle East. I suppose in Australia it was labelled Bodyline Bowling.

Any chance, by the way, of getting "Franglais" in *Punch* labelled MB Kington? It suddenly occurred to me that it would be nice to have my name in the old mag. I still think for the time being I had better segregate my ideas from the Monday meeting, otherwise I'll be accused of plagiarism. The other day, for instance, I lit on a Reagan quote to turn into an e e cummings poem which you also dealt with the week after.

Had lunch with Merrily Harpur[8] the other day, who told me I'd missed Dave Allen at the lunch. I once saw his stage show, which was clever, but I was taken aback at how filthy it was. I mean, filthy.

C U soon.

yours

———————

To ALAN COREN
July 1, 1983

Dear Al,

Thanks for your nice letter – not often I get letters from editors. Outraged pedants in Leeds, yes, but editors seldom. The other day I got a letter from a man who claimed to be the editor of a magazine in Leeds called "Outraged Pedant", but it was only about renewing my subscription. Charlie Douglas-Home never writes at all, and it's only by hearsay that I actually know his name. I haven't even met the man, yet. It's only by hearsay I know he's a man. So many women these days with men's names, you know. Jackie Collins, Susan George, Charlie George, Valerie Giscard . . .

I thought nearly a year ago that "Franglais" was beginning to flag, and thoughts of giving it up tap-danced across my mind, but for some reason or other it seems to be getting a deuxieme vent these days, so I suppose go on till someone shows the red card. Jeremy Robson[9] asked me in guarded tones the other day (he is so discreet in conversation that I seldom know he is actually asking a question) if, no, a fifth, you know, book might be on the cards. As it were. Well, er, actually, I said – it's catching – I think a fifth book of reprinted lessons might be a bit like claiming the golden goose. What I've always wanted to do one day is finish off Franglais Literature, or perhaps the Golden Treasury of Fr. Lit, in which each piece would be a tiny boiled down version of some classic. *Macbeth* in eighty lines. *The Importance of Being Earnest (Ernest)* in one short scene. *Decline and Fall of the Roman Empire* abridged into Franglais. Simple stuff. Think there's any point discussing doing this for *Punch* first? It would be harder work, but I'm not afraid of hard work. I just don't want to get involved, that's all.

yours

———————

To PETER McKAY[10]
September 13, 1996

Dear Peter,

I was touched to be sent an invitation for the *Punch* launch, but I was up in Edinburgh at the Fringe, partaking in a show I'd written intriguingly called "The Death of Tchaikovsky – a Sherlock Holmes mystery", and as we had easily sold 15 tickets that night I couldn't possibly justify flying south for the evening. I am told that over 1,000,000 gatecrashers turned up, so it was obviously a great success. I'm sorry I missed it.

Never mind all that – just a line to say that the new mag looks good, and that I wish you all the best. I wouldn't worry about old *Punch* people sniping at you. I worked at *Punch* for five editors, I think, and I have to say that as editors they were all pretty pathetic. The only truly distinguished thing any *Punch* editor prior to you has done was to write the play at which Abraham Lincoln was killed, and even that is generally forgotten. So if I ever tell you that you are the best editor *Punch* has had in living memory, don't be impressed.

yours from the depths of the country

———————

To SUE BRADBURY
June 3, 1997

Dear Sue,

If you want a mission statement (!), I would say that my aim is to provide a selection of the best of *Punch* over the years – not to be comprehensive (which is ridiculous) or to be historical (which is boring) but to provide articles, poems and cartoons which are funny enough in their own right to stand as the cream of British humour over the years. Funny because they were done by the best *Punch* artists and writers over the years, but also because they were done by the best outside talent that *Punch* could lure in from time to time. This was a larger pool of talent than people realised, ranging from Somerset Maugham to Anthony Burgess, and including entire serialised novels by Kingsley Amis (not to be included in the anthology!), as well as the first publication of the novel *I'm All Right Jack* by Alan Hackney which gave birth to the film.

Samples?

A very funny piece by Anthony Burgess on the adventures of a ten bob note.

Pieces by the underrated Alexander Frater who at his best was better than any of his contemporaries, yes, including Alan Coren.

A wonderful short story by the late lamented Stan Gebler Davies.

A parody by Kingsley Amis of the way Ernest Hemingway would have written science fiction.

Another parody of the way Beverley Nichols would have written *Lady Chatterley's Lover* written by the great James Cameron (a long way from his hard-hitting political journalism . . .)

A piece subtitled "A Day in the Life of the Dave Brubeck Quartet" by Brubeck's alto player, Paul Desmond. Desmond, a witty talker, was always being begged to write his life-story. He only ever wrote one chapter. It was for *Punch*. It was very funny. This is it.

The best cartoons, sometimes now forgotten, by Bill Tidy, Ronald Searle, Pont, Fougasse, H M Bateman, Phil May, Ffolkes, including one or two cartoons more talked about than reprinted (e.g. "I keep thinking it's Tuesday" and the cartoon of Churchill as a ga-ga old gent which got Muggeridge in such trouble).

The only book review ever written by Paul McCartney, also for *Punch*. On second thoughts, it wasn't that good.

Is this something like? Or can you boil it down? If not, I'll try again.

2

Columnist

By the latter part of the 1970s, Miles was seeking ways to spend more time on his own writing and so made various approaches to editors. After he left Punch *in 1980, he continued to contribute to the magazine, particularly his very successful "Let's Parler Franglais!" columns, but decided he wanted the challenge of writing a humorous column on a daily basis for a national newspaper.*

In 1981 he approached Harold Evans at The Times *and was initially turned down. Undeterred, he lobbied the editor by sending him a piece every day until Evans relented and gave him a daily slot on the obituary page. Miles was pleased with this location. There would, he declared, be no competition from the rest of the page. He suggested they call the column "Over My Dead Body", but that was rejected on the grounds of poor taste. Known as "Moreover", it became an instant success. Miles also made regular contributions to the sister paper,* The Sunday Times, *and, for a while, was their regular radio reviewer. He also wrote a weekly column for* Ms London *and then monthly for the* Oldie *and the* Lady. *He contributed to the* Spectator *and numerous other magazines. In 1987 he left* The Times *and joined the* Independent, *for whom he wrote a daily column until his death in 2008.*

To HAROLD EVANS[1]
May 1, 1981

Dear Harold,

Thanks for your nice letter. You ask if I might be prepared to write anonymously in the leader field. Well, no writer much likes having his name taken off the credits, but on the other hand I've been writing for *Punch* most of my life, which seems to be as near to writing anonymously as you can get. No disrespect to the old mag, but in the six months I've been doing a weekly TV crit for *The Times*, I've had more comments from people who have read me there than in six years at *Punch*. So, basically, no, I wouldn't mind. I'm used to it.

But there again, I've looked at several of your Saturday third leaders and (dear God, I have to be tactful here) I think they need kicking around a bit yet. I was suddenly reminded of what Bill Davis used to say as he strode up and down the corridor at *Punch*, wishing he were in the departure lounge at Heathrow: "The trouble with *Punch* is that it's a literary magazine!" At the time we used to think this was just the cry of the philistine who didn't understand half the words Alan Coren used, but I see now that he had sniffed out a good point, namely that most people in *Punch* tend without even realising it to adopt a kind of good-minor-writing style, a sort of leisurely raised eyebrow writing style which was peeking at itself in the mirror the whole while. And I think that when people try light-hearted leaders they seem to fall into a similar stance; a slightly arch, slightly Victorian attitude that to adopt a humorous pose is three quarters of the battle. It isn't; it's only the opening service. After that you've to surprise them with as many shots as possible.

OK, Kington, I hear you cry, let's see you do better. I'd like to try. Shall I suggest a subject?

But it was your passing mention of the Way of the World/Beachcomber idea that really got me excited. Cards on the table. That's what I've always wanted to do. Never had the chance. It beats me why British papers have almost allowed that tradition to die, the tradition of a space in which a writer was allowed to create his own unpredictable world, peopled with odd characters, breaking out into parody, invaded by tangents from other worlds . . . Myles na Gopaleen made a great job of it. Timothy Shy (though I only know his stuff from one wartime Penguin) was damn near as good as Beachcomber – in fact, I think I'm right in saying that Shy (Wyndham Lewis) was the bloke who first started Beachcomber, even before J B Morton. And in a curious sort of way, *Private Eye* still carries on the tradition. Forget their scurrilous gossip, malice, giggling vindictiveness, etc. What's good in *Private Eye* is their comic invention in such features as Dave Spart, Sylvie Krin, Ron Knee, Mr Thatcher, A Doctor Writes, E J Thribb, Bamber Gasket . . . cast of characters not so very far removed from Beachcomber's faithfuls, or Peter Simple's trendy awfuls. Sorry to mention *P Eye*. They haven't been very nice to you. But, like *Time Out* reviews, I always believe the opposite of their so-called fact stories. It's only when *Private Eye* states clearly that it's inventing something that I believe it.

Anyway, if you ever do find space for such a feature, that's me on the pavement in Grays Inn Road with my sleeping bag and primus stove having queued overnight to be considered. I have all sorts of ideas buzzing round, waiting to be exercised. I'll mention a few.

- I'd like to invent a high-up Scotland Yard Inspector who, instead of being the normal philistine, is keenly involved in the arts and approaches everything like a Peter Hall or Jonathan Miller. So, he would preview a forthcoming big trial at the Old Bailey as if it were theatre, improvised theatre, very excited at the cast involved and promising a new situation at each day's performance. Or, if there were a particularly boring show at the Hayward, he would announce the seizure of most of the paintings by the Art Squad, not because there was anything particularly offensive about them but because it was the only way of promoting any interest in the wretched show.

- An establishment pressure group with unexpectedly radical leanings. At the moment I like the idea of Stockbrokers Against Sexism; a group who are constantly distressed at the portrayal of stockbrokers as always being men. In fact, as they admit, there are no woman stockbrokers. But that is beside the point. It's the principle involved. We demand to be treated as any other liberated group. "Sir, in last night's TV play it was suggested crudely that stockbrokers find it difficult to establish deep relationships with other people. Those of us who have had the courage to come out and admit that we are stockbrokers find this deeply offensive . . ."

- Beachcomber used to print occasional extracts from a dictionary of modern times. Best definition he ever came up with was "Disarmament Talks: A series of informal chats about the next war". There's plenty of juice left in the idea. Some I have lurking in my mind are . . .

- Confrontation: a stage in negotiations when both sides sit in separate rooms, refusing to meet.
- Graphic Designer: a jobbing craftsman who is only mentioned in the credits because he lettered them.
- Opera: a series of loosely connected songs designed to make an evening's entertainment out of an overture.
- Pizza: the art of Italian flour arranging.
- A series of letters from readers describing My Worst London Experience. From a woman who had tried to get a minicab home to Streatham and ended up through the driver's ignorance in Dover: total cost £78. The most expensive night out in a theatre. The longest period spent trapped on Westway. Full of horrific detail, of course.
- An occasional series featuring Great Women in History, with potted biogs. This came to me when my son said by accident once that he'd seen Peter O'Toole in a film about Florence of Arabia. She'd be worth writing about . . . other candidates I have are Doris Godunov, Ivy the Terrible, Judith Iscariot, Ethel the Unready and of course the great Chinese leader, Charmian Mao.

And also any amount of one-off ideas based on things passing through the news. I wrote a super cricketing yarn last year at the time of increased aggro in cricket which started:-

"Middle and leg, please," said Jack.

"Find it your flaming self," said the umpire.

Jack felt sick. Last man in for England, 694 runs to get and ten minutes left. Could he do it? He looked round the field. The Australian fielders were tossing cans of lager to each other. One of them spat at him, not unkindly. Jack felt sick.

Never got it printed. Pity, really, especially as Jack did get the runs. Sadly he was mobbed by the crowd en route to the pavilion. The Man of the Match prize had never been awarded posthumously before.

And just before Easter, when I was idly looking through the

holiday announcements for any sign that it was originally a religious festival, it occurred to me that one could update bits of the Bible as backing for our modern feast . . .

"And Jesus took a chocolate egg and brake it, and said: Do this in memory of me. Go forth into the garden, and hide your eggs, and behold, shall not the little children come out to find them? Consider the bunnies of the field . . ."

Yes, well. Perhaps a little avant-garde.

I've broken Rule 3 of journalism, which is Never bore the editor with long letters. But I had to ramble on a bit to give you a vague idea. Vagueness aside, I'd be happy to provide a few sample columns. That breaks Rule 4: Never do anything without being paid. But a humorous column shouldn't obey any rules, anyway. It should make up its own.

    yours

This is a sample of the sort of column that Miles sent Harold Evans every day for ten days until Harold relented.

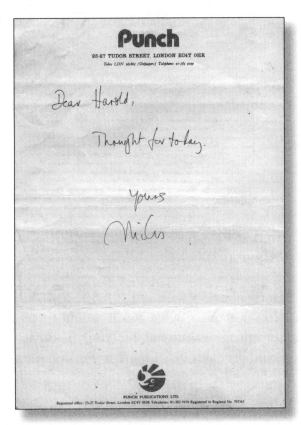

Those Bombs

" I can see no pattern in this at all. Prince Charles, Maggie Thatcher, Jill Knight
and myself share no common thread. A more eclectic group it would be difficult to
imagine. " - Roy Hattersley, after being sent a Jiffy bomb.

According to a poll, more than 40% of British voters would vote for a new party
formed by Prince Charles, Mrs Thatcher, Jill Knight and Roy Hattersley. The
More Eclectic Group, as it would be known, represents all shades of British opinion
except perhaps those who think that Ron Greenwood is doing a good job. Surprisingly,
the poll shows that Mrs Thatcher is more popular than Shirley Williams. In answer
to the question, " If Mrs Williams is a kind, competent sort of deputy head mistress
figure, how do you rate Mrs Thatcher ? ", over 53% said Yes.

In response to the question, " How do you mean, Yes ? " over 53% said, " As a sort
of bossy, confident headmistress figure, of course, of the kind we need. "

Even more surprisingly, 64% saw Prince Charles as a bossy, confident, headmistress
of the kind we need, and 73% saw Roy Hattersley the same way.

The full results of the poll are as follows:-

If an election were held tomorrow, who would you vote for ?

A white-haired, 67-year-old, English head of department who
hadn't got all his staff problems sorted out 12%
A quietly spoken Scots head of liberal studies 4%
A bossy, confident headmistress 23%
Harold Macmillan 61%

Eliminating the statistically irrelevant vote for ex-headmaster Macmillan, this
gives the new More Eclectic Group a clear lead of 27% , a remarkable mandate for
the bossy headmistress image and a vote of sympathy for people who have been sent
bombs. Speaking from his home today, Mr Hattersley said: " If that's the postman,
leave whatever it is by the front gate. "

Jill Knight is available for interview.

To HARRY
May 9, 1981

Harry,

Ever thought what fun it would be to pay the Queen to write
something sensational for you? The enclosed is the nearest one
could probably get. I think it works quite well.

yours

Chequebook Journalism Special

THE QUEEN WRITES FOR YE TIMES
The King I Married was a Mad Axeman Murderer!
An exclusive tale by Catherine Parr

Astonished. Dumbfound. That is the onlie word to describe my feelings, when I did learn the true nature of my late husband, King Henry VIII. So meeke and gentle a soul he had seemed before our marriage, devoted to his hobbies of falconry, minstrelsy and making war throughout Europe.

Nothing in my life had prepared me for the monster I found on my wedding night.

"Look ye here, wife," he roared at me. "I am sent by God as a holy mission to destroy those that are unfaithful and adulterous! Already have I slain two wives and thou shalt be the third, at the slightest sign of extra-marital nook on thy part."

Having said the which, he did draw aside a curtain in our bedchamber to reveal an execution-block, a chaplain with head bowed and an executioner in a black mask. This did so chill my blood that I swooned, yet when I came to myself the King had gone; for the purpose, the executioner did inform me, of having an evening with ye laddes.

So began my life of terror with ye Tudor Ripper, the which I can at last tell to the gentler readers of Ye Times. Of those nights when he would come back from an escapade, half-crazed with sack and breathing threats, not to mention ye garlicke.

"My wives have all been separated," he would leer at me; "sometimes by my Lord Cranmer with a piece of paper, sometimes by my axe. Thou canst truly say I have chopped and changed!"

And he would roar with laughter at his jest. But I, to whom could I turn? To the constabulary, perchance? Do not make me to laugh. I was truly a tragic prisoner in a royal love-nest terror situatione.

(Next weeke: The King tellst me – a male heir, or else! My

night of passion with ye Tudor Ripper. I find an axe beneath his pillow!

Only in Ye Times!)

Copywrighte Catherine Parr 1548

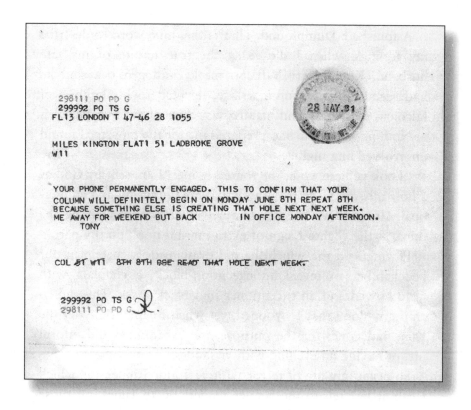

To CHARLES DOUGLAS-HOME[2]
June 21, 1982

Dear Charlie,

I had lunch today with John Grant, an event we first planned some time last July, and among other things he mentioned your plans for rejigging the middle of the paper. He stressed that nothing was concrete yet, but told me that you were thinking of taking my piece off the Court and Social page, putting it on the Opp Ed page, putting the diary on the Court page, perhaps bringing me down to three times a week . . . This all sounds quite interesting, not to say very interesting, but when I mentioned to John that I had one or two reservations – or at least points I'd like to put to you before you went over the top guns blazing – he agreed that you'd have no objection to my writing them down in a letter to you.

First, I would be reluctant but not muscularly so to leave the Obituary page. This is particularly because I am conservative by nature, partly because a quirky thing like my column tends to look more colourful surrounded by very regular, not so colourful features, partly because I know that even on a bad day I have a good chance of being funnier than the obituaries.

Second, I would be reluctant but not hysterically so to reappear opposite letters. It's a damn good page to be on, and an honour to be there, but there's just a chance that my stuff might look odd among the normal features.

Third (and all the way down to ninety-ninth), I think it would be a terrible mistake to write my piece just three or even just four times a week. There are lots of reasons for this, of which the money is the least.

The most trivial and selfish reason is that I like writing every day and would miss writing on a blank day.

A better reason is that would leave less margin for error. At the end of my first week of doing "Moreover", Michael Frayn wrote an extremely nice letter to Harry Evans saying he liked my stuff but that Harry should always remember that humorists have off days, maybe 3 in 5. I aim to score higher than that, but it's also true that not every piece a humorist writes, even if good, can appeal to everyone. Well, if I were writing three times a week and one or even two of those didn't strike home, the scoring rate would feel much lower.

John Grant assumed – as most other people do as well – that it would be a relief to write less often. Amazingly, I think it would be harder. I find it easier doing five shorter pieces a week for *The Times* than I did doing one longish a week for *Punch*. It's something to do with keeping the muscles warm and ticking over, or the juices flowing, or the production line going, depending on whether you prefer an athletic, digestive or industrial metaphor. Believe it or not, I really look forward every morning to filling that space in *The Times*, like a jazz soloist itching for the moment to step forward and do his sixty-four bars. I always have two or three ideas turning over in my mind for the next few pieces, and wouldn't like to wait too long for fear of them going cold.

As a concomitant of this, I think readers feel the same way: that a humorous column has to appear regularly and on consecutive days to establish and maintain a rapport with the invisible audience. This is something to do with the margin of error I mentioned, something to do with being able to vary the approach day by day, but most of all to do with a feeling that a humorous column is a bit like a tiny repertory theatre which presents a different play every day. There may be plays that the reader doesn't feel quite in tune with, but better that than to see the theatre dark on Tuesdays and Thursdays.

So I do feel very strongly that a column like mine, whoever writes it, should appear at least five days a week, Monday to Friday. It sounds arrogant, but I think it's just common sense. The best argument against is that the reader will tire of the tone of voice of one writer, but I think that is swamped by all the arguments in favour, and in any case I think I vary the tone of voice enough to avoid that danger. One might just as well argue that leaders should only come out three times a week because readers tire of a newspaper's opinions.

I hope you don't mind my saying all this. It's just that I feel it's working well at the moment, that I'm enjoying it, and that I wouldn't want to change the magic formula.

yours

———

To CHRISTOPHER WARD[3]
September 8, 1982

Dear Christopher,

Believe me, I am as touched as any journalist by flattery, that is to say a very great deal indeed, but I have problems. One is that I do not think *The Times* pays me the wonderful fee I deserve. The other is that I cannot imagine writing for anyone else.

This is nothing to do with thinking *The Times* is the greatest paper in the world. It has awful ludicrous faults. Sometimes I think it has little else. But I have been writing for the bloody paper since something like 1966 one way or another and I now feel part of it. It's like being part of a family; relations want to make you scream sometimes but you are stuck with them for better or for worse, and you'd lose something if you left them.

I am sure you would surprise me with the generosity of your offer. That is what worries me. I might accept it. So you mustn't mention money to me. I am stupid about money; I love the idea of it and do very little about it. Believe it or not, I have claimed no expenses from *The Times* for ten years.

Again, I recently went through a bad time wondering whether to accept an offer to do *Film 82* or not; eventually I turned it down. It was only later I realised I'd never asked how much they were going to pay me.

Now a question for you. Do you really think my stuff would look good in the *Express*? Or is there not a chance it would look a bit mandarin, toffee-nosed even?

On the other hand, I'd love to have a drink with you.

yours

———————

To NEIL KINNOCK
December 30, 1985

Dear Mr Kinnock,

Thank you for your card about my "Child's Guide to the City of London",[4] which quite made my Christmas, though I'm disappointed to tell you that it* aroused very little overt protest. Oddly enough, I did get letters from all the other party leaders about the piece. David Owen wrote to refer me to three books he had written on the subject. David Steel wrote to refer me to David Owen's letter. Mrs Thatcher wrote, offering me a peerage to keep quiet. Unfortunately, it is a time-sharing peerage and I would only get it a fortnight a year, so I indignantly rejected it.

———————

* the piece

45

The most disturbing reaction I got to that piece, and this is true, was a phone call from a man I used to know at Oxford and who was a close relation of the late Charlie Douglas-Home. Did I, he wanted to know, know much about the City of London? Not a lot, I said; I used some information and a lot of intuition. Well, he said, he had worked in the City for 20 years and the truth was even worse than my satirical picture of it – the conspiracy, corruption and general determination to rob the man in the street or to engineer booms and slumps were quite unbelievable. But if you start telling people, they think you're paranoid, he said. I think he was paranoid, but not much.

yours sincerely

––––––––––

To CHARLES WILSON
March 10, 1986

Dear Charlie,
I am breaking a life-long rule in writing to you, because my principle has always been to avoid contact with editors, who can only cause trouble, and stick to the sub-editors, the people with real power. I only met Charlie Douglas-Home the once, and that was by accident. "Been avoiding me, haven't you?" he said. "Yes," I said. That is all I can remember of the conversation.

But I am writing now to say, rather banally, congratulations on being made Editor – a bit late in the day, but it's nice to get a servile pat on the back late in the day, like getting a telegram from the Queen on your 101st birthday. It's good to see a real journalist in charge of a paper. Real journalism isn't something I know much about, being a humorous fantasist, but if you have ever wondered whether I still enjoy doing my five-a-week stint on the Opp Ed page, the answer is: Yes, I do, very much. I still get a real kick out of being given a small corner of *The Times* in which to be a licensed loony, and I hope it shows.

If I have one small criticism of your editorship, it is that I was a bit sorry that you and George Brock thought it wasn't time yet to print the piece I wrote about a fictional new paper called the Daily

Moreover. It was not written to exacerbate the situation – quite the opposite, in fact, as I thought it might defuse things with a bit of fantasy about a one-man paper. I still entertain hopes that you print it later, nudge, nudge.

Incidentally, I was in your home town Glasgow the other day for the first time in decades and I thought it was a smashing place, very civilised. I was even involved in a minor car crash in the environs of Glasgow Airport, and the other driver leapt out of his car and said: "All my fault, Jimmy."

That's what I call being civilised.

This is one of those letters that don't need answering.

Editors should get more like that, so there is no need to reply. Unless you care to explain how Hibs beat Celtic 4–3 in the Scottish Cup.

    yours

THE TIMES

Times Newspapers Limited, Virginia Street, London E19 BH.
Telephone 01-481 4100 Telex 925088

From the Editor

Mr Miles Kington
Flat 1
51 Ladbroke Grove
London W11 3AX

27 March 1986

Dear Miles,

I have learned today that you have won a 'commended' in this year's British Press Awards.

We tried to ring you today, but could get no reply. You may therefore first learn of it by reading it in the paper on Saturday.

Many congratulations, and thank you for the honour it brings the newspaper.

I hope I will see you to congratulate you personally before the Awards Dinner on Thursday, 22 May.

Yours sincerely,

Charles Wilson

Registered Office: Times Newspapers Limited, 200 Gray's Inn Road, London WC1.
Registered No. 894646 England

To JOHN TORODE[5]
August 15, 1986

Dear Mr Torode,

I would have replied to you before, but I have been in Edinburgh for the Festival, the cultural equivalent of a massive pile-up on the M1.

I like the sound of the paper very much, and I like the idea of writing for it. However, I have just this minute signed a renewed yearly contract to *The Times* (I am on that sort of freelance basis with them) and there is no real reason why I shouldn't honour it, and play out the year. I have to admit that I quite like writing five times a week for them, and until I come to my senses and ask to do less, I'll probably want to keep it that way.

I'm assuming, of course, that you'd want your recruit, whoever it was, to cut ties with their present base and move over completely. If so, I'd be very interested in getting in touch with you next spring, when my contract starts to run out, and talking about things then.

On the other hand, I'd like to become a reader of the *Independent* as soon as possible.

yours sincerely

———————

To GEORGE BROCK[6]
January, 1987

I have recently been made an offer by the *Independent* newspaper to become a regular humorous writer for them, and after carefully considering the offer from all possible angles I have decided to rush in blindly and accept it. It will probably seem extraordinary to you that after writing freelance for *The Times* for twenty years I should want to transfer my loyalties, so I owe you an explanation.

The heart of the matter is contained in the length of time I have been engaged to *The Times*. Although I have only been writing "Moreover" for 5½ years, I have been freelancing for you since the days when I was "A Correspondent", and sooner or later one needs a fresh stimulus. My first job for you was as jazz reviewer and I gave that up because I was getting jaded. After five years as your humorous columnist, I similarly feel that I very much need a change of scenery. I don't think I'm writing badly at the moment, but I have been feeling that it took a lot more effort recently – I was, in fact, getting restless, itchy-footed, and the offer from the *Independent* came along at just the right psychological moment. I think we all need a change of scene from time to time, a new adventure of some kind, and my mistake is usually to stay too long in the same place; staying 13 years on the staff of *Punch* for instance, was a step in the wrong direction, and I think a change for me now as a humorist is just right.

You might well rejoin that the *Independent* is bound to collapse within the year, that I will be out of a job and bitterly regretting the day I ever left *The Times*, and you may well be right, but one has to step out now and again, and I am prepared to take the chance. It is not for the money, nor is it solely to get hold of the word processor which *The Times* promised to loan me a year ago. Most of the time I have been very happy working for *The Times*, I have been given a lot of freedom and encouragement and I don't regret any of it.

Perhaps the worst that can be said is that we have come to take each other somewhat for granted, which is not a bad reason for a change.

Under my contract I am bound to give you three months' notice, which I now do. How you would like to handle these three months is a matter which you and my agent can easily settle during my absence in Burma.

yours

———————

To CHARLES WILSON
January 20, 1987

Dear Charlie,
Thank you for your letter before Christmas. I don't think much purpose would be served by our meeting for lunch except to have a

nice lunch, as I have already signed a contract with the *Independent*. But I think I owe you an explanation as to why I am leaving *The Times*. It is not to do with money, as you might have guessed from the fact that I never tried to ask you for more, nor is it to do with the fact that you moved to Wapping a year ago which is about two miles further from my home and thus a much further bike ride. Politics don't come into it at all; I think Rupert Murdoch's move against the print unions was long overdue, and the worst that can be said about him is that he decided to become as ruthless as they always have been.

It's all to do with feelings. I feel I need a move. I feel I needed to take a chance, I felt I needed a challenge. All my life I have been working for old and safe institutions like *Punch*, the BBC, *The Times*. I felt like taking a gamble on something new and good, and the *Independent* is new and it's bloody good. It sounds a bit arrogant if I say also that one of the things it needed was a spot of good humour, but that's how I felt. I quite realise that I may be making a big mistake, but I don't think so at the moment; at the moment I feel due for a shot of adrenalin.

I left the staff at *Punch* after thirteen years there and knew when I left that I had been there too long. Well, I have been freelancing for *The Times* for over 20 years now, so maybe I am due for a change there as well. I have seen editors come and go, five of them I think, and perhaps it is time that an editor saw me come and go. As you know, I have made a practice of totally ignoring any editor who happened to be in power, which is the best way for a humorist to operate, so I hope you don't take this as in any way reflecting on you – I don't think we have met since you became editor, so I have no idea what it has done to you or you to the place. I am very sorry to be leaving *The Times*, after all we have done for each other, but . . .

But this doesn't sound like much of an explanation, does it?

I really can't think of one big reason why I want to leave *The Times*. I think it may have something to do with the fact that the character of *The Times* is gradually changing, and leaving me less to do within it. People have said that *The Times* is changing politically, and I think it is, though as I do not give a fart for politics in this country, which are only party politics and thus extremely tiresome, this does not worry me. But it is changing in another way; the features are becoming gradually frothier and flightier, the tone of the paper is getting less earnest, and the human jungle is coming out into the open. Not a bad thing, perhaps, but it makes it harder for me to operate as a one-person fringe show if all around me are getting a little nearer to the way I work – except of course for Bernard Levin who gets more serious. (Do you know, I have never met Bernard Levin.) So I feel that my role in *The Times*, which was once to act as a foil to all the pompous and tragic stuff around me, is getting somewhat eroded.

There are other smaller factors too, irritations which have tended to build up over the years. I only mention them here because you may be able to spare other people from them.

1) The total inability of *The Times* interior messenger service to get things, or at least my stuff, to the right desk at the right time.

2) The way I was promised the loan of a word processor on a priority basis the week you arrived at Wapping, which I am still waiting for.

3) The increasing conviction that your syndication department is either corrupt or useless or both. I have often been told by friends that pieces of mine have been reprinted from *The Times* abroad, but very seldom have I been paid for them. Barry Humphries once said to me: "A lot of your pieces reappear in Australia, Miles – I hope Rupert is paying you for them." Well, he wasn't, and when my agent tackled your syndication department, they claimed that they had no idea such pieces were appearing abroad.

4) The reappearance of the dreadful Fourth Leader.

5) The absence of the occasional pat on the back. It would have been nice to be asked out once or twice, or get a progress report.

6) The occasional slightly inane censorship, especially when I made slighting comments about *The Sun*, a newspaper.

*

But all that is by the by. I've enjoyed working for *The Times*. You gave me amazing carte blanche. I think I did all right by you. It was a good double act and I don't see why it should be over for ever. Meanwhile, I'm going out on a new trapeze and that should be quite exciting too.

Why don't you ask me out for lunch after I've gone there, and I can tell you all the inside secrets of the *Independent*?

yours

———————

To GEORGE BROCK
February 16, 1987

Dear George,

Time has caught up with me, I'm afraid. I leave for Burma in less than 24 hours and the amount of things I have left to do does not easily admit of more *Times* pieces, so there will not be any. But there is a bit more to it than that. I know the one piece I have let you have was rather long, but then you've got a big paper there and I was slightly perturbed that you hadn't used it yet. It's now two weeks or less – less, actually – to the end of my contract with *The Times*, so if I gave you the pieces you wanted, you would be printing them after I had stopped being a *Times* writer and had become an *Independent* writer. I don't like that. It sounded almost from what you said at the weekend that you need more stuff from me just to back up a letter you wanted to send to the *Standard*, saying that I was still writing for you. Well, that's silly. Sending letters to the *Standard* is silly and saying I am still writing for you when my contract expires in ten days is also silly, and I don't want to get mixed up in it.[7]

It would all be much more sensible, I think, if we left things as they are. I have finished writing "Moreover" for *The Times*, which is what I was hired to do, so let's leave it at that. It was your idea for me to bow out early. Now I have and we might as well leave the curtain down on the stage. You can certainly use the wine piece I sent you if you like, but I would be equally happy if you sent it back.

Must rush now, to catch Philip Howard. It'll be the last time. End of an era.

yours

———————

To SEBASTIAN FAULKS[8]
May 26, 1988

Dear Sebastian,

As you well know, letters from colleagues are the best kind to get, especially if they're nice; Lenny Bruce used to say that the best laughter from a comedian was the laughter that came from the musicians in the band. So thanks. It makes up for not getting to meet Anthony Burgess and other great men. What's wrong with this typewriter? Why doesn't it separate all the words?

(I have a theory about this machine. For years and years, whenever I was drink and typed, the typing came out drunk. When I was sober, which was actually most of the time, it came out sober. But recently I think my writing, and the reactions of the machine, have got slightly out of phase. I think it is sometimes drunk when I am not. And vice versa, on occasions when the wine should have muddled my thought, but it flows beautifully. And once or twice I think my typewriters had a hangover when I have not. Don't tell anyone I said all this. They will think I am mad.)

I used to have an informal arrangement with Claire Tomalin at the *ST* that if she ever came across a book for which no reviewer in the world was suitable, she would try me. That way I got to do a review a year. The new regime seem to have inherited this, and I have done two pieces for them in the last year or two, one on a coroner's memoirs which was well worth doing, and this one which is not worth doing at all. I shall not be doing another one. That is because the review came out with the last paragraph neatly placed at the head of the piece. I rang up Nigella Lawson, who had commissioned the piece, to find out why and she said: "Oh, I am so sorry, I thought Simon Jenkins must have cleared it with you – he was the one who dealt with the piece."

This seems to suggest that at the *ST* the junior, Nigella Lawsonnia, commissions the pieces and the senior man, Simon, does the subbing. This I fail to understand. But I will not be risking it again. I felt uneasy, anyway, as the *Sunday Times* I think is such a rubbishy paper these days. And so is every other one. I haven't bought a Sunday paper in anger for years now.

yours

PS But isn't the *Independent* a nice paper? And there is one guy in Features who is sometimes flat.

———————

To SIMON JENKINS
April 4, 1990

Dear Simon,

From chairman of the B[ritish] R[ail] environmental panel to *Times* editorship in one fell swoop – congratulations! I don't think it's ever been done before. In fact, I checked with the *Guinness Book of Records* and they confirmed this. The other way round it's quite common – many an editor has fallen on evil days and taken a cushy BR committee to help with the train fare – but never going up. They were pretty cagey at Guinness, actually. Maybe it's because my opening remark was "Ernest Saunders here – I've got some facts which I think the Guinness Record people ought to know about".

Anyway, now, when people have stopped congratulating you, and started expecting you to turn the paper into a great paper again, even a good one if necessary, is when you need another message of congratulations. So here it is.

OK. Now get down to turning the paper around.

yours

Email to DAVID ROBSON[9]
1993

David – Well, I have seen the new design(s) now, and I have to say I don't like it – at least, it's not nearly as good as what went before. There seems to be a mad rush of blood to the head every now and then in paper and magazine design, which forces people to put in lots of rules and boxes if there aren't any, and to take them out if there are lots. In the case of the *Independent*, you seem to have filled up some rather pleasant open and fluid spaces with unnecessary Zimmer frames. It's a bit like putting formal flower beds in open park, or putting scaffolding on an unspoilt house. I expect one day someone will remove it all and call it another new design.

This is all by the by, as I have no say in the design, and nobody would listen to me if I did say anything. But I do feel I should have some voice in the way my own piece looks. I think someone should have mentioned to me that you were thinking of putting my photo on the piece, so that I could have strenuously fought against it – I can't think of any good reason for doing so. And if you were going to put a photo on my piece, despite my strenuous objections, I think you should have put a photograph of me on it – or, at least, a photo that looked more like me than the hungover, death's head, pallid-grin snap you have dug up from somewhere. I have pictures of myself taken more recently that make me look nicer to know. But for heaven's sake, if you are still rethinking the design as you go along, please rethink that photo. If nothing else, it takes up valuable word space. I mean this.

To JAN MORRIS
August 1, 1996

Dear Jan,

You will never believe this, but as I was penning my little article about Wilson and the Welsh, I thought to myself, "I hope to God Jan Morris doesn't read this, as she'll go on the warpath, and

I'll have to spend hours composing a conciliatory fax when I should be starting my first novel." And now it's all come hideously true.[10]

What you have got to remember is that I grew up in Wales and Scotland, not in England, so for most of my youth I was in a racial minority and an English one at that. Until I went to Oxford at 18 I had never lived in a place for any period where the English were in the majority. When I finally met them, I didn't like most of them, but that's not the point – the point is that I have been left feeling deep down that the Welsh and Scots are the majority and I am in an English minority, so although I do from time to time make anti-Welsh and Scottish remarks, I am the only journalist who ever does so from the viewpoint that the English are getting their own back on the master races (Welsh and Scottish). I might even feel the same about the Irish, as I was born in Ireland, but thank God I left there soon enough not to get a complex. I hope this explains everything. I do from time to time say some rude things about the English, but they never notice insults. They cannot believe that anyone would want to insult them.

Incidentally, I wish your projected Welsh showbusiness dinner well. I don't think I could face it. Not because it's so Welsh but because it's so showbiz.

So much for friendly small arms fire. I hope you are flourishing. I am about to go to the Edinburgh Festival under the artistic directions of my wife Caroline who, in her tax bracket as a theatre director, has persuaded me and another man to concoct a small Fringe show called "The Death of Tchaikovsky – a Sherlock Holmes Mystery". We discovered that Holmes's absence after the Reichenbach Falls coincided exactly with Tchaikovsky's still unexplained death in St Petersburg. At first we thought it would be nice to engineer Holmes's investigation of the mystery, but now it seems that Holmes was more involved in the death than you could possibly imagine, or indeed, want to know.

Thanks for writing. I'd rather get a pained fax from you than an unpained one from most anyone.

*

PS I have just noticed your letter in today's paper. You still don't explain what the Welsh Academy is. Believe me, I don't particularly want to know. I just don't think anyone else does, either. You are absolutely right about people laughing at the English. I am not sure how right you are about having to speak Welsh before you can comment on Wales. It would eliminate most of the population of Wales from contention. I did try to learn Welsh in my youth, in emulation of George Borrow, but in those days they had no very good language manuals and I failed.

yours

———————

To ANDREW MARR
March, 1997

Dear Andrew Marr,

This is an odd letter to write, because although I write for the paper most days we have never actually met, and the reason I am writing is nothing to do with my writing, but at the behest of a reader. A reader who says she has won an *Independent* competition and never received the prize – but I enclose a copy of the letter so that you can pass it on to the right quarters. She says she has written to you already and got no answer. I told her that editors have many better things to do than answer letters. She challenged me to name one. I couldn't think of one. So it's over to you.

Well, I hope we meet one day. I did receive an invitation to an editorial lunch at Canary Wharf one day, but when I calculated that I would spend about six or seven hours just getting there and back, I decided that no lunch was worth a lost day. In fact, I wouldn't even have time to write my *Independent* piece. I would then get fired for having gone to lunch with the editor.

Incidentally, I didn't meet the previous editor either. Mark you, he never asked me to lunch.

As I sat down to write to you, I suddenly had a strange memory of a boy I used to know called Marr. When I was at school in Scotland (at Glenalmond in the 1950s) he was one of the fattest boys in the school, until he came back one term very thin. He had had one of those operations which bypass your stomach or something, and most of his food never got digested. Anyway, he went overnight from being very chubby to being a beanpole, and nobody recognised him for a whole term, which meant he got away with murder. The other thing I remember about him was that he could play Grieg's piano sonata very well. That's all he could play. He never played anything else. He just practised this one work, which is quite difficult, and quite unpopular, though I have come to the conclusion that it is rather good. As far as I remember, losing three stone had no effect on his piano playing. Whenever I hear that work, I think of him.

If he was a relation of yours, I am sure you will find this fascinating. If he wasn't, I am sure you will wonder what I am wittering on about. I wonder the same thing myself.

yours sincerely

––––––––––

To SIMON KELNER
June 10, 1998

Dear Simon Kelner,

I know my agent Gill Coleridge is in touch with Ian Birrell at the moment about my contract, and I am not writing to you about any of that – I am just getting in touch to say hello, and to utter a word of caution about the new placing of my column.

Until now it has been a landscape shape, broad and shallow, over five legs. This was a nice flexible shape, because it meant that if I adopted some format such as a Shakespearean pastiche or a bit of mock-ballad, the length of the verse line could be easily accommodated, sometimes by widening the column width and using only four columns.

If you are going to stick to this shape, narrow and upright, over two columns, you have lost this flexibility. There is a case in point today. At the end of today's column, I have a couple of speeches which lapse into blank verse. The sub or whoever handled it has been completely unable to accommodate it in the narrow space available to him, and has made the blank verse run on as if it were prose, which makes nonsense of it.

Now, I know that being able to handle Shakespearean pastiche is not the main preoccupation of a modern paper editor, but one of the things about a column like mine and one which the readers seem to like, is the variation of format, which quite often gets right away from the ordinary succession of paragraphs into verse forms, dialogue, court proceedings, catalogues, etc. This is going to be much harder with the new, thin, upright column.

(While I am at it, I wonder if it is a good idea to try to pull a quote out of my piece and blow it up big as a come-on? If I write something fictional, as I mostly do, there may be times when it looks a bit odd . . .)

I just thought I'd add to your worries as the new editor. I'm not a trouble-maker, generally – I just wish I had been consulted before the new shape arrived, so that I could have made these points in advance.

Good luck!

    yours from the depths of the country

––––––––––––

To KANIKA UTLEY[11]
May, 1998

Dear Kanika Utley,
Thank you for your fax about the column in which I detail the trial of the postman charged with biting a dog in self-defence.

I am afraid you are going to have to prepare yourself for a bitter disappointment. My column is a daily humorous column, into which I often weave fantasy disguised as truth to tickle my readers' jaded palate. This was one such example – the postman never existed, and nor did the dog. I do from time to time invent curious court cases in order to make the law seem even more idiotic than it is. Recently I invented a case in which a man had trespassed on a construction site with large signs saying "THIS SITE IS PATROLLED BY FIERCE GUARD DOGS". In fact, there were no such dogs on the site, but the man had hurt himself falling over when he thought he was being pursued by a dog. He therefore sued the construction company for saying FALSELY that the premises were guarded by dogs . . .

I seem to be obsessed by dogs. This is not true. Nor by postmen. I am sorry if this message causes you a passing annoyance, but don't forget that your fax to me gave me great pleasure. I am afraid it is always pleasurable when someone takes your jokes seriously. Still, at least your senior producers seem to have been as trusting as you were . . .

yours sincerely

To RICHARD INGRAMS
May, 1998

Dear Richard,

I enclose the duly filled in form nominating my summer break reading and I understand that if I have named the correct three books I will win a holiday for two in blissful Bohemia, but that if I don't win I will have to keep my day job at the *Oldie*.

The normal bland tenor of my days was whipped up to a frenzy the other day when on two successive dates I was a) taken to an evening meet at the Bath Races and b) bidden to speak at a seminar at the Bath & West Show and I would tell you all about it except that I intend to spin the straw of the experience into solid gold for the *Oldie*. I fear I am in danger of drifting into a rural nightmare, in which the conversation round the dinner table is all about sustainable soil renewal and organic farming. Luckily, I still have a few books I can sneak off to and read when the going gets hard, such as Margaret Drabble's *Oxford Companion to Eng Lit*, which I noticed the other day ended an entry on Wyndham Lewis with the note "Not to be confused with D B Wyndham

Lewis, the Catholic biographer". A strange way to dismiss the man who started life by creating Beachcomber, went on to be Timothy Shy and ended up writing the only St Trinians novel with Ronald Searle.

I am writing an Edinburgh Fringe show based on the death of Tchaikovsky called, "The Death of Tchaikovsky, a Sherlock Holmes Mystery", which trades on two indubitable "facts". One is that nobody knows why Tchaikovsky died (cholera? suicide because of his homosexuality? – poor chap, Tchaikovsky was gay by nature and hated being so) and the other is that at the very moment of his death Sherlock Holmes was in the area, and could have been called in to investigate . . . But I have said enough. I have had lunch twice now with Anthony Holden, who wrote the most recent life of Tchaikovsky, and most illuminating they were too, even if I cannot remember much of what he said. The only thing I keep remembering from our conversation is a story he reported – from Harry Evans who apparently was dealing with Marlon Brando about his autobiography. Brando's first draft was all about ecology and North American native rights, and was unreadable. Evans sent it back, asking for much more kiss 'n' tell material.

Following which, Brando rang all the ladies he had been connected with to find out how far they had gone – he rang Ursula Andress and said, "Ursula, you remember we made a film together, and I just wanted to know, when we were making the film together, did we ever . . . you know . . . ?"

Strange.

Email to ANDREW MAYERS[12]
February 8, 2001

Dear Andrew, If music be the food of love, I'll have two rare Scarlatti sonatas and the Vivaldi salad, said Paganini once, and it's as true today as it was then. If Sean O'Grady asks what I'm writing about today, tell him I'm working on an anagram of Keith Vaz. Meanwhile, here is a quiz question. A GENUINE quiz question. Which street in Soho is named after Fanny Burney? This is absolutely genuine, and the first sub-editor who gets it right is wasting his time at the *Independent* and should go full-time as a pub quiz contestant.

Email to ANDREW MAYERS
February 13, 2001

Dear Andrew, I don't know if you read the piece which I did for the paper today, all about the old folk's home in which every resident was an eye witness of some historical event and where people paid to call in and talk to them – well, anyway, Channel 4's *Big Breakfast Show* phoned this morning to be put in touch with the place. Always gratifying when that happens.

And now for another slice of real life – today, life on our train system.

It should be dedicated to my step-daughter who caught the 2.27 train to London from Bath yesterday and arrived at 8 p.m. instead of the scheduled 4 p.m.

If Sean O'Grady should happen to inquire what I am writing about today, you may tell him I am rewriting *Pride and Prejudice* in the style of a World Wrestling Federation presentation, featuring Mister "Dark Dynamo" Darcy as the villain. If he should ask why, say I hope to make my fortune from it and get the hell out of the *Independent*.

PS The street in Soho which is named after Fanny Burney? It's D'Arblay Street. She married a Frenchman of that name and became Mrs D'Arblay.

To RICHARD INGRAMS
March 3, 2004

Dear Richard,

I thought I should write and say thank you for the lunch yesterday. But then I thought that you probably had nothing to do with it apart from being the figurehead – no cooking, no table setting – and that I should probably write and thank Mr Simpson, or Mr Swan Hellenic, or Helen, or Ben, or Barry Cryer, or Beryl Bainbridge, or whoever it is that really organises these things.

On the other hand, as you were trapped at High Table and didn't get out and about much, I thought it might be interesting for you to have an on-the-ground report from a punter, so I am going to write down as much as I can remember of which people I met and what those people said to me.

IN THE BAR BEFORE LUNCH

Marcus Berkmann:	Miles, I was going to write a fan letter to you about a piece you wrote for *The Oldie*, but then you mentioned me in another piece, so I thought you might think I was writing because you'd mentioned me, so I didn't write.
Me:	Ah. Was that the piece in which I said that you and I only ever met at *Spectator* or *Oldie* parties?
Berkmann:	Yes.
Me:	Well, here we are again.
Berkmann:	Yes.
Keith Waterhouse:	Hello, Miles. Didn't I see you at a party the other night?
Me:	Yes. You were receiving an award as the greatest living columnist.
Keith:	Was I? That was nice for me.
Christopher Sylvester:	I am working on a book about the social side of Hollywood. At least, I think I am.

	I have done a lot of work on it already. At least, I think I have.
Marcus Berkmann:	Hello again, Miles. I had come to talk to Christopher Sylvester to get away from you, but you seem to have had the same idea.
Me:	OK. I'll go and talk to Michael Fishwick then.
Michael Fishwick:	Miles! Hello! Do you know Victoria Hislop? Me: No, I don't think so.
V Hislop:	Yes, you do. We have met before.
Me:	Oh. Why are you talking to Fishwick? Are you writing a book?
V Hislop:	Of course. It's a novel.
Fishwick:	And you, Miles?
Me:	I am writing the totally fictional autobiography you said I would never write. It's coming on.
Fishwick:	I'd like to see some of that. How about writing a novel?
Me:	I shall never write a novel.
Fishwick:	But isn't a fictional autobiography a kind of novel?
Me:	(puzzled – saying nothing)
Bob Geary:	Hello, you don't know me. I'm Bob Geary. Have you tracked down Robert Thompson yet?
Me:	No.
Mavis Nicholson:	I keep seeing requests by people in "Books Wanted" columns for books about the Tour de France by Geoff, my late husband. I still have quite a few at home. I wonder if I should wait till the price goes up a bit more and then start selling them?
Joan Bakewell:	Luckily, I'm still being asked to sign a few of my current one.
Mavis:	By the way, Miles, when are they going to

	change that dreadful photo of you in the *Indy*?
Me:	Well, I keep meaning to ask Richard to change the drawing of me in the *Oldie*. It looks nothing like me at all. But I suppose because Willie Rushton did it, Richard thinks it's a good likeness.
Wilfred De'Ath:	Yes, you are right. I have lost a few teeth. No, I didn't get into a fight. Yes, someone knocked them out. In Cambridge. No, I don't want to talk about it.
Woman:	Isn't that Trevor Grove over there?
Me:	No.
Woman:	Oh. But Valerie Grove is here.
Me:	Yes.
Valerie Grove (later):	Trevor wanted to come, but he wasn't asked.
Edward Enfield:	Hello, Miles.
Me:	(in an unusually friendly moment, I attempt to give Edward Enfield a comradely hug. Edward Enfield backs away terrified at any suggestion of physical contact)
Enfield:	None of that sort of thing, thank you.
Berkmann (again):	I am writing a book about fatherhood. I have two very young children, and there are no books to tell me how to be a young father. So I am going to write one, before I forget what I have learnt.

UPSTAIRS AT LUNCH

Tony Blackburn:	(opposite me at lunch, eating a salad while everyone else has smoked salmon) I am a vegetarian, actually.
Me:	Aren't you envious of us eating meat at all?
Blackburn:	Not at all.

Me:	Don't you even miss bacon?
Blackburn:	How can I? I don't know what it tastes like. I have never eaten it.
Me:	How long have you been vegetarian?
Blackburn:	Since I was 4 or 5.
Me:	Blimey.
Berkmann:	(sitting next to me at lunch) Considering we only ever meet at *Oldie* or *Spectator* parties, we have met each other a lot today.
Me:	You don't have to talk to me if you don't want to. Who's the other side of you?
Berkmann:	Harry Enfield. He's sitting opposite his father.
Me:	I think that's very bad table planning.
Laura Gascoigne:	I am the girl sitting next to you, my name is Laura Gascoigne and I work for "Pandora".
Me:	What's "Pandora"?
Laura:	It's the diary on the *Independent*, the paper you work for.
Me:	Oh, yes, of course. Are you going to get a story out of this?
Laura:	Oh, I have written my story already. What I really want to do is ask Valerie Grove if she met and married Trevor while they were on "Londoner's Diary" together. Was it the first diary wedding?
Me:	She is sitting opposite you. Ask her.
Valerie Grove:	Well, he was on the diary but I was actually a proper feature writer.

LATER, AFTER TERRY WOGAN HAS TOLD A JOKE

Berkmann:	I never thought I'd hear that one again.
Waitress:	Don't go. We haven't done the puddings yet.
Berkmann:	I think I see an unfinished bottle of red

	wine on the top table. Cover me while I go for it.
Jeremy Lewis:	Yes, I rather think I am doing a talk on Smollett in Bath on Friday.
Me:	I'll come.
Lewis:	Well, that's one in the audience.
Me:	I might bring the wife.
Lewis:	That's two!

IN THE GENTS LAVATORY

Barry Cryer:	Miles!
Me:	Barry! I want to ask you a question. Richard Ingrams sent me a book called *Almost Famous* by Bob "The Cat" Bevan. It's all about how he is a very famous after dinner speaker. But I have never heard of him. Does he exist?
Barry:	Yes. But only in the closed world of sports dinners, where he is very famous. Outside that, he has no existence, no meaning.
Me:	Thank you.
Barry:	Not at all. Does anyone else in this convenience need advice on recent books? Then I shall return to the dining hall.
Me:	Hello, George.
George Melly:	Who's that? Oh, it's you. Hello.
Berkmann:	See you at the *Spectator* party, Miles. Unless you're staying for another drink?
Me:	No, I have to get the 4.15 from Paddington.
Taxi Driver:	Paddington? Jump in, squire.

You realise that I am sending you this letter as much to remind me of the day as to remind you. But it's worth doing. I occasionally write down records of exchanges like this, and when I come across them again years later, I cannot remember having exchanged a single line of it all. How much we forget.

3
Music

Miles learnt to read music and to play the piano as a child, and although he is principally associated with the double bass and jazz, a life without access to his piano and the world of classical music would have been miserable. Miles was passionate about jazz and listened to it, studied it and played it with complete dedication from his first encounter at school. He took up the trombone and formed a jazz band, and at home, he would sit in with a local dance band.

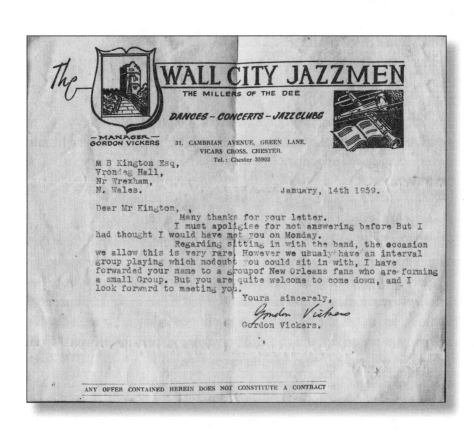

At Oxford, there being no vacancies for a trombonist, he switched to the double bass. It was in his early twenties, shortly after he had left Oxford, that Miles started his professional writing career reviewing jazz for The Times, *and as a double bass player, in 1972 he joined Instant Sunshine, a light-hearted cabaret group formed by a trio of medics, who became very popular after their debut at the Edinburgh Festival in 1975. Throughout his career he presented and reviewed a myriad of jazz musicians and programmes, on radio and television and live concerts, and compiled an anthology of jazz writing,* The Best of Jazz.

To ANGELA ASTOR[1]
June 28, 1977

Dear Angie,
    Well, here goes.

INSTANT SUNSHINE
    These four young men have . . . well, youngish men, anyway . . . these four men on the right side of 35 – all except Peter, that is, and Miles come to think of it . . . OK, these four ageing young men . . . try again.

INSTANT SUNSHINE
    "These" (*Scotsman*) "Four Young" (*Times*) "Men" (*Country Life*) have proved to be one of the most popular cabaret acts in England since Edward VII packed it in. Writing all their own material, often on the day of the show, they have become household names at 14, Upper Hitch, Carpenders Park and 51 Ladbroke Grove (garden flat, top bell). They will be performing hits from their LP unless the gramophone breaks down.

INSTANT SUNSHINE
    In 1975 they played three highly successful weeks at the Edinburgh Festival. Their two weeks' stint in the 1976 Festival was a sell-out. The demand for tickets for their week at the 1977

Festival was almost frightening. Their single day at the 1978 Edinburgh Festival could lead to national rioting unless the government steps in. ACT NOW! says the *Daily Mirror*.

INSTANT SUNSHINE

Formed fully ten years before the National Theatre and constructed entirely from old dinner jackets and guitars, Instant Sunshine have been kicking their heels for a whole decade waiting for a suitable venue on the South Bank.

Although they cost the nation £1,500,000 annually, the Minister for the Arts says: "It is money extremely well spent – I just wish I could get a receipt."

INSTANT SUNSHINE

Not a bad little band. For semi-pros, that is. OK, they need an agent and a tough choreographer. And a bit more variety. But not bad. Considering. If you like that sort of thing and I can't say I do.

To MARILYN LLOYD[2]
January 11, 1978

Dear Marilyn Lloyd,

Apart from myself, the other three members of Instant Sunshine are David Barlow, who plays guitar and spoons and sings in a deep mahogany baritone, Alan Maryon-Davis, who sings in a light veneer tenor and plays exotic percussion and does bird imitations, and Peter Christie, who has rather a nice voice and plays guitar and writes all our songs. I play the double bass.

The group started ten years ago when the other three were all medical students together, and used to put on Christmas shows for the hospital: this is known technically, I believe, as a kill-or-cure treatment. They named the trio Instant Sunshine for reasons which escaped them, and I, who was a friend of David Barlow, was asked to join the group about three years later, in the early 70s. The only regular job we have ever had was a weekly appearance at Tiddy Dols in Mayfair, an English tourist trap for rich

Americans and very good it is too; this job has now been going for about ten years, which must be some kind of record for a cabaret engagement.

Before 1975 we did a casual round of balls, minor festivals, parties and executive gatherings who couldn't or daren't hire a risque act, but in 1975 things swooped upwards when we risked three weeks at the Edinburgh Festival, where we ended up doing turnaway business on the Fringe. We went back in 1976 and 1977 and did better each year. We had hoped that this would make us world-famous, but it only made us world-famous in parts of Edinburgh. Still, over the same period we have also leaked on to radio (we have been the semi-permanent group on *Stop the Week* since 1975, have had our own show in 1977 and in 1978 have started a series on Radio 4 on Sundays at 1.40 p.m.) and TV (a long stint on a not very good Thames TV show called *Take Two*, a half hour show for STV and a slot in two series of *Oneupmanship*, the second of them now filming, always assuming the BBC isn't totally halted by strikes). In that time we have also made two LPs for EX1, the second of which ("Instant Sunshine – Funny name for a band") we are not ashamed of. But we frankly still most enjoy performing to a small audience in person, as we shall be doing for you.

The act is impossible to describe. It's a bit like Flanders and Swann, a bit like *Beyond the Fringe*, a bit like the LSO and a bit like the boring draw between Arsenal and Manchester City in 1968. We always dress in DJs even on radio – well, especially on radio actually as they can't see the stains there – and are basically four well-behaved anarchic irresponsible young English gents with a lot of good songs and some nice guitar playing. The double bass player is sensational. There is nothing wrong with us a damn good hiding wouldn't bring about and our big ambition is to be asked to appear on the Angela Rippon show, and refuse.

We also think that everyone should take their hols in England, because it's cheaper and many of the natives speak English.

We are all over six foot. In an age when not enough people pay attention to the importance of being born tall and then standing up straight, I think this is worth stressing.

As you can see, I am running out of true facts. If you want any more untrue facts, I can supply as many as you like.

yours sincerely

To THE RIGHT REVEREND, THE LORD BISHOP OF BATH & WELLS
March 7, 1979

My Lord,

This greeting seems somewhat formal, but when one has never addressed a bishop before it seems best to take cowardly refuge in the etiquette book. I write to you because I gather you came to hear our concert at Street (by our I mean Instant Sunshine's) and even came to talk to us afterwards, though I am afraid that none of us realised who you were. That sounds wrong; we wouldn't have behaved any differently, as we are always courteous until midnight, but it would have been nice to say hello personally. Oddly enough, David Barlow and I drove back through Wells the next morning and as we had never seen the cathedral at close quarters, made a frosty walking tour of the centre of Wells. A magnificent place. We were quite silenced by the splendour of it. Until we entered the cathedral and stood listening to the distant singing and said to each other more or less simultaneously: "Well, he came to see our show last night, so it's only fair we should come to see his show."

Ivan Sutton tells me that you may be coming to see us again at Exmouth. I very much hope so, even if you will be facing largely the same show, and that you might say hello to us again.

None of this is my real reason for writing; it's just that your mellifluous title got on my brain for a while and emerged as the enclosed doggerel. Nothing personal is intended; for all I know you never even touch after-shave; but having written it I thought it seemed a shame if the hero never got to see it.

yours sincerely

I am the Bishop of Bath and Wells
I wear the most delicious smells
Lime at matins, cologne at dusk
And late at night a trace of musk
For eau de cologne should never trespass
On a well-conducted vespers.
All my churches have a basin
Which I can wash my hands and face in
For great are charity, faith and hope
And greater than all of these is soap.
Before I grant my absolutions
I take the most divine ablutions
There may be other first-class preachers
But only one who smells of peaches
And leaves in every rural nave
A heavenly lingering aftershave.
Hear the organist thunder loud
And greet the sweet approaching cloud!
Hear him play as Handel would
Inspired by fragrant sandalwood
– See the conquering hero come
Smelling faintly of bay rum!
Tis I, the bishop! Magnificat!
Anointed with essence of kumquat!
Bow, ye watchers! Clear a path!
I am the Bishop of Wells and Bath.

———————

To STUART HARLEY[3]
August 8, 1979

Dear Stuart Harley,

Well, a strange letter to receive and no mistake, but strange letters are always more fun to answer than routine ones (a good lesson in life, that), so here goes.

I took up the bass because I wanted to play jazz. From the age of 8 I had played the piano; not badly, not well, but had got so used to reading music that I reckoned I would never be able to improvise on the piano. (I can just about now.) So I took up the trombone and learned to improvise, but then found that the trombone was about the hardest instrument I could have chosen. In addition, when I got to Oxford I found that an extremely fine trombonist had arrived the same time as me (his father was a brass band, or silver band, master from the Forest of Dean, so he knew most brass instruments backwards) and I realised there wouldn't be room for two of us, so I looked round for another instrument. I spotted a shortage of bass players, bought one and taught myself out of a book.

I had actually always been attracted to the bass, because of the way it moved under a jazz group, like the sea under a ship, essential but unnoticed. Very soon I found that there is a great pleasure (for me, anyway) in improvising behind other people, on the chords, without ever having to take a solo. I had never much been taken by the sound of the bowed bass, much preferring the plucked thing, so when, a week after I bought my instrument, I accidentally sat on the bow and broke it, I wasn't much bothered. I still cannot bow it, and am still not bothered, as I never play classical music on the bass. (Most of it is Rhubarb, Rhubarb.) I once had to take part in an amateur performance of a Brandenburg Concerto, and plucked the bass the whole way through. It sounded great.

I like the bass because although in classical music it is sometimes considered as a slightly elephantine and comic thing, in jazz it has had complete independence for thirty years and attained a state of free play it never has in classical music. That's listening to other people more, I suppose; for myself, I enjoy playing the bass because you're always in action without being the star; it's like being a wicket keeper in cricket or the straight man in a good double act. You can also, if you're good, make a heavy and ponderous piece of furniture move lightly and delicately.

I have called the bass it, but really it's more a sort of her.

You have to be sort of in love with the bass to understand why people play them. Beat them and they go sullen; flirt with them and they respond. At the best times you feel part of the bass and vice versa.

If you are seriously interested in the double bass, you ought to talk or write to bass players who have gone over to the electric bass guitar and find out what they gained, and lost. I could put you in touch with a couple, if you like.

I don't suppose this is quite what you wanted, but if you can make any use of it, you're welcome. If you want any more technical stuff, let me know. I might even be able to help you.

yours sincerely

———————

To CAROLINE STEPHENS[4]
March 19, 1980

Dear Miss Stephens,

Thank you for your letter. I shall enjoy Easter, knowing that the Prime Minister is listening to an all-English record, made by four all-English lads, singing words that no foreigner could possibly understand. If she hasn't got time, I hope you will listen to the record instead.

I don't know what else to say, really, except that the policeman outside your door was very nice. I've never seen anyone search a 12" LP for explosive devices before.

yours sincerely

———————

To HANS KELLER[5]
December 31, 1981

Dear Hans Keller,

I very much enjoyed meeting you at the Donats nearly a month ago. I knew I would because I have always enjoyed reading your writings, even though I also knew that talking to you would have the bracing effect of a brisk walk in a snowy wind rather than a stroll along the beach; you are not a comfortable person to talk to and thank God for that.

What you said to me then has bounced around in my skull ever since, and I hope you don't mind if I now report to you the scattered thoughts that it has provoked, especially in our glancing references to jazz. Now, I know that you are not interested in jazz and I can quite appreciate why, but I think you might be interested in why someone like me, who is (am?) thoroughly drenched in European concert music, should be drawn to jazz. More specifically, you asked me once or twice whether I did not feel that all music had a basic similarity whether improvised by a jazz musician or composed by a composer. And the answer to that, now that I have thought it over, is overwhelmingly no.

I am sure the answer lies in the fact that a music like jazz (or flamenco, pibroch music, or the blues) constitutes a language of its own. Languages tend to dictate or reflect the process of thought. A Frenchman thinks differently from an Englishman; a German-speaker from both. You yourself sometimes use English in a way which only a German-speaker could – I remember an article in which you contrasted understanding and "overstanding" in a way which would only make sense to someone who had had experience of the German language.

And jazz, for better or for worse, is a language which has to be understood on its own terms. Those terms are, I think, conversational in contrast to the literary terms of concert music. Beethoven writes; a jazz soloist talks. Now, writing endures, whereas talk fades into the air and vanishes when the talker goes home. If it were not for the fortuitous invention of the gramophone, jazz would hardly have a history and certainly no archives. As it is, the gramophone record has been a very mixed blessing for jazz; it has perpetuated, unchanged, sounds that should only have been heard once. But at least it has given a clear idea of the way jazz has arrived and changed.

And it is, I think, an example of a language which is profoundly antipathetic to your way of hearing. A composer is an architect who builds a structure, putting in all the steps without which his structure will fall down. But when a jazz musician plays a phrase, he knows what phrase the audience will expect next, so he plays a different one. The expected phrase is already present in their minds so he does not need to play it. He plays a variation on an unplayed variation.

I am sure you have had this experience with congenial conversationalists. You say something. You know the other person will say[:] Yes, but. So before he says it, you go on to the next step. Well, jazz is a bit like that. It is not an end product at all, it is a process. That is why Gershwin's idea of jazz, as you explained it, is so irrelevant or at least talking about something completely different. Anything that can be repeated faithfully as jazz is not jazz at all.

I wouldn't for one moment claim that jazz is better or worse than concert music, simply that it is very different. A jazz musician sets out to talk on a topic. That topic may be Gershwin's "The Man I Love". Often he talks balderdash, or repeats clichés he has mouthed before, or imitates previous talkers. But sometimes he is inspired and says things about "The Man I Love" which have never been thought of before and certainly not by Gershwin and never will be again. That's all.

They will never reach the height or profundity of a Beethoven Symphony, but then Beethoven will never talk in quite that way either.

You said to me at one point that a great deal of improvisation takes place in the playing of a Beethoven quartet. No doubt. But it is a completely different kind of improvisation. You would not expect when watching a West Ham game that the goals would occur at exactly the same place as the last game, even if at a different tempo. But that is how a Beethoven quartet works. (I think.) A real game of football provides an ebb and flow of action and reaction which is more like jazz. A Beethoven quartet does not allow for an inspired act of dribbling, long range shot or disobedience to the manager's strategy. Jazz does. That is what makes it fail so often and succeed so marvellously now and again.

From the way I have been talking you might imagine I thought jazz was the music of the future, but alas not; it is in the past already. Unless I am mistaken, jazz has been and gone. A language which has served its purpose and been replaced by something I find effective but cruder and duller. I feel the same about concert music, but more so. Where are the Schuberts and Mozarts and Brahms of

today? The fact that more people than ever appreciate the musical-
ity of Beethoven or Haydn is no compensation for the fact that
today has not produced another Beethoven or Haydn. Jazz is dying;
concert music is dead; all the rest is history. Well, that is not so very
bad, as it is a great time for archaeologists, and the great pulse of
history which archaeologists always ignore is still alive.

Some other day. It was very late when I wrote that last sentence
and I can not see even now what I thought I meant. But before I
send this letter off to you, and you toss it aside, or frown for a
moment over it, let me add one or two other points about jazz
which – for me – throw interesting sidelights on concert music.

The composer is not very important in jazz. There have not been
many; there have been few good ones; and none of them has influenced the music strongly, with the possible exception of Duke
Ellington. There have been no full-time composers in jazz. They
have all been players as well, and have usually written for the bands
they played in; more especially for the players in the bands they
played in. That meant when the bands changed, such composers as
Ellington and Charlie Mingus recomposed the numbers.

Jazz musicians do not on the whole write good melodies.

Even strongly melodic improvisers do not write good melodies.
That is because their style of improvising is different (more conversational again) from the style of writing melodies that very good
American songwriters used. The vast majority of songs or tunes
played by jazz musicians are non-jazz themes written by songwriters; very often it is not the themes that interest the jazz musicians as
Gershwin has done too much of the work already, the work of the
harmonic intricacy and rhythmic wit. (They prefer a simpler frame-
work, just as humorists find it hard to write about something which
is already intrinsically funny.)

Form has, if anything, become simpler through jazz's history. Jazz
of the late 1920s followed the ragtime tradition and favoured com-
positions with up to four or five different sections. Pretty simple by
concert standards, but quite tricky compared to later jazz which
simplified the average number to a single repeated 32-bar sequence.
They used that single sequence as the basis for some quite interesting structures through variations in tempo, key, mood and dynamics,

but it wasn't really architectural structure, more a sort of ebb-and-flow change.

Now, as I said before, none of this is likely to appeal to your musical ear. The sort of excellence you admire in music is the kind produced by geniuses who rise above the artistic shortcomings of any era. Jazz depends far more on the craftsman who brings his own particular variations to a language, even if they amount to no more than a new set of clichés. I think that temperamentally you are drawn to a different kind of music, and who can argue the rights or wrongs of temperament? I admire genius a great deal but I also think a world occupied by only genius is richly arid. Who wishes always to live on Everest?

I believe I've given the impression of someone who listens morning, noon and night to jazz but in fact I probably listen to more 'classical' music than anything else. My tastes are not extraordinary. I think Beethoven is a colossus (having disliked him till the age of 25). I think Mozart is over-rated but still wonderful. I prefer Schubert to all others. I think Chopin sings more beautifully than anyone. I find Liszt's music as good as anything Houdini ever did, i.e. beguilingly meretricious. I do not like opera much, because the concert style of singing (I mean the Western classical style of singing) strikes me as unnervingly artificial, much as you might find jazz saxophone maddeningly self-indulgent. (Odd how certain sounds or combinations can hit a blind nerve. String quartets I love; violin plus piano and piano duets I find hard to take.) And so on.

Yet I find myself perpetually drawn to composers who are obviously not geniuses. Weber, in his non-operatic moments. Smetana, Borodin, Bizet, Dvořák, here and there. Oddballs like Hummel and Moscheles. CPE Bach. Even, God save us, Gottschalk. And I don't think it's just because I'm attracted directly to the second-rate – I think it is also a reflection of my jazz interest in the craftsman. Weber's piano sonatas, for instance, have a different flavour from anyone else's because he had a different mind; also, sometimes, because he had trouble with his left hand and I enjoy hearing how he solved the problem.

All I am trying to say in this rambling letter, dear Hans Keller, is that while I value the ice-cool and brain-hot analysis that you bring to music, I believe it is only one approach. You have derived a great deal from music which I shall never know. But I have enjoyed music in ways which you will never appreciate.

There is nothing wrong with that. There are gulfs between cricket cognoscenti and football lovers which is not worth crossing . . . The other night I played bass in a band which Barry Fantoni got together for New Year's Eve, a peculiarly successful session. None of us, except the pianist, was professional. And yet during the five hours we played together there was a growth and unity which gave me more satisfaction than I would have got from listening to or even playing the equivalent time-value of Hayden quartets. The Haydn would be better music; ours was better music-making. You would not believe this – why should you? Neither you nor I will ever know what a flamenco guitarist gets from his music. How can we? I accept entirely your joy in Beethoven and even Schoenberg. I am sorry you cannot accept the way I feel about jazz. But of course it does not affect the way I feel at all. You are right. And I am right. They are just different kinds of rightness.

If I don't post this soon, I never shall.

One of the things about jazz that can annoy people most is the unrelenting tempo, which never varies, undergoes no rubato. It is absolutely necessary, of course, so that the infinitely varied shifts on top of the beat can take place that make the music swing. It doesn't work if the underlying beat is varying also.

Yehudi Menuhin was once asked on television by Oscar Peterson if he didn't find the unvarying beat of a jazz rhythm too constricting. On the contrary, he said; he had never felt so free in all his musical life.

I noticed today that you added a letter to the Anthony Burgess brouhaha. But you two, too, are talking different languages. You have nothing to say to each other. You are talking about different Beethovens. You, of course, are absolutely right. But he may be as well. Unfortunately the whole subject has religious overtones. I read recently a theory by a psychiatrist that religion has been replaced for many people by music, and it certainly rings true when I see people crying: No, mine is the true, the only Beethoven!

Jazz is a more modest musical language than Beethoven's tradition. I think modesty may be a quality we need more of.

You are too busy a man to bother replying to this letter, but I hope you will think about it en passant, at least to the extent of admitting that different kinds of music can be different, and radically different. I love concert music. I love jazz. Neither has much to learn from the other. What can an architect learn from a conversationalist, an actor from a footballer?

Now, back to Beethoven. Please give my regards to your wife.

yours sincerely

––––––––––––

To JOHN CHRISTOPHERSON
May 10, 1984

Dear John,

Stop writing interesting letters – I feel drawn to answer them when I should be doing something more dutiful.

Thanks for all the info on Feather, Mikado etc – I knew vaguely about *The Swing Mikado* and had forgotten all about it. I've done another tiny programme since for the World Service on odd versions of the National Anthem and wish I'd known about Carla Bley then – as you say one of the best. I did come across, though, a set of variations on "My Country Tis Of Thee" (same tune) by Charles Ives for church organ, which are wonderful – some of the harmonies are so crunchingly off it's not true, and he also turns it into a fairground organ tune. I'll look out for the Spike Hughes book. Oddly, I replaced him at *The Times* as a jazz reviewer in the 60s, though he hadn't been doing it for years – a time-lapse replacement. But he was still getting all the free jazz review LPs, and the arts editor thought it would be impolite to stop him receiving them.

That's the old-style *Times* for you.

A painter once said to me that only writers liked Magritte – painters never did. I see what he means. I like him. I also like Burra a lot. I also enjoy Melly's performances as opposed to his

84

singing – Sandy Brown said it all when he wrote that Melly was a great showman and a terrible blues singer.

I like modern jazz right enough – it's just that I started getting a migraine when everyone began imitating Coltrane in the 1960s and blowing free, and it took ten years for it to wear off. When even war heroes of mine like Stan Tracey went free, I almost gave up. But they've mostly returned to the paths of righteousness now, which suits me fine. Perhaps I can sum it up by saying that I find Bobby Wellins much more listenable than Art Themen – Themen is a fine player, but he needs editing so badly.

For me, the best time in Jazz was about 1960, when in my one big visit to New York I heard Teagarden, Ornette Coleman, Monk, Mingus, Zoot, Red Allen and Monk, and loved them all. Jazz lost its nerve slightly thereafter, with the rock onslaught, and has never quite recovered it. Don't tell anyone I think such foolish things.

My son, aged 15, has started stealing my Miles Davis records from that era. That's the kind of crime I approve of among the young.

yours sincerely

───────────

To KENNY DAVERN
December 4, 1985

Dear Kenny Davern,

Thanks a million for letting me sit in on bass at the White Hart, Bath. I have recorded all three numbers in my head and play them back quite often, and may I say that you get better every time I listen back? I don't often get to play jazz these days, so needless to say I have been walking on oxygen ever since. I have also learnt the chords of "Wrap Up Your Troubles" meanwhile, so if we ever meet again . . .

In return for the two knock-out LPs you gave me, I enclose a paperback collection of my *Times* humorous writing which has been published this week. A poor swap, but I think you might enjoy some of it. By coincidence, there is quite a large section devoted to a visit I made to Louisiana a couple of years back, including an account of the Alvin Alcorn Trio which still reads quite well. That was the last notable group I sat in with . . .

I must get out of the habit of ending paragraphs with a row of dots.

Quite by another coincidence, the piece I have written for *The Times* this Friday coming is also about jazz in a round-about way, being a frivolous suggestion for a rewrite of Shaw's *St Joan* as a portrait of a girl singer with a big band. Green Dauphin St, yet.

I would have come to hear you at the Pizza Express on Wednesday, but alas I had to be in Oxford in the evening. Hope it went well. I have taken to heart what you said about bass players and amplifications; it is something I have often thought myself, vaguely, but now I am thinking about it definitely. I'd sell my amp, if I could. Unfortunately, I never had one.

I will write to you in New York one day, partly to let you know how we're getting on here in the Third World, partly to ask you for Dick Wellstood's address. I want to tell him that even if he is giving up the piano, he has to go on writing sleeve notes, at which he is a past master. And if he has become the kind of American lawyer who sues everyone for £13m, I want to be on his good side.

OK. Time to listen to "The Man I Love" again.

yours

―――――――

To HUMPHREY CARPENTER
January 30, 1986

Dear Humphrey,

Yes, Vile Bodies' second tape was much better – like Charlie Parker and Duke Ellington, you seem to perform better in front of a live tent. Lots of nice bits of arranging and instrumental flashes of fervour. The trumpet seems to vary between wild and pretty smart, but that is no doubt some thing to do with the personnel problem you mentioned. Still not enraptured about the vocals, but I guess a big time band like yours has to have the vocal glamour. Trouble is that we white guys can do a pretty fair copy of 1930s jazz playing, but it sounds a lot more English when it comes to singing. People tend to either try and sound black (Nat Gonella, Kenny Ball etc) or come out very English – Temperance Seven, etc. In the middle is an awkward place to be. Here's an idea, though, I have occasionally heard standards sung in a foreign language, which adds a dash of exoticism to proceedings. There was a Glenn Miller radio broadcast the other day from about 1943, on which some bloke sang "All The Things You Are" in German, and sounded quite weird and good. And there's an Alex Welsh record from a Berlin concert on which one of the band sings something like "I Wish I Had A Talking Picture Of You" in German – great.

Funnily, enough, last year in Edinburgh I was living right bang opposite Jimmy Boyle's Mandela Theatre, and even went a couple of times to the midnight attraction of 1986, the Brighton Bottle Orchestra. It was a nice theatre, it was well-attended, and it's a good place to be, even if a touch far from the centre, though it's a bit brave to put on anything at midnight. What am I talking about? If it's good enough, anyone will go anywhere anytime at Festival time. Well, I've done about eight years of the Festival so, yes, I suppose I do have some advice. Get in touch any time you need it. I'm looking for an excuse to come to Oxford for the day. Phone me up and make an offer I can't bear to refuse.

"Doing the New Lowdown" is a nice tune, isn't it?

    yours

———————

To PETE KING[6]
January 22, 1989

Dear Pete,

I'm not very good at asking favours, so I don't do it very often, so I don't get much practice, so I was amazed when you said on the phone yesterday, Yes, I could just about squeeze five of you in on next Friday for Art Blakey, you bastard, But this is to say Thanks, and I am ever so grateful. And I have received assurances from all of our party that they will obey the golden rules of Ronnie Scott's Club, viz

1. Not to shout out the punchlines to Ronnie's jokes
2. To accept what the waitress brings
3. Not to die during the last number of a set
4. To accept any coat given you by the cloakroom person
5. Not to be surprised if you find people at the next table closer to you than the people you came with, and to talk to them instead if need be
6. To clap at least one bass solo during the evening

You have to remember that now I'm living in the country I'm doing my best to turn into a country yokel, because you pay less income tax and lower rates, but this does mean that you get to hear less jazz. Next weekend I have bought tickets to go and hear a band at Warminster Arts Centre with Barry Beckett and Chris McGregor aboard, and I know I'm only doing this because they've taken the trouble to come to Warminster – if I were still living in London, I'm sure I wouldn't bother, as being in London means being blasé but it's so amazing that any jazz group should visit Warminster, that I have to go. Warminster, you probably haven't even heard of. It's a sweet old town on the edge of Salisbury Plain, which suffers from having the Army nearby, testing shells and nuclear weapons nearly every day five miles away up on the Downs.

The daily timetable of Warminster goes something like this.

9 a.m.	Shops Open.
10.34	Somebody buys something.
11 a.m.	Close for lunch.
3 p.m.	Reopen. Traffic lights change. News comes through of 1964 World Cup Final result.
5 p.m.	Closedown.
6 p.m.	Soldiers arrive in Warminster for evening off! 546 pubs open and get full immediately! Fighting breaks out!
11 p.m.	Closing time, Warminster totally destroyed. All soldiers taken home in ambulance! Royal Military Architects start rebuilding Warminster.
5 a.m.	Warminster rebuilt as before.

9 a.m.   Shops open.

Etc etc. So you can see that the visit of a jazz group to Warminster is something of a sensation. There may even be dancing.

There's an old bloke I sometimes meet in Bradford on Avon who plays hot violin, aged a few hundred years, called Matt McCoomb, who occasionally drags me aside and tells me tales of jazz in London during the war, when he was starting out.

"We used to have George Shearing on gigs sometimes," he told me. "He wasn't the best pianist around, but he was available. The best pianist was . . ." (And here he named someone I have never heard of, probably dead) ". . .but if we couldn't get him we'd get George Shearing. Trouble with George was, he was mad about boogie woogie just then and he'd play it at any possible opportunity, which is a bit of a liability if you're doing a ballad."

He would say, "I suppose we'd better have George Shearing if we can't get anyone else."

He nudged me then.

"He's done very well for himself since, mark you." He nudged me again.

"But I tell you something, I still don't think much of George Shearing's playing."

You can see we get some very intellectual jazz discussions down here.

Thanks for the table next Friday, Pete. Any time you want a table for 5 in the country, you just let me know.

yours

———————

To STEVE MARTLAND
January 19, 1990

Dear Steve Martland,

Very much enjoyed your segment on the *Late Show* on post-modernist music. I suppose it was partly because my prejudices coincide with yours, but also because I think we're both right – and it was very stylishly and originally done, he said patronisingly.

I was saved from a lot of worry in the early 1960s by a book called *Serious Music – And All That Jazz* in which Henry Pleasants related how he had worked as a contemporary music critic for years till suddenly he had woken up one day and said to himself: All this music I am praising is crap. I haven't enjoyed anything for years! He went on to pin most of his faith in jazz, rock, etc . . .

At the same time I read a book called *The Business of Music* by Ernst Roth. It was the first time I had ever been invited to a book launch. Boy – was I excited! I combed my hair, brushed my shoes and read the book before going. Surprise, surprise – nobody else there had even looked at it. It was by an old Vienna émigré who had once believed in Schoenberg (and published him) and gradually come to realise that he had been sowing the seeds of a very arid and hard harvest. He could see nothing ahead in art music but intellectual senility. He could see nothing ahead in pop music but visceral rawness. Oh, for a bridge, he cried. He died soon after. I sometimes wonder if I am the only person who ever read his book. I wonder if he would feel hopeful about today's scene. Personally, I am pinning my faith on a serious, intellectual Cajun composer emerging. And there again, music for <u>forty-four accordions</u>? Still, make a great *Late Show* . . . Me, I am basically a jazz bloke and it's too late to redeem me, but I like the Reichs, Glasses, Nymans etc and aim to get into them a bit more . . . No need to answer this. And now you don't have to read Roth's or Pleasants's book.

yours

———————

To KEITH FLOYD[7]
1995

Dear Keith,

I was once rung up by a Jewish guy who wanted to fix his son's Bar Mitzvah and hire Instant Sunshine for the occasion. I have never been to a Bar Mitzvah, but it seemed an odd idea to me to get a cabaret group for a religious function, so I asked him how long he wanted us to play for.

"Four hours, maybe more."

"We have never played longer than two in our lives," I said. There was a pause.

"People like to dance longer than two hours," he said.

"We never play for dancing," I said.

There was another pause. "What do you play for?"

"We play for people to listen. They sit in seats in a theatre or after-dinner situation, and listen to the clever words we sing. After fifty minutes they usually plead for an interval. We are ready for one ourselves."

"So you don't play for dancing?"

"People would hurt themselves if they tried to dance to us."

"Or background music?"

"Would you hire Flanders and Swann for background music? Would you hire the King's Singers for not listening to?"

"I think I don't want you for my son's Bar Mitzvah."

"I think you don't."

Keith, I think you may be labouring under a similar illusion, which can only lead to disillusionment. We are a cabaret turn, and if people don't shut up and listen, we are lost. There comes a certain point in parties when people don't want to listen – after dinner, when they get rowdy and fond of liqueurs, for instance. I suspect your party might reach that point quite early on. I think you think we are a jazz band. We're not. I could get you a jazz band, but it wouldn't be Instant Sunshine. You could get one from your way, I'm sure. Much though I'd love to be an integral part of your July 14, I'd hate to sabotage it . . .

To DAVID BARLOW
January 15, 1997

Dear David,

I am sending you a letter to wish you all the very best for your QEH [Queen Elizabeth's Hall] gig because it is cheaper than sending you flowers and also because, if you wish to mention me at all, you might care to read out this heartfelt tribute from me to the group.

"I would just like to say that I very often look back on the twenty irreplaceable years spent with the group and ask myself the old, old question: when am I going to get paid? Not many people are privileged to spend twenty years in the company of three top doctors, and nor was I, nor can I honestly explain how it was I came to leave the group. It was all, if you remember, to do with some business about fraudulently prescribing drugs, and it was all very patiently investigated by the BMA. What I still do not understand is how it was that the only non-doctor in the group was the only one to be struck off and I had to leave.

"Well, a lot of water has passed since then, as you know I have forged a new career out here in New South Wales, where I play double bass with three singing and banjo-playing urologists called You Find Your Own Kangaroo, Mate! I have now been with them for four happy years. I haven't been paid yet, but these are early days. I did have a reminder of the old times recently when after a concert a man came up to me and said, 'You won't remember, me, Kington, but I'm a friend of Barlow's, an old Tommy's man, you couldn't lend me twenty quid, could you?' I could, as it happens, but in memory of Instant Sunshine I pretended otherwise.

"Good luck tonight, and if there's any money left over after the drinking, remember your old chum."

Go on, I dare you.

love

―――――――

To RUSSELL DAVIES
May 10, 1999

Dear Dai,

I must write and tell you before your fifty-two weeks are up how much I'm enjoying *Jazz Century*. It's absolutely wonderful. I haven't done much thinking about jazz for years, but what you say forces

me to work out my ideas about the music all over again, reinforc-
ing some prejudices and shaking up others. Better still, I think of
new things or old things I hadn't thought of for years. When you
were talking about triplets the other day, I remembered Chris
Barber once saying to me that if the group had a whole bar's rest
in a very slow number ("Snag It", he was thinking of, I think) it
was much easier to count accurately if you tapped off a triplet
to each silent crotchet rather than just tapped a very slow four.
Nothing to do with what you were talking about, but good advice
all the same.

And so many records you play that I didn't know about. I knew
it all once. Now I don't know nothing. But mostly I like even more
what you say. It's all very wise. You don't hear much wise radio.
Dave Gelly used to sound wise on Radio 2. Maybe that's why he
doesn't appear there any more.

One thing. I was delighted to hear Cassino Simpson the other day;
partly because I first heard him with Omer Simeon playing some
lovely stuff in the late 1920s and partly because I actually have an
LP of some piano solos he recorded INSIDE the mental institute in
Elgin, Illinois, in about 1940. It must be quite rare because I once
requested it on *Jazz Record Requests* and they hadn't got it in the
BBC Library. Any interest in hearing it? Or have you got everything? If you have never heard it, it's good stuff and some of it
quite wild.

Have you finished doing the series yet? Or, like all journalists, are
you a week ahead of delivery?

Incidentally, I traced your address via Humphrey Carpenter and
Emma Kingsley. I can't say I am sorry or glad about your move
from Cambridge to London because I have never known anything
about your private life at all, but I hope it all works out. See you
one day.

yours

To ANDRÉ PREVIN
August 13, 2001

Dear André,

This is another episode in what must be one of the most scattered correspondences ever.

Ten or twenty years ago I got a postcard out of the blue from you, saying in effect that you had finally played through Clementi's Sonatas, and they weren't worth it.

Having a sneaking suspicion that you were right, and that just when you think Clementi is going to do something good, he spoils it all. I never answered your postcard, not least because you skilfully left no address on it.

(You should always have had a sneaking sympathy for Muzio Clementi on at least one count, i.e. that he like you was forced as a boy to be uprooted from one country to another. I have never quite understood the reasons for it, but when he was about fourteen he was more or less bought from his family in Rome by an English squire called Peter Beckford and transplanted to the depths of Dorset in England . . . Strange episode . . .)

However, as I have never quite abandoned Clementi to obscurity, I am trying one last suggestion. Out of curiosity, I once bought a book which offered a selection of his instructional pieces called *Gradus ad Pamassum*. Most of them are pretty dry and mechanical, and not playable by me, but one of them develops in a way which tickled me as being a bit swinging in its own way, so I thought the least I could do was photocopy it and send it to you. The first twenty bars just play around with a five finger idea, but after that, just for twenty bars or so, it really seems to come alight for a moment.

I look forward to receiving your dissenting postcard. Either way I shall never refer you to the man again.

I note occasionally that you are moving effortlessly into a boyish old age. I surprised myself in 1987 by marrying again and having another child and moving to the country, and embracing mud and water instead of tarmac and brick.

Although people occasionally say to me that if only I'd accepted all the offers I'd got, I could be famous and on TV every night, I much prefer the way I live.

Hope this gets to you all right. I'll be in touch again about AD 2010.

yours

"from the man who finally gets round to answering your letters just when you'd given up all hope . . ."

———————

Email to TIM JOSS[8]
May 25, 2003

Dear Tim,

I never acknowledged your previous e-mail, which followed up my idle inquiry as to whether there were any people in music history known solely for being dedicatees. Holberg is the obvious example. Nobody knows any plays written by Holberg. He only survives through Grieg. Some of your suggestions were good – Haffner, Rasumovsky, Waldstein – but Sylvie and Lile Marlene don't really count. They're fictional. Elise MIGHT count. But I have a horrible feeling I am up a small diminishing side stream. What I need is names like the Rokeby Venus. Everyone knows who Venus was BUT WHO WAS ROKEBY?

Don't even think about it any more. I'm not.

That was a very instructive experience for me, at the Greek clarinet thing the other night, me being the only person I met who wasn't bowled over by it. You, Nod, Lucy, Caroline – all deeply impressed. I was deeply impressed by your being deeply impressed. Trouble was, I was keyed up for something like the Bulgarian bands I had heard, playing very complex stuff, very dance-like, very sparkling. The Greek stuff was very simple and dirge-like by comparison. Wedding band? Funeral band, more like. Also, when Lucy Duran said how wonderful the polyphony was going to be, I expected lots of different lines weaving in and out of each other, which is what I reckon polyphony should be. I didn't hear that. I hear more polyphony when I am playing with my trad jazz band.

Don't get me wrong. I am not asking for my money back. What I heard was actually quite impressive. But what I heard was a Greek singing group doing some quite doleful songs with bits of violin and clarinet here and there. If you were not told who the leader was, you would find it hard to believe it was the clarinettist. You'd think it was the bank-manager-looking singer. And it was very heavy music that I heard. I think you all heard the music you were TOLD you were going to hear. For instance, it was shameful the way the tambourine player milked the audience for an ovation for doing very little . . .

I think it is quite funny that I should be out on a limb on this one. I don't mind, though. I like being out there.

———————

To ANTHONY THWAITE[9]
September, 2003

Dear Anthony Thwaite,

What a pleasant surprise to hear from a distinguished person on such a minor matter. And you can be sure that if a d.p. writes a letter like that, he is bound to be right, and I am sure that Larkin was a tiny drummer. I still maintain however that it was a most unsuitable instrument for him. Which may be why he didn't persevere. I myself tried the piano and the trombone before I ended up with the instrument that suited me: the double bass. Whereas all drummers are extroverts, all bass players are quiet, serene, unassuming, happy, contented, saintlike and extremely annoying people. I think that just about sums me up.

I think also that I was unkind to call Larkin's opinions "predictable or frightened". What I think happens in jazz appreciation is that after a while you get to a natural cut-off point in the development of the music, following which you don't appreciate the further ramifications so much. I certainly found this during my stint as a reviewer. All the free jazz stuff in the 1960s I couldn't stand. Didn't like Coltrane much. Got fed up to the back teeth with fusion music in the 1970s and with the way that Miles Davis was going. But to my enormous surprise jazz started back-pedalling a bit in the 1980s and 1990s and now, when all that forward-looking free jazz sounds a bit old-fashioned, a lot of the younger guys are doing much more traditional things and not thinking it's unnatural. I am enjoying new jazz a lot more now than I ever did, for the shameful reason that it's not as modern as it used to be. I think Larkin might have too. Even though his cut-off point was a lot earlier than mine. I don't think he ever really enjoyed much that was post-1940, so he must have had bad moments when he was sent all that modern stuff.

You probably can't stand jazz or are bored witless by it, like most people, so I'll shut up. Incidentally, I have a tiny spot in the Larkin story. I once got him to write a book review for *Punch*, of a Cole Porter book. I came across a reference to it once, in his letters, something like "I'd love to come but I'm busy with a blasted book review for *Punch*" or something like that.

I expect you're all fed up with Larkiniana by now. What are you on to now? I see from the map (I'm also a map bore) that you live on the Diss–Norwich road, which is not so terribly far from where my daughter has moved to – a village called Hopton in the flatlands a few miles south-east of Thetford. When she comes here, she thinks we live in the mountains, and when I've visited her, I do too.

Very nice to hear from you. I was much cheered by your nice remarks about the column. I never get any feedback from the paper, so I depend on readers for my ego-boost. (One day, after I'd sent in what I thought was quite a funny piece for the paper, I said shyly to one of the subs who'd rung me up: "What did you think of today's piece?" "Fine!" he said. "Fitted perfectly.")

yours sincerely

To IAN CARR
March 16, 2004

Dear Ian,

Greetings! Our paths have drifted apart over the years, though I hear you and read you and listen to you with pleasure whenever I get the chance, and indeed the reason I am writing to you now springs from something you wrote in your Keith Jarrett book.

It's about the obscure pianist John Coates Jr. I came across this guy about ten years ago on some obscure label I found when in Canada. It was a solo album recorded badly on a bad piano at the Deerhead Inn (is that right? I'm quoting from memory) but which I thought was refreshingly different from most modern pianists. I have come across one or two more by him, Japanese imports usually, and accumulated them. I have never heard him mentioned on British radio or met anyone who liked or disliked him, so I was taken aback when I found him given passing treatment in your book, but in very curious terms. It was almost as if Jarrett was saying, through you, "Hey, people say I copied this guy Coates but I didn't, so forget it! And forget him!" It is true that there are points of overlap between their styles, but I think I could tell them easily apart, so I am not sure where the note of worry came from.

I remember thinking when I read that bit of your book, years ago, "I must ask Ian if I ever see him again if there was more to it than meets the eye, like some terrible vendetta between Jarrett and Coates," but as I never run into you, I never did. On an impulse I suddenly have, after all these years. I rang up Jazz Services and said I was a mighty important journalist and they should give me your address, and blow me down, they did. So much for security. Mark you, I HAVE NOT GIVEN YOUR ADDRESS TO ANYONE ELSE. But there again, no-one has asked me for it.

As you can see from my rural address, I have been cut off from the lifeline of London jazz for many a year, but the good air of the country more or less makes up for it. I beaver away at being a humorous columnist for the *Independent*, wondering if I will ever get a proper job, and knowing that I would turn it down if I was offered one. I am married a second time and have a 16 yr old son by that marriage, which keeps me young and active. It seems to keep him young and indolent. Should be the other way round.

Are you well and happy? I stumbled across an unofficial web site of yours on the Internet which said that Nucleus was getting together again. True? I'll help reform the Nucleus audience and come and see you.

I can't remember if you ever knew Nigel Stanger, from Newcastle, who was a great mate of mine and died a few years back. It's extraordinary how when we were young we used to scoff at old people who looked at the obits every day, and now even Neil Ardley is not immune. I sometimes think of Ronnie Scott's advice on staying young ("Mix with older people") and wonder where I am to find these older people.

To STEVE VOCE
March 17, 2004

Dear Steve,

I should have known better than to write a disobliging piece about Glenn Miller. It never pays off to disoblige. Noblesse ne des-oblige pas. Not only did I get your letter about Woody, I also got ticked off by Nat Peck in a published letter for misquoting him about his days with Glenn Miller. Fairly, in both cases. Not so fairly in yours, as I was only trying to suggest that Woody Herman was not a star soloist in his band, not that he was a lame duck . . . But I think it is quite true what I said about bandleaders often being the least remarkable musician on show in the band. Some didn't even play (Lunceford, Andy Kirk) and some of course were leaders because they were star soloists, but when you think of bands led by Eddie Condon, and John Kirby, and Fletcher Henderson, and Stan Kenton, and Ted Lewis, and maybe even Ken Colyer – well, I think that they were leaders because they were good leaders, not great players.

The nearest I have been to your neck of the woods in 1,000 years was when I was dragged up last year to Blackpool by Scottish cous-ins who had become hooked on the Autumn Jazz Party run there by the Barrons. Were you lurking thereabouts? I had never seen a lot of these guys in the flesh before – Dick Hyman, Marty Grosz, Randy Sandke, etc – and most were pretty good. Dick Hyman is amazing, but he was in his tour-of-the-world mindset – bit of Tatum, bit of James P – and never quite settled down to being himself. Hyman did a duo session with Roy Williams, which Williams would have sparkled in some years ago, but this time round he sounded as if he had lost it. I hope I am wrong.

The last live jazz I saw was the Esbjörn Svensson Trio in Bristol. Bit of a knock-out. I wish I had gone to see Richard Galliano last week, though. Do you know his stuff? Have you noticed that the accordion is creeping back into the modern end of jazz? Extraordinary.

We have the Bath Jazz Festival coming up in May, or at least the jazz part of the Bath Music Festival. The music is all booked by a guy called Nod Knowles, who is very good, and convinced that European jazz is alive and very good (and cheaper than American musicians) so come every festival we have a great battle between his pro-European troops and the "Dear Sir, Jazz is an American music – where are the Americans?" brigade. Last year he had an Italian clarinettist called Gian-Luigi Trovesi, who was wonderful, and this year sees the return of John Rae's Celtic Feet who I also think are great. It's nice to know that my arteries haven't totally seized up yet.

I also still play double bass in a band now and then. But fun though it is to play with, I would never recommend anyone to listen to it.

Finally, I am sorry that you say Mr Fergusson has 50 obits still queuing up to get in. I have to try to get my late father-in-law in as well. My heart sinks.

cheers

———————

To DICK HYMAN
January 16, 2007

Dear Mr Hyman,
Thanks you for your letter about my pieces on your playing in

the *Independent*, receiving which was the most pleasant and unexpected thing to happen to me all year. I know it is only January 16th, and that if it turns out to be the highpoint of my year I shall have had a fairly low key 2007, but it's a good way to start.

Many years ago I used to be the regular jazz reviewer for the London *Times*, but I gave up in 1980 when I ran out of adjectives. The final straw was when I went, in some trepidation, to review a Cecil Taylor concert and fell asleep in the middle. I knew then that I had been doing it too long and it was time to get back to real life.

But I do remember that when you give people good reviews, they very rarely write and say thanks (but why should they?) so your letter was like a ray of sunshine.

The odd thing was that my real writing job has always been as a humorous writer. I worked on the staff of *Punch* for a long time, where I once met Paul Desmond and persuaded him to write a piece for the magazine which, I believe, is the only chapter of his projected autobiography that he ever got down on paper. My only claim to fame in jazz history.

I also once got a letter from Norman Granz, but not about my jazz stuff – it was about my humorous column, which he liked very much. Amazing. I sent him back a friendly letter, and the next time he was in Britain, he invited me to come round and see him at the Festival Hall. I found him in a huge dressing room all alone with Oscar Peterson. We shook hands all round, I asked Oscar Peterson if he still got nervous before the big event and a little later I left. I can't remember anything Granz said – I was only very conscious that not too long before I had written a rather sniffy review of Oscar, saying that an evening's exposure to his non-stop piano playing was rather like getting in the ring for ten rounds with some relentless heavyweight. If he had read it, and harboured a grudge, I was half prepared for him to get up and take a swing at me. If he had I would have fallen like a log, come round and said: "See what I mean?"

I tell a lie. I have just remembered one story Granz told me.

It was about André Previn. He was making an album with Previn, I think, backing Dinah Shore singing. Anyway, he said that Previn was playing very restrained and tasteful backings, somewhat out of character, when suddenly on one tune he started getting very florid and rococo. Granz looked round, startled, and realised that some famous pianist (it may have been Peterson himself) had just come in the studio and Previn was going into show-off mode.

This letter has been all about me. It should have been about you. But you know what I think about you from those pieces. We did meet, once, when you were at Blackpool. I was with my Scottish cousin, a big chap in kilt and huge grey beard. We sat at the same dinner table one night, and I couldn't think of a single intelligent question to ask you. So you were spared.

Thanks so much for writing. Don't ever stop. Playing, I mean.

    yours sincerely

4

Broadcaster

In 1976 Miles gave a talk on Radio 3 about Alphonse Allais, a nineteenth-century French humorist. This marked the start of a prolific broadcasting career in radio and television. His easy-going conversational style, his ability to talk with interest to anyone, whether they spoke the same language or not, meant that he became much sought after by producers. Had Miles chosen to do so, he could have sidestepped from his career in writing and made a very successful one as a broadcaster.

To JOHN HOWARTH[1]
August 20, 1980

Dear John,

My old mate. How are things? I am finding it hard to write without you at my shoulder ("Why don't we have Llama[2] falling out of a helicopter? Come to that, Miles, why don't we have you falling out of one?") and I hope you are finding it hard to film without my words of encouragement ("No, you bloody well can't have a seconds of pudding"). I reckon Peru was a grand old adventure, and I suppose I should have written a book about it by now. Come to think, I'm meant to have written a book; or at least one-seventh, because the BBC wants all seven writers to collaborate on a Great Railway Scripts of the World thing. I've asked for extra appearance money for Llama, and they're going to let me know.

Some of the pictures I took with my typewriter have come out and as some of them include you I am ~~throwing them away~~ sending them on to you. In fact, the ones of you and Roy seem quite good in places. I've sent him the good ones.

I also got round to getting down the Bolivian bit in print, though they cut a lot of it, and in case you didn't see it, I just happen to have a copy by me which I enclose.

I'm finding it hard getting back in the group, mainly because of this other bass player they've hired, but I've got out my book of Scott Joplin rags and am working several up on the piano. Next time we meet I shall hire a piano and murder them for you. Don't forget, either, that I took seriously your threat to ask us up to Basford Hall. The children are longing to see the secret passage. Let's wait till the weather turns nasty.

yours

———————

To EDUARDO VERA C.
September 5, 1980

Dear Eduardo,

Thanks for the card (great picture) and all the news you sent.

What news? Well, no news, except that you wanted to hear from me, so to show that I have not forgotten you, I am writing this letter. In English, I am afraid, because to write it in Spanish would take longer than the train from Cuzco to Puno.

Life in England has seemed rather ordinary after Peru. I've spent most of the time on holiday with the family, or doing a bit of sailing. But at least it's warm and we have had no revolutions or military take-overs; not yet. Unemployment here has now reached 12%, which I think is the worst since the 1930s, but on the other hand that means 88% employment, which seems pretty good. Our most exciting time after we left Cuzco was arriving in Bolivia the day of the "golpe", and getting mixed up in lots of road barricades, shooting, curfews etc. I wrote about it for *Punch*, and here it is for you to read. In English again. Sorry.

I've seen a lot of the film (there's about twelve hours of it, eleven to be cut out) but the one bit I haven't seen yet is the fantastic scene in the picantería where this fantastic Peruvian (only he's really a Uruguayan) steals all the attention. Either we'll make it the star sequence of the film, then get you over to appear in your own show.

Or we'll leave it out. Some of the film of Cuzco and Macchu Picchu is really very good. Not as impressive as you, though.

Give my regards to President Belaúnde. I hope he is doing all right. And have a pisco sour on me at the Abraxus. You can send me the bill.

    yours

To MONICA SIMS[3]
January 19, 1982

Dear Monica,

As Simon Elmes has probably told you, I have asked to be dropped from the Monday morning team of archivists, and as you have once or twice said you enjoyed my stuff, I felt I should write to tell you why.[4]

The over-riding reason is lack of time, coupled with a slight feeling of staleness. To do one of these quarter hours properly takes a full three or four days, at least, and with all the commitments I have at the moment I found I was being forced to cut corners slightly, which left me unhappy. You'd think that with practice it would take less time, not more, but after three or four years it's harder to work round the good stuff which you've used before, and takes longer to delve into untrodden parts of the archives. Being honest with myself, I just didn't have the time to do it as thoroughly as I would like.

The staleness comes, I suppose, from dealing repeatedly with the same format, and I found by the end that though I enjoyed the actual listening, tucked away in an archives booth, as much as ever, I found the scripting and packaging getting increasingly irksome. This was something to do, too, with the expectation that that spot should be jokey. It seems odd for a humorist to object to jokiness, but I think there is so much of interest in the archives, of all flavours, that to restrict one's self to a bright Monday morning undemanding banter instead of letting the extracts do it for you is hard work, and not always the best approach.

I do like working for radio very much – much more than TV – so I suppose in a way it's better that I should get away from the archive spot in order to come back some other way, if the chance ever arises.

I must also place on record my gratitude to Simon Elmes, who has taught me a great deal about broadcasting and who was very patient when I turned my scripts in late. I have sent him a copy of this letter, by the way.

yours sincerely

———————

To CLARE[5]
January 24, 1982

Dear Clare,

Thanks for your (nice) card. Of course you did most of the work, and dug up the interesting stuff that made it work, but thanks anyway.

It was pretty instructive for me to see my to-camera piece, because I realised when I saw it that that isn't the way I should do it. My daughter, who watched it with me said: "You usually have smiley eyes but on TV they are sort of cold and dead." Like, the Jack the Ripper of BBC 2. I know what she means – I was sort of giving a picture instead of communicating, thinking that being casual would be informal, whereas it wasn't. (This is just nit-picking; the spot was basically fine, eyes apart.)

A cameraman of my acquaintance who saw the programme said he would probably have shot my face from not so low down, and not done the occasional zoom in, which is interesting, as I think it did make me look as if I was pontificating too much. Much more interesting, though, was watching *Nationwide* the other day with no sound; I suddenly realised that all those pros are constantly moving and gesturing the whole time, their features working and acting out. If you look at it consciously, it seems odd, but must work. As I write this letter, I am waving my arms all over the place.

I wouldn't be pondering on this if I didn't have the *Film* prog coming up; obviously I want to make a good showing, i.e. not make an idiot of myself, and I must rush to get in touch with Barry Brown to do a bit of a work-out with autocue.

I wonder if anyone ever dispenses with autocue and learns their script?

I think I'll start practising in the mirror in the mornings when shaving. Normally I devote this time to trying on new moustaches. You know – you leave the shaving cream around your mouth till last, then carve it into the shape of, say, Sean Connery's whiskers and say: "If you so much as lay a finger on that girl, Mr Goldfinger, this island will be wiped out by nuclear weapons." Actually, I've got quite good at Connery's accent now (mid-Atlantic, with a tinge of Edinburgh).

Actually, maybe I'll try presenting the *Film 82* in his accent. Be different anyway.

Thanks for all your help and beavering around. You were great fun to work with.

     yours

To SUE FREATHY[6]
April 11, 1982

Dear Sue,

It is inexcusably rude of me not to have answered your letter of Feb 1 before today, which gives you some idea of what a rotten client I'd be. It's probably the nicest letter I've ever had about TV face – I mean, a letter from an admiring viewer in Newton Abbot is nice (to choose at random one of the five towns in Britain I've had letters from), but to get a letter from an agent . . .

However. There are two inhibiting factors. One is that I am sort of affianced on a literary level to Anthony Sheil, who also have a telly department who I guess would handle my comings and goings on the box. Not as efficiently as you, but enough for the purposes of my TV career which, to pass to factor No 2, I am a bit uncaring about. Even if they offer me *Film 82*, and they seem to be trembling on the verge of doing so, I doubt very much if I'd take it. I used to say, it would be easy to turn down such an offer. Now I feel it would be crazy to take it. I think I could actually do it quite well, and I'm objective enough to see that with a bit of tutoring I could probably be quite a good telly person, but for all sorts of reasons I don't want to be. I don't want to be recognised in shops. I don't enjoy doing TV particularly (don't hate it either, just find it a bit wearisome). I don't watch TV much – never, to tell the truth, saw Barry doing the film programme, so it doesn't mean too much to me. On the other hand, I love writing and like the smell of print, I'd rather be my own master on a small scale than a TV puppet on a big one.

This probably means I'll never be rich and famous. Pity. I'd like to have been rich and famous, just for a week. But that's impossible with TV. Trouble is, I guess, I'm a bit old-fashioned and puritan.

One day I'll no doubt regret being so high-minded, but not now. Meanwhile, I think I'll get your letter framed.

yours

———————

To ROGER LAUGHTON[7]
Spring/Summer 1982

Dear Roger,

At the risk of endangering a beautiful friendship, I have to write and tell you that were you to be serious in your offer of a stint with *Film 82*, I don't feel I can take up the offer.

The main reason for this is that it would involve working from next September through well into the spring (April, I think you said) and on reflection this really doesn't fit into what I have to do already. It could, more or less, co-exist with my *Times* pieces. It couldn't co-exist with a book I have agreed to do by next July, or with my other regular commitments. It would bugger up a trip which Instant Sunshine is planning (has planned) to New York in

October, for three weeks. And it would tie me down too much for anything else that might pop up.

Now, obviously all these things could be worked around some-how. The publisher would agree to the publication date being postponed. The group might gracefully postpone the NY trip for the sake of my chance of stardom, etc. But all this would only be worth doing if I really, really wanted to do the programme, and I have one or two doubts about that.

1. You said that *Film 82* is an exercise in journalism, that I am a journalist, etc. Yes, but I am not really that kind of journalist. I enjoy thinking on my feet, creating little humorous corners of the world, making little armed raids on idiocy or perhaps sanity, being anyway uncommitted. Even when I've been on TV, it's always been as a guest, an odd figure, not a telly person. I feel that going on *Film 82* would mean a change of direction, and not one I'm ready for.

2. The time. Barry Norman "had got it down to" three days and a couple of evenings. As someone in the office said, that means he had Thursday, Friday, Saturday and Sunday to himself. Hmm, I expect to have Saturday and Sunday to myself. What it really means is that I might have two days a week to myself. That's not enough; not to keep writing, that is.

3. Psychologically, I don't think I'm ready. Two years ago I went freelance in all sorts of ways. I left *Punch* after twelve years. Sally left me after seventeen and I suddenly stopped being desk-bound, wife-bound, whatever-bound. (Your sending me to Peru was the biggest catalyst for all that, and I want to say thanks again.) But *Film 82* would mean going back to a desk, getting married again. I don't really want to, deep down.

4. Three weeks on *Film 82*, though absorbing, I found a hard grind. It's not going to be a less grind over six or eight months.

5. Without wanting to get involved in an argument about TV with you, I really am not committed to the medium yet, as you would like me to be. For instance, you may not believe this, but when somebody said to me right at the start that I shouldn't try to copy Barry Norman's approach, I had the perfect answer (which

I was too cowardly to give). There was no way I could copy him, as I'd never seen him doing the programme. I haven't even seen him do *Omnibus* yet.

It's a shame in lots of ways. The money I expect would have been a fortune. The people in the office are all smashing to work with. People quite seemed to like me. And I fear you will think I'm letting you down dreadfully. Even so, I think I am doing the right thing.

I wish I could explain myself better.

But I know I'm right.

Speak to me, Rog.

––––––––––

To SIMON ELMES[8]
December 23, 1982

Dear Simon,

This will come as a shock to you, I am afraid, but I really can't go on with the archives, at least not for a while. You know I expressed strong doubts last summer, then agreed to come back for an autumn stint. Well, my doubts are much stronger now. The law of diminishing returns has set in and I find it harder and harder to get a programme together. The store of directly comic material in the archives gets more difficult to find, and I don't like Ebdon's and Worsnip's tactics of making stuff seem funny by setting up jokey intros. My own bent, as you know, is not necessarily to make the archive quarter hours funny, but that seems to be what's wanted.

There is another problem which is simply that I have been trying to do too much recently and I must cut down if I am not to go round the bend. The archives programmes take more of my time proportionately, as regards end product and money earned, than anything else. And it should take even more than it does – I should spend at least a day more, longer perhaps, than I do at present, rooting around listening, but I simply haven't got that sort of time at the moment.

I shall miss the listening, but I won't miss the script-writing or recording, which is getting harder and harder.

I fear this may put you in a quandary, though not an insoluble one, but you have probably sensed that I am not happy at the moment, and I really think it's the best thing. Honestly, I find my heart sinking at the thought of another archives session at the moment, and that's no way to approach anything. I really mean this.

yours

———————

To ALAN HART[9]
April 16, 1984

Dear Mr Hart,

I gather that it was at your suggestion that I was approached by Martin Everard of "Presentation" about the possibility of doing a pilot programme of a weekly digest of BBC-TV output; as I had turned down the idea, I thought it was only polite to write and say briefly why I had decided to kick fame in the teeth.

In a sentence, it sounded a good idea, but not for me. I might be wrong, but I felt it needed a more sober and statesmanlike presence than I would want to offer, a bit too closely identified with the BBC. If I'm known for anything at all, it's for being mildly off-beat and I'd like to stick to that.

I think, for example, that if ever I got involved in a chat show (I'm going to float a couple of ideas here, which you can keep carefully filed in your wastepaper basket), it would be nice to try something different. In my twelve years at *Punch* (dear God, was it really twelve?) I rubbed shoulders with a lot of humorists, cartoonists and comedians, and realised then that the one thing they weren't very good at talking about or even cared to talk about was humour. And yet whenever funny men appear on chat shows, they are summoned to talk about humour. (Not true, actually, of Clive James, who has a better idea of how to handle funny people.) They should be asked to talk about anything but humour; then they might be funny.

Some of them will always be deadly serious – John Cleese always is. I'd be tempted, if ever there were a show featuring only funny people; to call it *The Sad, Sad Show*.

Even more predictably, guests on chat shows are always asked to talk about the thing they're famous for, which is the one thing they are sick of. Oh, they've always worked out a good set of stock responses, but there's more to life than routine. The odd thing is that many celebrities have a pet interest which they're seldom asked to talk about, and on which they might be much better value. I remember that Warren Mitchell is a keen jazz clarinettist as indeed is Woody Allen. Spike Milligan likewise blows a lusty if slightly out of tune trumpet. Terry Jones is nuts about medieval studies.

Kenneth Lo, the Chinese cookery expert, is nuts about tennis – he played for the China Davis Cup team in 1936 and still wins the Aged Veterans Cup at Wimbledon. I think there's a good seed-bed here for a show called something like *Second Strings*.

And, though only as a one-off, it would be fun to do a programme which took snippets of chat shows, political discussions and actually analysed the way people reacted under questioning. How politicians evaded the issue. What they did when they didn't know the answer. How celebrities steered the talk back to home ground. How they always told the same stories whenever they appeared. How a long sentence could be boiled down to a meaning of five words.

Well, there are a few ideas. Actually, since I started this letter I have been rung up by someone called Laurence Rees of Documentaries who is thinking of getting me to present a series based on how foreign TV sees Britain, which sounds much more my kind of line. So you can easily disregard this whole letter. But having written it, I'm damned if I'll not send it. Thanks for thinking of me in the first place.

yours sincerely

To KEITH FLOYD
November 27, 1985

Dear Keith,

Well, I watched your sprat, scallop and bass programme finally tonight and I thought it worked a treat. Your no nonsense approach, rather like a conductor chatting with the orchestra all through Beethoven, is amazingly refreshing, especially as you can tell you're not doing it aforethought, but flying by the skin of your pants. There are rough edges here and there, and I think they add to it. It was also, which I think is even more important, the only cookery programme I've watched after which I could remember every detail of the cooking process. Nearly. Only criticism is that we never did learn what Rick thought of nouvelle cuisine. I couldn't make out if it was because he was being too tactful or if you didn't give him a chance. Neither, probably. You should be a star.

Well, you are a star, but more people should know about it.

I had a great evening after I left you on the train. I was going to see a New York clarinettist called Kenny Davern who unaccountably was playing at the pub just down the road. He asked me to sit in on bass for three numbers, and it went well. Just as I left the stand he hissed: "Wish you were the bass player tonight, not the other guy." I've been walking on oxygen ever since.

I'll be in touch about lunch. Meanwhile, I hope you take over the *Wogan* programme all right.

yours

———————

To GILLIAN HUSH[10]
February 9, 1987

Dear Gillian Hush,

I was just listening, not ten minutes ago, to your and Phil Smith's programme on Lancashire lorry drivers, and just wanted to say how great it was. Lovely reflective voices, measured story-telling, quirky little insights, bits of unabashed poetry – wonderful. And none of

117

the frills that people so often put in – music, sound effects, voice overs, explanations. Just people talking about what they're doing and talking really well and somebody doing a good editing job too.

I am engaged at the moment in going out to Burma to do the script for a film for the BBC – one of their Great Journeys of the Whatsit – on the Burma Road, and I can distinctly remember saying to the producer on our recce, as we reclined in some buffalo-infested dive, that what we should be making films about today is the real routes of the world, the lorry routes. I have seen with my own eyes the route from Amman down to the Red Sea, a regimental trooping of lorries across an empty desert. I know a bloke who has just driven across the Sahara and there again, he says, there is a main road lined with burnt out trucks, discarded tyres and bric-a-brac. The other day there was a horrendous crash on a motorway through Yugoslavia which apparently is known locally as Death Road and which also links Europe with the Middle East . . . That's where the action is today, that's the modern equivalent of the Silk Route or whatever. Don't you think our film is a little irrelevant? I said. After all, there is no Burma Road today. The border to China is closed.

Maybe, he said, but what people like to see is the picturesque, the old-fashioned, the last steam that or the horse-drawn this.

I'm glad you ignored his advice and went for the real roads.

Don't get me wrong. I'm quite enjoying the idea of going out to Burma. But I think we'll be lucky to get anywhere near as good a programme as yours was. When people say how much better radio is than TV, it's programmes like yours they're thinking of.

yours sincerely

———————

To JULIAN HALE
July 8, 1988

Dear Julian Hale
I should never get involved in the briefest correspondence about

taste in humour, especially with an experienced producer like you – the BBC can bat all day without giving away a wicket. One favourite device is saying that there is no accounting for humour and another is producing a letter from someone who loved the show, both of which you did. (A third is saying, "which proves we're setting it about right". I bet you were tempted.) So I shouldn't even write back. But I am. Partly to say that all forms of humour are valid but they are not always apposite and I think Phil Smith, Glyn Worsnip and even John Ebdon used inapposite humour for their archives slot. In Glyn's case, it usually took the form of a remorseless succession of puns – I can remember him saying, after a discussion on bulls, "Well, that beefed up the conversation a bit." In John Ebdon's case it often depended on taking things out of context. I can remember him saying a propos of a goldsmith who was making gold taps and gold baths. "Well, what about the toilet, then?" and the goldsmith saying immediately: "Oh, we keep that in the safe and bring it out when we need it." Ha ha. Except that by chance I had been listening to that very record in the Archives the week before, and the goldsmith was talking about something quite different, and quite interesting. But Ebdon preferred the cheap laugh.

That is what I meant by Phil Smith saying that working in the BBC was rather like being in some terrible solitary confinement prison which a genuine prisoner had just been describing. He was diminishing that bloke's experience. If you had a news item about 190 people being burnt to death on a North Sea platform, and Phil Smith said "Yes, my sausages usually end up like that", would you think it was funny? It's exactly the same joke formula. What I'm really saying is that the archives contain wonderful stuff and to make quick and easy pub jokes about it doesn't enhance it. You're meant to be promoting the Archives, judging from your title, not amateur comedians. So when you write to me and say you are "sorry that I felt Phil Smith was unfunny", you don't get the point. I am sorry that Phil Smith was trying to be funny at the Archives' expense. He shouldn't be remorselessly trying to be funny; it's the mistake that Glyn Worsnip made, and which you don't seem to understand either. No need to answer this, as I couldn't face another stonewalling BBC letter, but I really think I have a valid point. I shall get the copy of my letter out often and agree with it.

yours sincerely

———————

To MELVYN BRAGG
July 12, 1988

Dear Melvyn,

I think that was rather a nice letter of yours. Russell Harty would have enjoyed being defended after his death like that.

I met John Arlott the other day for the first time, on Alderney. He said: "Until very recently I have been getting *The Times*, the *Guardian* and the *Independent* every day, and not reading any of them, I just don't have the time. It's ridiculous. So now I just get the *Guardian*, and I don't read that either."

I saw your *South Bank Show* on boogie woogie, one of my great loves, and although it was a bit busy it got a lot of good stuff in. Francis Smith, one of your experts, is a bloke worth doing a programme on. He is the most wonderfully entertaining talker about any of his specialities – blues, boogie, book covers, illustrations, etc – and he is also a world class cartoonist under the name of Smilby. Recently he inherited some small wealth on condition he changed his name from Smith to Wilford-Smith. Did it without hesitation. Now lives in Herefordshire, near my favourite town, Kington. It's the only place in the world where they pronounce my name properly, and don't call me Kingston. I was mentioned in a Swedish paper recently and they called me Kingston there. What is this universal desire to put an s in Kington and why haven't I bowed to the majority and changed my name to Kingston? No, wait – there's a letter coming through the mailbox. It says . . . hold on . . . leave you £5,000,000 on condition you change your name to Wilford-Kingston.

yours

To LEONARD G. PLAYFORD[11]
September 20, 1988

Dear Mr Playford,

I hope you haven't forgotten writing to me about your historic drive up the Burma Road to Kunming and back. I loved your letter, which really conveyed what a trip in a lifetime it was for you.

My trip was a little less exciting. I went with the BBC to make a film of *Great Journeys* they are currently embarking on (they have discovered that if you put the word Great in front of something ordinary, people buy it, which is I suppose why British Rail now advertise the Great British Breakfast, though I have never spotted anything very great about it). One of the titles the BBC had fallen in love with was the Burma Road, so off we went to film it, despite the fact that for most of its length it was out of bounds to us, and to the Burmese as well. In fact, the Burma Road has not been open since the war, except to the local tribes who come and go quite happily when they are not engaged in border warfare against each other or their local government.

However, if you interpret Burma Road loosely as the route taken over hundreds of years by anyone passing between China and Burma, from Kubla Khan to Marco Polo, then there is quite a lot you can say and film – you can include the Irrawaddy River, for example, or the train up from Mandalay to Maymyo – and so we found ourselves filming furiously either end of the Burma Rd to make up for the fact we couldn't film it in the middle. We found people who had helped build the Road (one Chinaman who still hadn't been paid for his work) and people who had gone up and down it. We met a policeman who had been in charge of the checkpoint on the Road where it passed from Burma to China, and who had had lunch with Chiang Kai-Shek, though he really didn't have much of interest to say. And so on. Tali has been cleaned up a lot since you saw it, the gates repainted and revivified for tourists, but we were lucky enough to find one old walled town just off the main road almost unchanged – pigs in the main street, not cars.

Personally I hate travelling around with a film crew – from the point of view of getting to know the country, though they are usually fun to be with – and I would much rather have done a trip like yours. But I always think it is better to go with a TV crew than nobody at all and stay at home.

Reading your letter again, there are some questions which come trotting into my mind. Of course, I would love to know why you were there in the first place and how you drove and whether it was just for pleasure, but other questions too. Who were the military authorities who told you what to do – British or Chinese? Where did you stop overnight? What happened when the bandits stopped you? Was there a generally accepted currency? If the Yunnan Highway was different from the Burma Road, how was it different and was there any traffic down it? Could you pass along the Burma Road if you were not attached to a convoy? Ah, so many questions. If you have the time and energy, do please jot down a few answers – I would come and pick your brain but I am 100 miles away.

Otherwise tell me to get lost.

One fascinating book I found a good companion on the journey was an old volume called *Down the Old Burma Road* by a man called Bradley. He had walked and ridden from Kunming to Burma while going on leave in 1931 – he was a medical missionary of some sort – so of course he was going that way long before the Chinese found it necessary to build up a supply route against the Japs. But the book hadn't been written till 1941, presumably to cash in on the newly fashionable Burma Road, and it is a very dry but well written and human account of what must have been a hell of a trip. If I come across a spare copy, would you be interested?

I am sorry I have taken so long to answer. I won't bore you with excuses. You may be interested to know, amused even, that the recent dreadful events in Burma have made our film look startlingly idyllic. People will switch on to find out what's going on there and we will show them only shots of sunny countryside and happy people. Perhaps I will rewrite the script to make it look as if we knew all along what was going to happen . . . "One can smell the fear underneath the smiles of the people . . ."

yours sincerely

————————

To MICHAEL GREEN[12]
January 12, 1996

Dear Michael,

I was vaguely surprised to get a tape of the pirate sketch from the *Million Pound Radio Show* from you, as I couldn't remember having talked to you about it, but I am glad you sent it to me as, although I had heard it once before and thought it was very funny at the time, I had forgotten all about it. Well, it's still very funny. Oddly enough, I recently exchanged postcards with Dillie Keane about something, and she mentioned that she too had had a copy of the tape from you. I am now working on a theory that you are sending a copy of the tape to everyone you know as a sort of controlled scientific experiment to see what people's reactions are to a random stimulus . . .

I have long nurtured a similar idea, which would involve all the hundreds of business cards I have collected off people met in stray encounters over the years. These cards are all carefully stacked on my desk upstairs (the one I can no longer use because of all the business cards on it) and my intention is to write a generic letter which I would send to all the people mentioned on the cards, asking if they could remember the occasion of our meeting and if they still wanted to do business. It might get some humorous feedback. On the other hand, it could just get a lot of people calling round selling me double glazing.

I am not sure what reaction you wanted from me about the pirate sketch, but I do think it is a superior example of the sketch formula in which one convention (modern management) is imposed on another (piracy). Monty Python used to do it all the time – impressionist painters and bike racing, hairdressers and climbing

Everest – but in their case the juxtaposition was nonsensical. The pirate sketch actually makes a point. The point is that piracy would not benefit from modern management techniques. This strikes me as entirely valid.

(For some time now I have been telling my son stories about a character called Fatty, King of the Pirates, who leads a pirate gang which is interested only in food and which, when it captures a ship, goes straight to the storerooms for biscuits and sausages. One day I am going to write it all down, get it published and not make a fortune.)

I knew there was something I wanted to ask you. Is there any news of the idea which Anne-Marie Cole and I worked on before, the Miles Kington Interview, and which I believe she has suggested another series of? I really enjoyed doing those interviews with historical characters, and I think they worked well, despite the cumbersome title – I'd love to do some more.

yours

———————

Fax to DAVID ROBSON
February 12, 1996

URGENT

David – I have had a word with Steve Cole, the producer of *In Search of the Holy Foreskin*, and although he is delighted that you should be interested, he cautions me to caution you that it won't be an easy piece to write. This is because he had great difficulty setting up the filming there, and when we did actually get to film there, found that unsuspected obstacles had been put in our way. There is no reason to think that they wouldn't be put in your way either.

To resume the story. Steve came up with the idea of the film based on a 1984 story that the foreskin of Christ (the relic of his circumcision) had been preserved in the church at Calcata, a small hilltop town between Rome and Siena and stolen from there, or at least from the priest's house while it was removed from the church during refurbishment. Through various intermediaries in Italy he established that nobody wanted to talk very much about the story, because, as far as he could make out:

a) The Vatican was rather embarrassed about the whole business of having a foreskin on its hands at all
b) There was a strong feeling that the priest might have stolen the foreskin himself – not that he particularly wanted it, but that he might have wanted the jewelled reliquary it was contained in; there was already a suspicion that he was nicking stuff from the church previously, as things had been vanishing . . .
c) Calcata itself was a divided place at the best of times . . . divided between imported arty townsfolk and the natives.

So when we got to Calcata as arranged we were not surprised to find that the priest had scarpered taking the church keys with him. This is not quite true. We were an hour late for our appointment with him because it is a hard place to find, and there are no road signs in Italy on B roads, and because the bloody film crew hadn't thought to buy any detailed maps of Italy, and the priest had gone after an hour in high dudgeon and low relief and didn't reappear while we were there. But we didn't expect to find nobody in the town prepared to talk to us about it all.

Nobody, that is, except one of the local "hippies", a woman who was actually a qualified architect who had been instrumental in saving the old town. The story of this seems to be as follows . . .

The ancient hilltop bit of Calcata, which is ever so charming and quaint, was threatened by a scheme to pull it all down and build a new housing scheme. The locals were not averse. But some crafts-people from Rome who had moved in to do their pottery, gemwork, macramé, etc, fought against this move to pull down their adopted community and won a stay of execution, with the result that the old part of the town is now a hippy township, echoing with 1970s music, full of long-haired folk and dogs, with portraits of

Jimi Hendrix where you would expect Jesus. There was even a tiny shrine to Laurel and Hardy which I spotted.

Now, to most people in Italy if it means anything at all, Calcata means the town where town meets country. My son has been in Rome for a year, working for a TV station. When I mentioned Calcata to him, he said, "Oh yes, the hippy hilltop town, I've heard of that." He hadn't heard of the holy foreskin connection. The only place where the two (hippy and foreskin) connections came together was when the architect turned out to be well briefed on the foreskin theft and agreed to talk to us about it BUT ONLY IF SHE WERE NOT IDENTIFIABLE ON SCREEN. We duly filmed her from behind on or in a veil or whatever, and when we asked her why the secrecy, she said she had talked about the foreskin theft on radio recently and received death threats as a consequence, and was now rather frightened.

Who from? No idea. She may even have been making it up to ask us for more money (and she was not backward in asking for advances). But the whole thing was very spooky, sitting in that semi-deserted Italian square with this veiled woman rehearsing her suspicions to camera, and the occasional hippy craftsman coming out to dry his stained glass whatsits, and the shadows getting longer and longer and darker in the square, while way up in the light blue sky a very small toy plane went over every five minutes starting its descent to Rome airport and our only access to the old church a small window way up in one of the adjoining lofts which was full of pigeons and pigeon shit . . .

There's a good piece to be written there. Very good piece. But having mentioned it to you, I think it has to be written by someone on the ground who can speak Italian and do some first-hand investigating, which rules me out on both counts. I rang you up because the Channel 4 PR guy was pestering me to try to coincide a piece with the March 5 transmission, but quite honestly it would be much more worthwhile taking your time over it and getting a good piece in your own time rather than gratifying Channel 4's requirements. I don't know what your deadline is but I am out of this country all next week, so it's hardly likely that I could do it anyway.

I append four pages of scratchy information on the subject, one from a book on relics by David Sox (sic) and two from another book on relics by James Bentley, a delightfully roguish cleric who accompanied us on the trip and got through more wine than anyone. If you want to ring me to talk about it, do – Steve Cole, who works by day at HTV, would also willingly talk to you, and being the producer he is naturally better informed than the mere presenter (me).

yours

To ROY FISHER[13]
December, 1997

Dear Roy,

Thanks for your fax/letter/proof that you can write all right. You have the advantage of me in one respect. I didn't know *Holy Foreskin* was due to be repeated. Let me know if you learn any more . . . It was a strange experience making that film – the producer knew exactly what he wanted, a complete expose of priestly fraud, but there was never any hope he could get it, so he kept filming stuff which would look good in such a film and we ended up not with a whodunnit but a didanyonedoanything . . .

One odd benefit of our trip to Italy was that we did go inside the famous Assisi basilica before the late quake, but I have something of a blockage about almost all Catholic extravaganza. It's in such wonderfully florid bad taste that I can't really see it, and I'm afraid I can't remember much about Assisi. The oddest thing we saw in Italy was the Virgin Mary's house in Loreto (which was flown there by angels) and the body of Santa Rita of Cascia, patron saint of lost causes, which still hasn't really rotted after 400 years or more. I have a little tag on my key-ring saying (in Italian) "Saint Rita Protect me" given to me by a nun, which I superstitiously keep on my key-ring. If I am ever found dead and unidentified, they are going to get the wrong idea about my religious background.

I haven't seen Barney Bates since his terrible accident, but then I have hardly seen anyone in London. He is/was a terrific player. I once played with him at the Chelsea Arts Club in a band led by Barry Fantoni (not a great player), and Reginald Bosanquet – no less – knocked a whole bottle of red wine inside the upright piano, by mistake. Half an hour later the middle three octaves of the piano had gummed up. So it isn't just pianists who have accidents.

yours

———————

To JUDITH WINNAN[14]
December 8, 1997

Dear Judith,

I hope this is seven leagues nearer what you want than before. Otherwise I shall be staying up all night tonight rewriting . . .

"Mummy, why's Daddy staying up all night?"

"Ssh, dear, he's trying to introduce a note of gaiety and informality into what the lady in Cardiff calls a wooden script."

"Is that very difficult?"

"Impossible, dear. Now go to sleep or Lord Raglan's good arm will come and get you."

"Mummy, when you lose an arm, does it go to heaven before you do or does it wait for you?"

"No, dear. Its friends have a whip round and buy it a house in the country."

"Arms have houses of their own?"

"Yes. They are called alms houses."

yours

To GERMAINE GREER[15]
November 23, 1998

Dear Germaine,

I have been trying to get in touch with you for a few days, but all the contacts I had for you – *Guardian*, *Oldie* – said, as they suggested numbers, "These look rather old to me . . ." so eventually I followed *Private Eye*'s advice and tried faxing you via your agent . . .

For a year or two now I have been involved in co-presenting a Radio 4 programme called *Double Vision* with Edward Enfield (father of Harry, but a person in his own right). It came into being when they wanted a holiday replacement for *Loose Ends*, and we have now done three or more series. The format is simplicity itself. Edward presents himself as a crusty old fogey and disagrees with everything I say under the illusion that I am a thrusting liberal, unaware that I am the last of the young fogeys, and I indulge in the pleasure of disagreeing with him. We enlist our guests' support in whatever matter we are discussing and they either take sides or go off at a tangent, or publicise a book they have just written, or, failing that, publicise a book written by someone completely different. At various times in the programme we work in some archive material or even a song or two . . .

(The programme had a curious genesis. Richard Ingrams was meant to be presenting an afternoon of *Oldie* material at the Salisbury Arts Festival and had enlisted me and Enfield to do some of the reading. At the last moment, he backed out and left me and Edward to do the whole ninety minutes, even though we had never met before and didn't know what we were meant to do. So we busked it, interviewing each other, telling anecdotes, plunging into nostalgia, exchanging prejudices and so on. Quite [by] chance the afternoon was recorded by Tony Staveacre for a Radio 2 Arts programme, and later, when he was asked by Radio 4 if he had any ideas for a *Loose Ends* replacement, he played them this tape and they fell for our partnership. Oddly enough, we had gone on to do it at other festivals, always without Richard Ingrams . . .)

Enough. Would you like to be a guest on the programme? We are thinking specifically of Dec 18th, which is a Friday. We record in Bristol which is 90 minutes from London by train and we would be through by 4 p.m., having met for lunch at 1.30. On that day we hope to tackle lots of topics beginning with h-, such as history, heritage, heirlooms, hotels and hunting.

Let me know if you are quite interested, or alternatively if you think the idea is hateful, horrible, heinous, half-baked, etc.

Even if you can't do it, why not let me have a contact number so that I can annoy you again?

yours

———————

To MELVYN BRAGG
January 23, 2001

Dear Melvyn,

Before, during and after lunch with Michael Heath the other day, I felt the dawning of an idea which I would like to be involved with and which might well appeal to you in a South Bank context. Namely, The Death of the Cartoon. There are still some cartoonists left, but Michael's habitual groaning about the lack of opportunity, lack of respect and lack of money which cartoonists get made me realise that, for once, he wasn't just groaning – it was true. Even when you and I were lads, there were cartoonists who were household names – Giles, then Bill Tidy, Larry, Steadman, Scarfe, to name only the English ones. We could even venerate French artists like Sempé, Bose, André François . . .

No more. I challenge the average young art lion to name any fine young cartoonists. They don't exist. Michael Heath said he thought that Robert Thompson is the best of the young guys, and I know who he means, but I bet most people don't. The markets have dried up (*Private Eye*, *Spectator*, *Oldie* – not much else) and the concept has dried up. For a long time people would quote cartoon captions (curate's egg, bang went sixpence, I keep thinking it's Wednesday, and so on) and would talk about things in cartoon terms (a Thelwell horse, a Searle St Trinians girl, a Pont situation) but not any more.

What do you reckon to the idea of a programme in which I went in search of the remaining great men (Searle is still alive – there's Trog, Langdon, Larry, Tidy . . .) and tried to work out why the single cartoon is an endangered species? This is just an exploratory letter. I would be happy to suggest lots more ideas, and talk about it. I think I'd be a good guy to do it, because a) I knew most of the cartoonists via *Punch* b) I have done television and can handle it c) would like to get back on the screen before all my hair goes d) I am not a cartoonist myself and have no professional jealousies and hang-ups. We could leave those to Heath . . .

Let me know if you think it's a good idea and which address you like to be written to at.

Oops. I never said, How are you? How are you?

yours

———————

To HELEN BOADEN[16]
September 25, 2001

Dear Helen Boaden,

I was quite disarmed by your patient letter of Sep 20, above all by the fact that you should even bother to answer my piece in the *Independent*. After reading it I can see, step by step, why you came to many of the decisions which you did. But I suppose that a listener like myself gets a different picture, because we get the fait accompli without the reasoning behind it, the judgment handed down. And we did get a diet of soft muffled wallpaper instead of the usual sharp background scenery, and were deprived of our usual Radio 4 for what seemed an awful long time.

Still, even after following your reasoning, I do feel that actions like dropping the Provincial Lady because she referred to the

Manhattan skyline is taking things too far. I really feel that nobody out there in audienceland would dream of comparing someone's arrival in Manhattan in 1939 with Sep 11 2001. (After all, the Provincial Lady wouldn't have seen the World Trade Center either . . .)

It's a curious thing, this good taste and bad taste question. I was once told that airlines never show films on board like *Airplane* that feature plane crashes. Yet outside a plane the same film is, presumably, harmless. I once tried to tape a showing of *King Solomon's Mines* only to find it had vanished from the schedules. I rang up HTV to find out why. Oh, they said, it was out of respect for people's sensibilities – there was a scene with machetes in the film, and in view of the recent tourist killings in Uganda . . .

Well, yes, maybe someone would connect the two, but I doubt it. And if that were true, how can anyone ever show any film about car crashes, because 6,000 people die on the roads every year? And . . . But this is an endless argument, and in any case there can be as few disasters as bad as Sep 11th, which tended to break all known rules.

Ruefully, I remember once taking part in several editions of a BBC TV game called *Scoop*, which was the first effort to get a *News Quiz* type programme on TV. The run coincided with the Falkland War. Every week we had to recognise stories in the news. No week was the War even mentioned, even though it dominated the headlines. It was too serious to be funny about. But it did make the programme look strangely remote from reality.

It was odd hearing from you, because I had been fully intending to get in touch with you. James Boyle once dropped me a line, suggesting I drop in to see him one day, an invitation I didn't feel totally inspired to take up. But I was going to reverse the process with you, and suggest I might crave an audience one day, I've done a lot of stuff for Radio 4 over the years and would like to see if I could be useful again in the present century. This is not that letter. But I would like to send it soon, just as soon as the memory of my article fades . . .

Meanwhile, more power to your arm. There's a lot of cracking good stuff on Radio 4, and I'm afraid I hold you directly responsible for it.

————————

To ANNE VALERY[17]
July 1, 2003

Dear Anne,

I don't know how I never knew that you and Quentin Crisp were soul mates, but it stands to reason, both of you being ex pupils of the Soho University of Life. I can't remember how I first became aware of him, whether through his stage appearances or his first book, *How To Have A Lifestyle*, which I still think is one of the wittiest things ever penned. I knew him a bit, through writing (at *Punch*) and showbiz (the group I played in sometimes criss-crossed his path, especially at Edinburgh, and just plain fan-worship I turned up at his place in New York once) and I wish now I had tried to correspond with him, but really I would just have either tried to show off or been in awe of him, so it is just as well I didn't. Anyway, to think that he mentioned me to you is wonderful. I wouldn't send me the letter. Far too risky.

Either have it photocopied your end, or wait till I see you one day and we'll do it together. Then I'll put it in my cuttings book. I don't actually have a cuttings book, but I could always buy one.

Yes, I was a week in Spain, doing research into the late great General Franco. This is for a Radio 4 series of 3 half-hour programmes. That came about because I did that programme on General de Gaulle last year which they liked, in which I managed to catch a light but respectful tone towards le grand Charles which appealed to them, and they thought I could do it again with little Franco. Well, YOU know – you were in the de Gaulle programme, for heaven's sake. Franco is very different. We had a talk with a man called Paul Preston who has written a 700 page life of El Caudillo, which took him 10 or more years, and at the end of it he loathed the man as much as when he started.

Anyway, the young woman who is producing the programme (Julia Adamson) took me out to Madrid to talk to lots of people who had worked with Franco, fought against him, suffered from him or admired him, and we are building up a good stock of interviews. But one thing she is slightly short of is personal stories by people like you, so do let me put you in touch with her. Oh, and tell me all about Alicante.

When was this? What happened to you? What kind of trouble were you causing this time? Didn't you know that General Franco had a country to run? How could you have been so ungrateful as to try to disrupt his efforts to make Spain a better place? Honestly, Anne . . .

We are working on the whole thing in July, so there's time yet, and it would be great if you were the only interviewee who was in BOTH programmes . . .

While out there in Spain I read one of Gerald Brenan's books, the one written in about 1959, when he was touring Spain when it was still poor and hungry, just before the tourists brought "prosperity". His picture of Franco's Spain is grim, grim, grim.

We flew up to Galicia for two days to visit Franco's birthplace, and to meet a man called Fraga who once was in Franco's cabinet and is still running Galicia. He's at least 80. People find it very hard to give up power. He must know that if he gives up, he will shrivel up and die.

I had never seen Madrid before. It's a fine old place. After a while, you begin to think that most Southern European cities are roughly the same, especially in the Paris/Rome/Madrid belt, with the same grand back streets and the same grand public buildings, but Madrid is a superior example of the genre. Bloomin' hot, though. Forty degrees most days. My brother is just back from Saudi Arabia and says it was 50 degrees there.

We talked to some grand old women, especially one who had spent all the Civil War in an anarchist commune, amazingly unharmed by the fighting. She fled over the Pyrenees at the end of the war, carrying her 2 yr old son with her, through mountains scattered with dead and dying bodies. Unbelievable, what some people can do.

    yours

5
Books

The World of Alphonse Allais, later reissued as A Wolf in Frog's Clothing, was Miles's first published book and was the translation of a collection of the writings of his hero. During his lifetime, Miles published twenty books and three, including How Shall I Tell The Dog written while he was dying, were published posthumously. He read widely, taking up some writers with a passion, only to grow disenchanted later. Allais was a constant, so was H. L. Mencken, Myles na Gopaleen and Lewis Carroll. Just before his death, Miles was enthusing about Noël Coward.

To D. J. ENRIGHT[1]
December 9, 1974

Dear Mr Enright,

At last, the long-awaited first batch of translations from Alphonse Allais. I say "first batch" because I would like to add some more to the pile before you decide whether to go ahead with a full book's worth or not; at the same time, I would like to hand you the first fruits now so you do not give up hope entirely of ever seeing anything from me.

I have two reasons for wishing to give you some more samples. One is that I have not yet licked the problem of finding the right translating style. I am quite pleased with what I have done, because there are bits which I do not wish to change at all, and I never thought I would even get that far. At the same time, I can see that there is a slightly wooden taint hovering over the whole lot of it, a mid-channel feel of conflicting cultures, and I would ideally like to eradicate it if possible. It may not be possible. The rhythm of Allais's French, which seems so natural, is entirely different from the rhythm of English humour, and I suspect that if I were to make his pieces read as if they were original English productions, I would stray too far from the original.

Secondly, the selection I have given you is not as varied as Allais himself. I have leant towards the kind of anecdote I myself enjoy very much – the rather sardonic accounts of everyday anguish, usually involving disappointments in love. There are also examples of his other preoccupations (scientific inventions, railway companies, Christmas, Saki-type children – before Saki, I should add) but no examples of other things which should figure in an Allais anthology. For instance, his constant return to the subjects of how to build a Channel crossing, how to do Britain down, how to combat the imperial strength of Germany, how to write the worst shaggy dog story in the world, how to replace the present uneconomic and dull system of burial and how to add some fun to the Paris Exhibition of 1900. Even that list sounds dull; what I mean is that every time I glance through the pieces I have already translated, I immediately think of one which I haven't done which seems even better, and that is encouraging.

Another encouraging thing is that although I have seen most of the selections that have appeared in France in book form, I have not yet seen one that combined the best or even the consistently good of Allais. Like all journalists, he wrote a good many duds. If we produced an Allais book without duds, it would be the first ever. Nor have I ever seen one which grouped small sections of pieces on one preoccupation. For instance, he returned now and again to the then current French feeling that Britain was too big for its boots, too rich and successful (comme c'est loin, tout ça) and sabotaged us in a series of wicked suggestions. One was that being on the verge of exhausting our coal supplies we had made the whole island hollow and were about to float away. Which, he suggested, in a second article, was the <u>real</u> reason we had connected Britain to every other country in the world with soi-disant telephone cables. Which, he suggested in a third piece, provided a wonderful chance for the French to cut our mooring ropes and attack us. Which, he suggested in a fourth piece . . . and so on. Because half the charm of

Allais is not that he is a belly-laugh producer, though he can be, but that the accumulative effect can be irresistible. (As a bonus, he often rounded off his columns with little fabricated fillers, usually answers to fictitious correspondents, which could easily be used in a book to save paper. For instance . . . (and I quote from memory) . . . "To Madame la Marquise de G. – I am truly sorry that my last delivery of prussic acid tasted off. If the whole shipment was indeed corked, I shall gladly refund your money.")

To try and give you a slight element of surprise, I have for the most part avoided the pieces I quoted from in the *Listener*-reprinted broadcast, though I would like to use all of them eventually.

Nothing much else to say, you will be relieved to hear. I shall look forward to hearing what you think about this prior batch. I myself cannot still make up my mind about Allais. A lot of him seems dated and pioneering by today's standards; a lot of it seems splendid and fresh by any standards. Some of it seems still ahead of its time; I can think of at least two stories which are so scabrous I cannot bring myself to translate them.

A last thought: I am already improving and changing the submitted 14 pieces before you, so do not think they are the final version.

yours sincerely

———————

To MICHAEL PALIN
January 31, 1980

Dear Mike,

I was sent a book recently called *The Ascent of Rum Doodle* by a publisher in Sheffield called Geoff Birtles – the firm is called Dark Peak. It's a sort of *Three Men In A Boat* version of mountaineering. Actually, it's more Pooterish. No, wait on, it's more Victor Hugo in a lighter mood. Anyway, I thought it was jolly funny. And he happened to mention to me on the phone t'other day (they really speak like that up there, isn't it wonderful?) that he'd sent you a copy but had no idea if it had got to you. So being quite keen on the book, I thought I'd drop a line and say, Well, read it anyway, even if you're not going to buy the TV, film and fishing rights. It's quite fun.

I think you're smashing. Take this as a Valentine Card.

yrs

Mls

To W. E. BOWMAN
February 22, 1980

Dear Mr Bowman,

I was absolutely delighted to get your letter and find that you are still in the land of the typing. I have been boring everyone in the office stiff about how good *Rum Doodle* is, and it makes a change to be able to bore the author. I know that writers don't generally like to be talked to about books they wrote twenty years ago – the latest one should always be the best – so I'll just say that it's gone on my shelf of classics and leave it at that. I have persuaded the Lit Ed of the *Sunday Times* to let me do a short review of the reissue for them, but although I've written it and they've said the piece is fine, I couldn't say for sure when they'll print it. This Sunday, I hope.

I also very much liked your piece of Welsh nonsense. I grew up in Wales and bought a copy of the *Mabinogion* at an early age, which helped. I showed it to several members of the staff. Two quite liked it; one, the youngest, thought it was terrific and should go straight into the mag; one, the editor, and oldest, didn't really like it very much. He has forfeited all my respect. However, and this should please you as much as it displeases him, we received a letter this morning from a reader in Felixstowe saying that the editor's latest piece was the funniest thing he had ever read except *The Ascent of Rum Doodle*. Ha!

I think one thing that put off Alan Coren was your occasional weakness for puns like Cwm Cwm Mlad, and I must say that your straightforward parody of Welsh place names without jokey second meanings did strike me as funnier.

Knowing publishers, I suspect you may not be getting much, if anything, from the reprint of *Rum Doodle*, but any publicity that comes from it might help to get other publishers interested in your non-published stuff, of which you seem to have a healthy or perhaps unhealthy pile. I very much hope so, anyway.

yours sincerely

———————

To NORMAN THELWELL[2]
December 11, 1982

Dear Norman,

And here, as Eamonn Andrews would say, is someone you haven't seen for forty years, someone you thought was living in Western Australia . . . I haven't seen you for a while, for the very simple reason that I left the staff of *Punch* 2½ years ago and that is the only place where we were likely to meet.

Geoff Dickinson tells me you are thriving to the point that you are sometimes tempted to give up work altogether, which is bad news for me as I am about to suggest some drawing to you. I'll take a deep breath, tell you about it and you can think it over and tell me to get stuffed.

I have agreed to do a book for Rainbird/Hamish Hamilton entitled something like "Nature Made Ridiculously Simple". The idea for the book was born twenty years ago when I was living in a garden with a large unknown tree. Unknown to me at any rate. I pored over tree books and eventually identified it beyond reasonable doubt as a Robina Locusta or False Acacia. The only snag was that three months later, when autumn came, the tree dropped walnuts all over the lawn.

I don't blame the walnut for looking deceptive. I blame the tree book for printing so many trees which look similar. In fact, the more I look at nature guides, the more I find it difficult to identify nature. A flower which is plainly a Greater Ragwort always turns out to look like the Lesser Ragwort, the Horned Coltsfoot and the Buckinghamshire Hawkweed.

What the world needed, I realised in a flash of intuition about 1977, was a guide to nature which reduced categories, not increased them. So from time to time I have written pieces which brought the number of species down to ten in every category. When I did birds, for instance, I turned all birds of prey into the Motorway Hawk whose natural habitat is the hard shoulder, all songbirds into the Invisible Songbird, which always sings in the next tree to the one you are staring at, and all gulls etc into Big, Fat, White, Sinister, Very Cynical Sea Bird which now flies inland not because of bad weather but because he has located a new rubbish dump.

The publishers now want me to expand the idea into a book to be brought out for Christmas 1983, and I have said yes. They also want me to get it illustrated by a cartoonist. I have said, Hmm, I'm not so sure. The trouble is with having books illustrated by cartoonists is that normally the drawings get desperately jokey, and that would be wrong for this book. The drawings should be almost straight, with a smile playing round the edge rather than a belly laugh in the middle. They should also be done by someone who can draw well and who knows nature. And there don't need to be very many of them, as I would like to use photographs as well.

What I have in mind is composite drawings based on those pictures that people like Shell put out, with a nature scene containing different bits and pieces; by the side they have a numbered silhouette version of the drawing so that you can refer to a key. I realise that it would probably be damned hard work to compose a composite picture, but as I said, there wouldn't have to be very many. Ten at most, I would think.

After much cogitation I can only think of two artists known to me who combine all the necessary wit and technique. You are one, the other is George Adamson, and I would indeed approach George if you said no. If he said no, I think I'd plump for all photographs. See, I'm being very honest.

But I'd rather you were interested in the idea. If it appeals at all, please let me know and I'll send you some of the material. If you are far too busy or not attracted by the idea, let me know that too.

If I had to sum the book up, I'd say it was aimed at all those thousands of people who at some time have gone out into the country with a little guide to animal tracks, which in books are always immaculate and clearly outlined, and discovered to their horror that real animal tracks are always blurred and smudged. My chapter on animal tracks will deal only with blurred animals; it will be the only book in history which faces up bravely to the fact that animals do not walk tidily.

I wouldn't suggest the idea to you if I hadn't noticed that a lot of your recent drawings, including the excellent ones based on your own estate, are in exactly the style I'm thinking of. You wouldn't have to draw a single gymkhana horse . . .

Anyway, so much for business. I hope you flourish. I keep very busy doing a daily bit for the *Times*, and hardly ever go to *Punch* these days. When I'm there, it feels like a jolly boarding school which I stayed at too long – nice, but to be avoided for a while.

Oh, and Happy Christmas. Visualise this letter decorated with Dickensian robins.

yours

———————

To DOTTI IRVING[3]
July 26, 1984

Dear Dotti,

It's not every day you get a letter from me. It's not every day I write a letter. In fact, I haven't written a letter since I last proposed marriage to Iris Murdoch. (She never answered. I have since learnt that she forwards all mail from strangers to Beryl Bainbridge. That may explain the letter I once got from Beryl, saying: "Yes – name the date!") But the fact is that the cheque I sent to British Telecom has not got through the post and they have temporarily cut off my line. It's wonderfully restful. I may never pay a phone bill again.

Anyway, thanks for your letter, full of amazing statistics about the *Franglais* books having sold more copies than there are people with French O Levels in this country. Well done, Penguin! I wonder why Robson hasn't given me any money for years? At first I thought that the way the sales figures slid down for each book reflected descending quality, but I realise now it reflects the amount of time they have been out. At least I hope it does . . .

The cover is not bad, really. I can't see it selling more than 3 copies, but if Penguin will insist on publishing everything I write. Here is a letter for Liz Buchan by the way.

Dear Liz,

I am sorry I did not come up with the goods, back and front, for *Nature*. This was because I was crossing the Kalahari Desert on a camel, making a TV film called "Terribly Alone in the Kalahari except for four cameramen, two sound men, back-up Land Rover and a mobile catering unit", and there were no post offices nearby, also I had blurb-writer's block. BUT you have done as good a job as I ever could, so this has been a good thrill and challenge for you.

yours, Miles

I realise it's going to be tricky cutting it out and handing it over, so perhaps she could read it over your shoulder. I don't in the least mind doing a few *Nature* interviews. You mustn't be misled by my curt, foul phone manner into thinking I'm curt and foul.

You were looking incredibly glamorous the other day. As soon as I have managed to break off my engagement to Beryl Bainbridge, we ought to arrange lunch.

love

———————

To SUE LIMB
January 19, 1988

Dear Sue Limb,

Now here's a funny thing. The other day I was in a bookshop in Stroud, being on my way to Scotland by car, and I picked up your new book from the counter ("Signed Copies" it said, though I couldn't see any unsigned ones to pick up) to leaf through it, having enjoyed your novel very much. I was put on to your novel by contact with Roger Limb, your composer sibling, who wrote the music for a short series of half-hour train films I did for the BBC. Well, I didn't do them; they did them and I wrote some words for them but you know what I mean. The reason I was driving to Scotland was to stay with some cousins who live in a ramshackle castle in the back of Perthshire, and Stroud was our first stop – when you consider that we were coming from Bath to Perth, and were making a bookshop stop at Stroud already, you'll wonder how we ever got to Scotland. The odd thing is that my cousin's children were completely captivated by only one thing in those train films and that was Roger's music. Every time they see me, they burst into a remarkably faithful rendition of loud Scottish humming of Roger's infinitely flexible theme. And they did this again this year. I wish children didn't have such a long memory; they make the humming of Roger's theme tune sound like a condemnation of my script. Which is exactly what they intend it to be. The reason that we stopped at a Stroud bookshop was that my stepdaughter had got in a panic about an essay about *Richard II* she had to write, and wanted any book about the play, and thought Stroud might provide the answer. (It did, actually.) She also wanted to read the play again, so we had the bright idea of reading the play out loud in the car going up. I still haven't the faintest what the play is about, but I can distinctly remember playing at least three noblemen in the back seat simultaneously. We got as far as Cumbria on the first night and stayed in a pub overnight. I used to think pubs were just for drinking in but now I'm enlightened.

Anyway, the funny thing is that when I waved your signed copy at the woman behind the counter and said: "I'll take it, do I get my money back if I don't like it?", she said: "That's a coincidence – Sue Limb herself was standing at your elbow when you picked that book up." "What a shame," I said, "I've always wanted to meet her, does she live hereabouts?" Woodchester, she said. So that's where I've written to. I wonder if it reaches you.

I've just started your book. It looks very good. I hope you don't mind me writing . . .

———————

To HILARY BRADT[4]
December 9, 1990

Dear Hilary Bradt,

My God, I remember that visit to the London Book Fair. I was blackmailed into it by my publishers, Unwin and Hyman, who thought that having an author around would help to sell copies of *Steaming Through Britain* (subtitle: Maybe This Time People Will Spot That I Know Nothing About Trains) and they may well be right, but it also means an author standing around for 40 minutes, half of it at the wrong stall (we had already helped ourselves to a drink and an ashtray at this likely-looking stall which turned out to be the stand of the Remainders People), talking to the most utterly empty-headed people on earth (publishers' underlings who have been with the firm for two weeks and old men who should have been fired years ago), and so if only you had introduced yourself, I would have fallen on your neck with cries of: "My God, at last a human being, let me take you away from all this and give you a good night out at the Remainders Stall" and you would have backed off, horrified. Moral: Always go over and introduce yourself to someone. It can't be worse than not doing so. I wish I'd followed that advice myself.

Not having done the *Observer* piece yet I don't want to waste all the detail, but suffice it to say that I thought Madagascar was wonderful. All we did, really, was go by train from Tana to Tamatave, excurse a little up the coast to Mahambo and beyond, fly back through a cataclysmic storm to Tana, do the train trip to Anstirabe, spend four or five days in and around Tana, and back home. Oh, and stay overnight at Perinet. I had determined to be the first writer in M not to mention lemurs, but alas, I was taken to see a gang of indris. They were great. What really made the trip for me was that my French was better than average, so I talked to a lot of Malgaches . . . Malagasy . . . Malagies . . . people who live in

Madagascar. And I was delighted to find a) that Maurice is French for Mauritius b) some damn good local wine c) a praying mantis in the gents loo at Tamatave. Though I have to admit that my French isn't quite good enough for "Excuse me, but do you mind if I bring my wife in to see the praying mantis on the back of the gents loo?" Amazing what sign language can do, though.

It's been my great good luck in life to get to three countries which seem to have the same bewitching effect on most people – Peru, Burma and Madagascar. OK, I know people go crazy over Bhutan, Bali and Mexico, but the first three are good enough for me, and it's odd that our paths should have crossed unwittingly in two of them. Yes, I enjoyed writing that PERU FOR BEGINNERS piece. There's quite a good story behind that. But I'd like to get in touch again after I've written the piece – I have a superstition about not blabbing stuff out till I've written it. Your book was very valuable. My wife took along, alas, Dervla Murphy's *Muddling Through Madagascar* which she enjoyed while feeling that Murphy does invite disaster the whole time and loves whatever the opposite of luxury is. I thought that the verb to describe this might be "Dervling" as in a new book called "Dervling Through Denmark". There should be a whole series, said my wife, like Impetigo in India and Herpes in Hungary. After 'Foot and Mouth in Finland and Moravia' we gave up.

Sorry about the typing. Sunday afternoon. What's Sunday afternoon got to do with it? I don't know but it seemed like a good excuse at the time.

––––––

Email to ANDREW GOODFELLOW[5]
January 8, 2001

Dear Andrew,

I can actually remember Basil writing *Accustomed As I Am*. He left *Punch* (and left his office to me – at last I had a room of my own!) and drifted away from full-time comic writing into the speech 'n' talk circuit. But whenever he had good material he couldn't resist writing about it, so eventually he couldn't help writing a book about the speaking game. I remember reading it and thinking that the good bits were terrific.

I was especially taken by one episode, when he describes a disastrous trip to Wigan, or somewhere Lancastrian, which involved his train splitting in half at Crewe and him being in the wrong half, having a drink in the buffet, and coming back to find all his stuff gone . . . then arriving just in time at the venue and speaking in an L-shaped hall, in which he was in the small half of the L and most people couldn't see him so didn't listen . . . and then staying the night with some people who weren't expecting him, from whom he had to borrow pyjamas as all his stuff was on the train still . . .

The point of all this is that when he next came to the office, I asked him if that awful story had really happened. He looked at me fastidiously and said: "Miles, as a humorous writer you really ought to know that you NEVER ask anyone that question. However, as it is you, I will tell you the truth. Yes, it all really happened. Not, however, all in that precise order, not all on the same day, and not a lot of it to me . . ."

I still think that's about the best summing up of one kind of comic writing I ever heard.

None of this answers your question. Basil died and so did his wife, and the only offspring I can remember is a son called Toby who had moved to California, and whom I never met. Would the *Punch* library be the best place to ask? Presumably they get queries about estates and things, don't they? Alan Coren always knew Basil better than I did – he might be a good source.

yours

PS I was very unfortunately not able to get to H F Ellis's funeral, which I much regret. I know Tony Staveacre got there, but haven't heard a match report from him.

To BILL BRYSON
January 17, 2001

Dear Bill,

Hey, how nice to hear back from you. I am glad we form a mutual admiration society. I am sorry to hear that there may have been a piece or two in which I took your name lightly, but I can't remember how or when now. If so, I am too old to fight duels, so I apologise.

Mention of *Rum Doodle* brings memories flooding back, but such is my feeble recall that I can't remember what the memories consist of. To the best of my recollection I was first introduced to the book by T.E.B. Clarke. Name ring a bell?

Clarke was the scriptwriter of many of the best Ealing comedies – *Lavender Hill Mob, Passport to Pimlico*, etc – and by the time I met him was well past retirement, but had a strange urge to write for *Punch*. He wrote two or three pieces for me while I was there, all very good, and then drifted out of my ken, but not before urging me to read *Rum Doodle*, because, I think, Bowman was a friend of his, and he thought the book should be better known. I read it and loved it, and I do dimly remember proselytising for it, if not writing an intro for it, but the only copy I now have in my possession, published by a climbing firm called Dark Peak, has no intro by me or anyone. But I got it down this afternoon and started rereading it, and I started laughing at it all over again. Not all of it is as good as the other bit, but when it is good it is so good . . . I chiefly remember the proliferation of porters, don't know why.

How did you come to meet Mrs Bowman? I'd love to meet her. Well, if this project comes to aught – and I am happy to do anything you want – I shall have my wish granted. Don't think you have to arrange anything in Bath for me. These days, Bath is only 100 miles by train from London, or two days' travel.

I had a passing whim to make contact with you when I saw you were coming to Bath, but generally it's bad enough for you having to be nice to strangers on these tours without having to be nice to old friends and acquaintances as well. Bath is a strange old place; it looks and feels great, but it is the centre of the most terrific smugness, self-satisfaction and inertia, like a land created by giants now occupied by pygmies. I am glad to say that although the word Bath appears on my address, I am actually across the border in Wiltshire and free of their gravitational pull.

(Recently there has been a reordering of postcodes round here, because the Royal Mail has decided it wants to do a lot more postal sorting in Radstock, so it is giving people new postcodes and asking them to remove the name "Bath" from their address. Horror! Consternation! Radstock is an ugly old mining town – Bath is a World Heritage Site! The value of my property will plunge, think people, if I can no longer put Bath down on my address! And my insurance premiums will go up if I am put in a postal area where more robberies occur! All this is wonderfully true. You can't beat good old-fashioned British snobbishness. It would make a good article. In fact, it almost has.)

yours

———————

To MICHAEL MITCHELL[6]
July 10, 2001

Dear Michael,

Just to be on the safe side, I enclose a hard copy – or what we used to call a few bits of paper – of what I take to be the genuine Sempe introduction.

But really I want to thank you for the magnificent edition of *Candide*. I have always thought Voltaire was a great man – well, not always, because there was probably a time when I thought Richmal Crompton was the best writer in the world, but I can clearly remember that I first fell under Voltaire's spell in a big way when I was spending what we would now call a gap year in New York in 1960, as a callow 18-yr-old, dodging in and out of jazz clubs and having a look at baseball and being propositioned by all sorts of American homosexuals.

Somewhere I acquired a pocket book version of Voltaire's Tales and carried it around till it fell to bits. I then came across Voltaire again at Oxford, doing French. He was in all honesty the only author we studied that I ever wanted to write like. We spent two or three weeks on him alone, and when the dry tutor said, "We'd better move on now", and I pleaded with him to spend another week on the great man, and he said, "No, that's all we need for the syllabus – time to move on to J-J Rousseau now . . ."; well, that's when I conceived a deep dislike for syllabuses and for J-J Rousseau.

Anyway, thanks for a brilliant present. Not many people would go to the lengths of printing a present specially for someone. And as it won't fit in my pocket there's no danger of it falling to bits.

Please pass on a meaningful message to Caroline. (I realise I said that because my son and I are currently laughing at the dying words of Pancho Villa, the Mexican patriot. Apparently someone leant over him as he was dying and said: "Any famous last words?" And he said: "Tell them I said something interesting . . ." and died.)

yours

———————

To MARK BALDWIN[7]
January 28, 2002

Dear Mark,

How nice to get a snap reaction to a piece from anyone about anything, but especially from you on that day, the very day I got a threatening e-mail from a Scottish friend about Burns, saying that they would reveal the fact that I had been to a Scottish school and should know better. As threats go, I have known more frightening ones.

It's always a bit dodgy when a nation pins its colours on one national writer, as with Burns. I remember once attending a literary do in Swansea where people were going on a bit about Dylan Thomas, so I ventured my opinion that Thomas's *Under Milk Wood* was really way ahead of anything else he wrote, and that he was a very funny writer and rather an over-rated poet, drunk with his own verbosity. There was a subdued chorus of rage, and teeth were bared. I was attacking the only nationally known Welsh writer of the last century. A lynching was imminent . . .

Once had a very strange experience about Dylan T. I was on a TV book programme with Caitlin Thomas, the widow, and Nigel Nicolson, the elderly gent (God knows what I was doing there) and Nicolson said to Caitlin: "People think of Dylan Thomas in so many different ways – as a poet, as a drinker, as a Welshman, as a lover or husband . . . How do you remember him now?" She leaned forward and said: "To me . . . Dylan Thomas was (pause) an utter shit" and leaned back again, satisfied. I almost cheered, her timing was so immaculate and everyone's breath was taken, and their flabber gasted. I said to the producer after we had finished recording: "Great moment of TV there," and she said, "Yes, but we can't possibly use it." Still, I thought, at least I can remember it . . .

Ever since our visit I have been using abebooks.com to great effect. You have changed my life. Yes, now we have too many books and my wife wants a divorce.

yours

———————

To MARTIN NEWELL[8]
November 13, 2002

Dear Martin,

Well, I agree with everything you say. Funny you should mention the washbasin idea. I have just come back from my first visit to Barcelona, the city famous for the buildings of Gaudi, the architect who happened on the idea of making everything look as if it were built from vanilla ice cream which had been out of the fridge just a bit too long. It's actually quite eye-catching, though it must have been hell to build . . .

SCENE: A BUILDING SITE

Gaudi: What's wrong with this window sill?
Builder: Nothing. It's finished.

Gaudi: But it's not meant to look finished! It's meant to look as if it's melting! Now, unfinish it!

Builder: Sí, señor, if that is what you want.

Gaudi: And don't talk to me in Spanish! We are Catalan! Talk to me in the native tongue!

Builder: Yes, sahib.

Anyway, if you go to the lavatory in a Gaudi building, you will not find a Gaudi urinal. Oh, no. He did not have the courage to build Gaudiesque urinals. That would have splashed everywhere.

This is barely relevant to what you were saying about poetry, but it all ties in somewhere. When Kim Howells the other day was being rude about the conceptualists' "cold manipulative bullshit", and pulled the wrath of the establishment down on him, he was right in a very blunt and tactless and simple way. When people wrote against him saying that the point of art was to shock complacency, did anyone point out that nobody is more complacent than Serota and Saatchi and the whole modern bullshit tendency?

I was invited to go and speak at the recent Aldeburgh Poetry Festival, and get involved in a debate in which I would be asked to oppose contemporary poetry, which I agreed to do. Then I came to my senses and backed out. I really don't care enough about contemporary poetry of the Motion/Raine variety even to want to oppose it. I had a card from someone who was there, Hilary Macaskill, saying that I had missed nothing. And I agree with you about light or comic or whatever we call it verse. Great living stuff. I was rereading a sort of autobiography by AP Herbert and came to some very trenchant stuff about light v pompous verse which I'll photocopy for you if I get the chance . . .

I remember when I was at *Punch* getting Clive James to review a book of 2nd World War verse, the soldiers' stuff, not the literary magazine stuff, and he came to me and said, "Can we use the word 'fuck' in *Punch*?" and I said we never had yet, and he said "Well, you ought to now, because I want to quote a poem which includes it." I asked editor Alan Coren, and he said, "Well, we have got to go through the barrier one day so, fuck it, let's go through it now," and the poem we printed was:-

> I love you in your negligee
> I love you in your nighty
> But when moonlight flits across your tits
> Well, Christ all fucking mighty.

I guess you know it. Never mind. I thought then and think now that it was one of the most perfectly crafted poems of all time. This was not the opinion of one of our directors, a puritanical Scot called Drew Webster, who almost had a heart attack when he heard about the intended breakthrough and tried to fire Coren before it could be printed, and failed.

I know what has been tickling at the back of my mind.

Philip Larkin's introduction to his collected jazz reviews, All That Jazz or All What Jazz, or something. I haven't read it for a while, but it's a very interesting manifesto, as I recall. He says something like that all art has two impulses: to please the artist, and to please the audience. If it's all one, it's incomprehensible, like *Finnegans Wake*. If it's all the other, it's Top Twenty pop rubbish. Where art works best is along the borders where the artist is having a good time and the audience knows what he's doing and likes it. I think the way he puts it is that things work best when the language talked by the artist and the language understood by the audience overlap as much as possible. I have regularly seen that introduction been lambasted by superior Arts Council or academic persons, but it's quite possible that they are not entirely right.

I think it would be a bad idea to exchange lots of long letters agreeing with each other, but I liked getting yours and liked writing this, even though I should have been working. And I do like your stuff. How do you keep coming up with it?

(Old jazz story I heard somewhere. Two well-known jazz pianists, one I think is Alan Clare, are on a tube train. Bass player gets on looking absolutely miserable, soaking wet from rain, lumping double bass. One pianist says: "When we get off, let's ask him the question." Other: "OK." They get off next stop, and one says to the dolefully dripping bass player, "Here, mate, how do you get that under your chin?" Bass player explodes: "Fuck off, you ignorant etc . . ." Two pianists go off into the night, highly satisfied with the reaction.)

your rural pen pal

———————

To RONALD SEARLE
October 2, 2003

Dear Ronald Searle,

Some years ago you drew the cover for the paperback of a book of mine – it was a set of translations of pieces by Alphonse Allais, which ended up called either "A Wolf in Frog's Clothing" or "A Frog in Wolf 's Clothing" (I could never make up my mind which was the better way round, so I could never remember which had been chosen) published by Methuen – and for all those years I have been wishing I had made known my appreciation.

As I was invited to the opening night of your show at Chris Beetles's gallery in Mayfair on Tuesday, I thought I might meet you there. In fact, I aggressively approached all the elderly people there who might have been you, backed them into a comer, grasped them by the lapel and said roughly: "Own up, you are Ronald Searle, are you not?" Showing a variety of emotions from pleasure to terror, they all denied it, so I am forced to write to you instead.

I was an assistant editor on the staff of *Punch* for years and years, and finally Literary Editor, and I expect I knew some of the people who, when younger, you might have known (Peter Dickinson, Russell Brockbank, Bill Hewison, Basil Boothroyd) but really I was in love with your work even before then. I can remember *The Rake's Progress* and even before that the parodies of the American-ised classics you did (*Macbeth* in one page etc). For a long while, in my teens, I thought that *By Rocking Chair Across America* was the funniest and best drawn book I had ever read, which shows you what sort of a queer teenager I must have been at a time when other lads were drooling over the sexy bits in *War and Peace*.

I am now in the job of doing a daily humorous column for the

Independent. Someone told me once when I was at *Punch* that a humorous magazine was the last place a humorist should be.

Too much competition. Where a humorous writer should be was in a worthy, serious and if possible boring daily paper. I see you are happily ensconced in *Le Monde*, so you may agree . . .

I hope you are well. You probably won't have any time to answer this. If you don't, I shall be obliged to write again, with a completely different letter.

yours sincerely

———————

To GEORGINA MOORE[9]
August 19, 2006

Dear Georgina,

Thanks a bundle for the lovely hospitality last week – Oloroso's was quite a place, and I don't think I would ever have got there if it had not been for your initiative. All it needed was a savage thunderstorm or two to crash against the windows romantically. On the other hand, then we would not have been able to sit on the basement stairs of Channing's Hotel, furtively smoking – the barman must have wondered if his job was really worth it if all his customers immediately dragged all the furniture out into the area and ignored him. Oh, and thanks for the couple of cigarettes, too . . .

We had a bit of hard time the next day – we got to the airport in plenty of time to embark, but our flight to Bristol didn't materialise and we were told instead to get on a flight to Birmingham, so that we could be taken from there to Bristol airport by minibus. Got home about seven or eight instead of three or four, which by today's standards is nothing, but it was still anti climactic. Still, it was the only dreary part of our Edinburgh trip.

Do you mind if I take this opportunity to say something about *Someone Like Me?*[10] It has always slightly worried me that Headline have gone through the pretence of treating it as a kind of autobiography. I mean, the fact that it was handled by the Non Fiction editor is odd in itself. And of course it is a kind of autobiography, but what it is chiefly meant to be is fiction. And funny fiction at that.

It is as a humorist that I set out my stall, and it is as a funny writer that I try to impress the crowds at literary festivals. But I have never really got the impression that Headline were always selling it primarily as a humorous book. I think that was the unconscious reason behind my opposition to the idea of the little boy's photo on the paperback cover – that the photo of a real person made it look more like a true autobiography than the hardback did, rather than less.

And again, the whole point of the book is that it is all made up, but I can clearly remember when I did radio interviews for it that someone from Headline, maybe Val, was a bit nervous of me admitting that it didn't all happen and asking me to pretend that it was sort of real, which misses the whole point.

I am not sure if I am explaining myself very well, but I know that I still find it more often in the Memoir shelves in bookshops than in the Humour shelves, which is a bit depressing. There are millions of worthy autobiographies out and about, but there are very few really funny books at any moment, and I think the book would be getting a better chance of stardom if it were pushed more along those lines. As, for instance, it might towards Christmas this year, when it will be there for the first time in paperback. Perhaps it might be worth my while finally meeting your man George in this connection.

Well, I have had my little Speaker's Corner moment, and I think it was probably better to write it to you now than cast a cold gloom over the evening by bringing it up at the dinner the other night and spoiling the occasion. Let me know if you think I am wrong but give it a thought before you disagree.

And now back to cheeriness and fun and laughter, and to say that it was lovely to meet you properly (and Caroline asks me to say how much she enjoyed meeting you), and I hope we meet again ere long.

yours aye

6

Agent

Gill Coleridge became Miles's agent in the late 1970s when she worked at Anthony Sheil Associates. When, in 1988, she moved to join forces with Deborah Rogers and form Rogers, Coleridge and White, Miles moved with her. He valued her highly and considered himself very lucky. A warm relationship existed between them and with her assistants, Clare Roberts, Harriet Gugenheim and Lucy Luck, with whom he had regular contact.

To GILL COLERIDGE
January 24, 1982

Dear Gill,

I was in such a nervous fluster the other day that I consider myself lucky to have left behind only a pen. I think it was brought on by wearing a suit.

I probably haven't placed on record yet how grateful I am to you for all your apparently effortless but really very hard work, and what an extremely good agent you seem to be. That "seem" doesn't look very gracious, but goodness, you are the only yardstick I have to go by. I think what I really mean is, I'd like to place on record how nice it is to work with you, and can I take you out to lunch again one of these soon days? I'll bring something to leave behind.

On Friday I went with my children and my elsewhere wife to *The Seven Samurai*. What a film. Something for everyone. My son went home practising sword fighting. My daughter said: Gosh, that village was so sweet – I'd love to live there.

Tonight they took me to *Arthur*. It's not half bad. Some of the dialogue was very sweet 'n' sour . . .

Prostitute (to Dudley Moore, bitterly): My mother died when I was six. When I was twelve, my father raped me.

Moore: Well . . . well, at least you had six relatively quiet years.

Idea to pass on to TV Janet. Kenneth Robinson told me that he interviewed the two Ronnies last year, and both had been enjoying "Moreover" – good lads. I reckon from seeing a couple of their shows this winter season that they need a few new script ideas (and the critics seem to agree), and as I often get good sketch ideas which I never send anywhere, do you have a channel to them and similar?

    your

—————

To GILL COLERIDGE
February 5, 1988

Dear Gill,

Please excuse this hand-typed letter, but every time my agent goes free I like to write and congratulate them and assure them that I am not got rid of so easy. No, sir, you may think you are leaving Kington's problems behind, but not so. After all, I am one of the few writers who never ring you up at midnight and pour out worries to you.

At this time, though, I would like to raise another question: Who can the agent pour out her worries to? Who can a new freelance agent turn to and do a bit of wailing?

Well, you may be interested to know that I have just set up an agency to look after agents. Yes, Kington Associates are providing an entirely new service – agent-sitting. We think we know your problems. (After all, we caused most of them.) And we think we can look after and represent you in the market place. Until now, agents had to fight alone and unprotected but now there is someone to look after you.

If you are interested in being represented by us, just get in touch, and we will take you out to lunch. When was an agent last taken out to lunch and pampered? Right. You can, pay, if you feel like it, but we'll do the rest.

Sorry, must go now. Hilary Rubinstein is on the other line.

He's crying. Must rush.

I think you're going to have a lot of fun.

yours
with lots of love

PS Cyril Ray is going to contact you for permission to reprint my last piece in *The Times* for the *Compleat Imbiber* 1989. I have told him I am all for it.

———————

While still at Punch, Miles conceived an idea for a book The World Atlas of Prejudice *in which he would compare humour and its origins around the world. He sold the idea to Christopher Sinclair-Stevenson at Hamish Hamilton, collected a healthy advance fee and then spent the next ten years almost-but-never-quite writing the book. He even made two radio series exploring the idea, but finally had to admit defeat and pay the fee back, which he did, in kind, by writing* Motorway Madness.

———————

To GILL COLERIDGE
April 30, 1988

Lord love a duck, don't take on so, it's all my fault, I'm only sorry you had to be involved. I have done the honourable thing and challenged Christopher to a duel. He has written back rather sarcastically and said he doesn't think I would turn up for a duel in time, not by a couple of years. So I have done the only honourable thing and arranged for a duel in a couple of years' time. Perhaps you could work out a contract.

(Incidentally, I'm always amused by the idea of a "contract killer". I always visualise the hirer, the killer and the killer's agent sitting around hassling over the contract for the killing. The small print about, non-completion, the option on further murders, the overseas broadcast news rights, etc . . . Could make a good sketch.)

SERIOUS PART OF LETTER STARTS HERE.

What I am going to do is this. I am going to have a final refusal to give up, because I don't want to let the auld fellow down completely, and I am going to have a mighty thrash through May to produce some good finished material. I will deliver this to you near the end of May and you can pass it on to him and he can do what he wants. If he chucks it back, at least it is done.

It's an odd situation. This relationship with H H was going to be quite fruitful and it's never worked out that way. The two books they did of mine never quite took off, and I don't think they did either of them particularly well. Hmmm . . .

Anyway, let me have a bash during May and if it doesn't work out we can meet on June 1 and talk about life and money. Sorry you weren't in the other day, and many thanks to Deborah for the loan of her enormous upper room – I deduced from photos etc that she and Michael Berkeley are one and the same person, which is nice, because my Caroline did a programme with M B on the Bath Festival and we both found him a good bloke, not at all like the usual artist or TV fraud. The Bethan-Bill-Bryden thing sounds quite fun. I'll tell you about it. No, I'll tell her about it and she can tell you, that way we'll save postage and R C and W will go into profit.

love

———————

Fax to DIANA[1]

I do believe you're right. Somewhere lying about are two valuable contracts. I will institute an immediate search for them, but you have to understand that I live in conditions of controlled chaos and terror – why, only last night two Rottweilers burst in to my house and then shrank back in horror when they saw the pile of unsigned contracts on my carpet. The other day I found a contract for a writing a piece for *The Times* for £2/10/-, marked PLEASE SIGN AND RETURN IMMEDIATELY. It was dated 1962. Perhaps I should sign and return it to you.

Fax to GILL COLERIDGE
1989

Dear Gill,

The thing about Merlin Unwin and the train book is that, fearful that I would not be able to get to all the railway lines in person, I have been busy for the last two months building extra replicas for my garden, and the adjoining field, thinking that if I made descriptive pieces on them in miniature and then sort of enlarged them for the book, nobody would ever tell the difference. Alas, the last few weeks, very bad weather has rather put paid to my plans. The grass got browner, the wood drier and drier, and there have been very many fires, scorching entire lines and often consuming whole stations. This means of course that if I stick to my original plan I shall have to describe most of these lines as in the grip of ferocious forest fires and holocausts, and those readers who are familiar with the lines will be aware that nothing of that sort has happened.

As my agent, you must advise me if this is a risk I can take.

love

PS If you really do want to publish my collected Faxes – and I think it would be a first – this might do.
PPS I am thinking of writing a piece about the disease which strikes quite normal people, urges them to write a first novel late in life (this year already Ben Elton, Howard Brenton, Patrick Garland, Julie Burchill), while established novelists seem to be giving up and writing history (Barnes, Theroux). Any other ace examples I've forgotten? So far it's a slightly dull list.

Fax to GILL COLERIDGE

1991

Dear Gill,

I don't know when you heard from Merlin, but I had a long chat with him last, let me see, Thursday and I undertook then to get it all in by end of November which seems on schedule even as I write. My trouble has been an old one – finding it much harder to deal with fact than fantasy, and getting a great mental block about the final version – but you don't want excuses from me, just assurance. Madam, you have my assurance. The Kington Assurance Co has been in business for 180 years now, and we have covered all the major events in the past two centuries. We assured the world that the First World War wouldn't happen. We assured them that the Second wouldn't. Finally, we tumbled to what was going on and assured them that the Third World War would happen, and sure enough, it didn't. Kington Assurance Co. The only one with a complete 100% record. Never right once?

I took some stuff along, completed, for Merlin, last, let me see, yes, still Thursday and he did at least profess himself delighted with that. I had no idea it was their lead item. Wow. Blood rushes to Kington's forehead. Falls forward and knocks himself unconscious on fax machine. Fax machine, activated, drags Kington's tie into maw and starts reproducing it. Four hours later, he is found nearly chewed by fax machine, with 400 photos of his tie on the floor. Sensational trial of the century: "FAMOUS HUMORIST SUES AGENT FOR GRIEVOUS BODILY HARM WITH A FAX. JURY ASKED: CAN A WOMAN IN LONDON STRIKE A MAN IN BATH? EVEN GILL COLERIDGE? JURY OUT. STOP PRESS. FAMOUS HUMORIST AWARDED VERDICT, BUT GETS ONLY 10p! AGENT CLAIMS 10%!"

I think I'd better get back to my train book. Honest, it's on stream now. But you don't want assurances from me. You want action. OK.

love

———————

Fax to GILL COLERIDGE
October, 1991

Dear Gill,
    This is in answer to Michael Doggart's letter or fax or whatever

we call them these days about a train book to be called *Little Trains of Britain*. He says that Merlin Unwin put the idea to me. He is quite right. What he didn't mention was my answer to Merlin, which was: "Merlin, I'm afraid I see *Steaming Through Britain* not as my entrance to the train writing world, but my exit from it."

I feel that *Steaming Through Britain* was a good book because it had good photos and because the text was different – personal, light and not too fact-laden. I think this trick would be hard to pull off again, and I don't feel I have anything to prove or achieve by trying it a second time. But specifically I have several objections to the proposals Doggart puts forward.

1. Delivery by March. Between now and March the railways he mentions are hardly open at all. It would be crazy to research a book on little lines before they open for the season. You could only get someone to do it who was desperate for money, highly imaginative or already conversant-by-heart with the lines.

2. The choice of lines seems uncomfortable to me. 7 of the 10 are in Wales or the Isle of Man. A bit one-sided, surely? And the Bure Valley Line, less than a year old, might be a bit raw and commercial to take in yet – though that would certainly provide good copy.

3. The division of labour between a bloke doing background colour and a bloke doing background history etc seems likely to be fraught with friction to me.

4. Whoever writes this book would certainly like to be consulted in advance about the lines chosen. There are lines on the list I wouldn't want to cover (one already covered in *Steaming*) and others on the spare list I'd love to write about.

5. I'm already doing a book for Collins to be delivered by spring next year. Doing another seems an unrealistic demand even by Collins's standards.

6. If this is a Collins book, why is it copyright Julian Holland Publishing?

*

I'd be grateful if you could pass these thoughts, and my definite No, on to Mr Doggart.

love

———————

To CLARE ROBERTS
June 21, 1996

Dear Clare,

I have read all three copies of the contract and they all seem fine to me. However, I suggest that you add the following extra clauses in future contracts.

11. If it be found at the end of the year that the contributor has not taken all the extra time off due to him, this shall be added to the next year.
12. If, after a few years, the contributor has accumulated enough time to take a year off, he can take a paid year off.
13. If, however, the contributor is found to have taken too much time off, then that's just too bad.
14. The contributor shall not have to go to Canary Wharf to meet the editor, etc, unless given extra money, a map, a compass, and basic survival kit.
15. When the contributor and the *Independent* finally part company, the contributor shall be entitled to write and publish a book entitled "My Years of Hell at the Indy, including The Day Andreas Whittam-Smith Put His Hand on My Knee at Lunch".
16. The contributor shall not be required to take part in any group activities such as an *Independent* Pub Quiz Team, *Independent* Cricket XI, *Independent* Fancy Dress Ball, *Independent*-led Emergency Government, etc.

If you could sign three copies of this letter and put them on file, I'd be grateful. Incidentally, a man called Jack O'Sullivan rang me from the paper the other day and said that in my absence a gratifying amount of readers had rung up to see if I had left. He then said: "Are you back now?" so he must be Irish.

Fax to GILL COLERIDGE
September 27, 1996

Dear Gill,

I should have answered your letter long before now, but I had that well-known writer's disease, displacement activity or cowardice or procrastination. The name of the disease varies according to the doctor you go to. Dr Caroline Kington, who normally attends me, calls it "Why don't you just ring Gill up for God's sake and talk to her?" syndrome, but I don't think it will ever catch on under that name. She tends to favour the "displacement activity" syndrome prognosis – i.e. if she finds me making bread, she says: "So, what should you be doing?" Or if I am playing the piano, she stands at the door and says, "I think it is high time you finished off that radio script." Logically, this means that if she now comes in and finds me writing this, she'll say: "Shouldn't you be baking bread or practising the piano?" but it never works that way round. It's a mystery.

Well, to get to Prejudice at once, my idea is to cash in on the Jane Austen craze at once and call it "The World Atlas of Pride and Prejudice". You just wait and see how their greedy little eyes will gleam at Penguin.

Penguin: It's a great idea, Gill. But how do we know this Kington guy is going to deliver?

Gill: You don't. You have to take him on trust.

Penguin: We already tried that. As a result, he has been running round with £10,000 of ours for ten years.

Gill: Fifteen.

Penguin: You should know, baby. You've been handling Kington longer than anyone has been working at Penguin. Incidentally, why did he never do the book?

Gill: Why does smoke go upwards? Why doesn't Hamlet

kill Claudius? Why haven't they invented self-adhesive postage stamps? Why is the place you start an airline flight called a terminal? Where is . . . ?

Penguin: Yeah, OK. I get the picture.

Gill: I have a corpulent dossier of faxes and letters from Mr Kington explaining why he can and cannot do this and other undertakings. They make merry reading. In fact, I think they would make quite a nice slim volume . . .

Penguin: Am I to understand that you are suggesting we publish a book of Mr Kington's excuses?

Gill: Good heavens, there's more to it than excuses! There's gossip and libel and recipes and songs and old Wiltshire sayings . . . !

Penguin: Nuts to you, sister.

Gill: Incidentally, may I inquire why you are talking like a low budget Damon Runyon character?

Penguin: Certainly. I am a new American employee here at Penguin. Or am I the new owner? Something like that, anyway. etc etc etc

I am not sure if you have actually mentioned motorway verse to them. That would be my preferred option. Good heavens, did I really write "That would be my preferred option"? That's the kind of pseudo-business English I can't stand. What I meant was, that is what I would like to do. I would really enjoy getting down to that.

(I had a call from a businessman yesterday who found my machine on and left a message starting, "I am sorry if I called at an inappropriate moment." In the old days we would have said, "Sorry you weren't in . . .")

If you think they would be interested, I would certainly produce, lickety split, some more verse and the desired introduction. The other idea swanning round in my mind (have I ever mentioned this to you?) is a book collection of interviews along the line of stuff I did for Radio 4 under the title "The Miles Kington Interview". This was a series of scripted interviews with famous dead people from Nostradamus to the Empress Josephine, from Oscar Wilde to the

Mona Lisa. On the original radio recordings the subject were played by some remarkably distinguished people – Miranda Richardson as Mona Lisa, Robert Stephens as Nostradamus, Simon Callow as Oscar Wilde, Bill Paterson as John Brown, Jane Lapotaire as Empress Josephine etc – but I think the scripts themselves would stand up very well on the page.

You said they wanted an answer soonest, and I suppose the answer is that if they are not interested in either idea (and both ideas are half written already, don't forget), then I shall have to get down to repaying the money in instalments as you suggest which will be painful but possible, and would mean my having to give up buying second-hand 78s till the next century. Failing which, we could have lunch together.

love

To HARRIET GUGENHEIM
December 6, 1996

Dear Harriet,
Thank you very much indeed for the delicious BBC cheque. I am glad you sent it on and I am sorry I sounded bilious last time I rang up about the late *Independent* cheque, but it was that time of month and year when lots of regular bills fall due and I start to worry. I don't want to burden you with my woes but among my other regular standing charges are:-

1. Regular payments to Princess Margaret, or she will go public with our little secret
2. £300 to keep my entry in *Who's Who*
3. Weekly payments to Andrew Marr in order not to have to go to Canary Wharf for lunch
4. Regular back-handers to the Tory, Labour AND Liberal Democrat parties (should get a knighthood one way or another!)
5. Yearly subscription to such magazines as *Loaded, Male Bonding Monthly, Body Building Weekly* etc

6. Regular payment to Michael Howard in return for freedom to insult him without a libel suit etc etc etc

Hope you understand.

To HARRIET GUGENHEIM
September 2, 1997

Dear Harriet (again),

I think I may have done the wrong thing in sending you a surly fax earlier today.

Let me explain why I did it.

Sometimes over the years Gill has told me about authors of hers who badger her about things. They ring her at home to complain, sometimes late at night. They take her out to ill-natured lunches. They send vandals round to write "WHAT ABOUT THE TV RIGHTS IN NEW ZEALAND, THEN?" in lipstick on her car. In fact, I came to assume that this was the kind of writer that agents respected so I have felt guilty from time to time that I was so apathetic in this respect.

At last this morning I found a good excuse to act like these other authors. Well, it didn't get a good audience response.

So badly did it go down, in fact, that you have spontaneously decided to go away and avoid me for two and a half weeks. OK, I respect that. So much so that I am going to pass on my top travel tips to you.

The first one is borrowed from Sir Les Patterson, who once said truly that you always take too many clothes on holiday with you and not enough money.

My own tips are as follows.

1. In order to gain respect from the people sitting next to you on a long-haul flight, plug your earphones into the plane's sound system at the first opportunity. After listening for a few moments, start cackling with laughter. Do this for two minutes, then unplug your headset, shaking your head as if you cannot take any more hilarity. They will spend the rest of

the flight furtively trying to locate this source of comedy on the plane's in-flight entertainment.

2. Do not remove the airline's free cutlery, face wipe, salt, pepper, etc, and keep it for a time when they will be useful. That time will never arrive. The most that will happen is that you will later decide to use the free face wipe and open it, only to find it is actually a sachet of sugar.

3. The only places you want to spend traveller's cheques at will be the only ones that do not accept them, and if they do accept them they do not accept your sterling cheques.

4. If asked, say that you knew Princess Diana quite well.

5. That in fact she was one of your best friends.

6. But you never liked her that much.

7. When out walking in strange areas, carry a Harrods carrier bag with a small quantity of dirty underwear in it. If you are mugged, this is what they will take.

Have a nice time. If you get a fax on holiday saying WHERE IS MY CHEQUE? it won't be me.

––––––––––––

To GILL COLERIDGE
January 30, 2001

Dear Gill,

Welcome back from your tropical Christmas holiday in . . . come to think of it, I've forgotten where exactly you were going for your tropical Christmas holiday, but it doesn't matter, because it leads me straight on to my new idea. I've been talking to lots of people about where they went for Christmas, and a lot of them did the same as you, went away to the sun, and I couldn't help thinking: "Poor people! Having to go all that way and take all their Christmas gear with them! Well, you know, Christmas isn't Christmas without all the right equipment, and the thought of packing all your crackers and artificial tree with you is unbearable . . ."

So this is the idea. A chain of Christmas shops in the tropics, and

subtropics, to come to the aid of all pale Northern Europeans flee-
ing south for Xmas! Don't take the stuff with you – go immediately
to Kington's Kristmas Kabin on arrival and get all your crackers,
holly, Santa Claus outfits, tinsel, carol tapes, Christmas pudding etc
after you have arrived!

We'd make a fortune.

I know what you're thinking. You're thinking there's a snag.

And you're right. When you set fire to brandy in the tropics on the
old Christmas pudding, you can't see it for the brightness of the sun.

I've already thought of that.

I've done a deal with a cheap French brandy firm to produce a
special Cognac de Noel that burns with a fierce orange flame, and
gives off lots of smoke.

But there's another snag, isn't there? It's a very seasonal trade.

What will a Kington's Kristmas Kabin do the rest of the year?
I've thought of that, too. Sell drugs.

The passers-by and the police may think that that powdery white
stuff on the window is artificial snow, but you and I know better.

It's cocaine.

Nobody has ever thought of searching the artificial snow on a
Christmas window.

Why should they start now? Forget books.

Kington's Kristmas Kabin is where the money will be. I'll come
and have lunch with you before the end of February to iron out
some of the details.

love

———————

Fax to HARRIET GUGENHEIM

Dear Harriet,

Just to give you the final rundown on the BBC 'n' jazz situation.

1. The Head of Music at Radio 3 is deeply offended by what I
   have been writing about his jazz policy.
2. I have been deeply offended by his so-called jazz policy.

3. We are so deeply offended by each other that nothing short of a duel could possibly settle the matter.

4. His secretary has rung my secretary to challenge me to a duel.

5. I have no secretary.

6. Using an assumed voice ("Hello – Miles Kington's disabled secretary here") I have offered to let him fight my agent.

7. He has refused to fight you and wants to fight me.

8. I have agreed this reluctantly, as I am a very busy man and my death would postpone several urgent projects beyond their deadline.

9. We have agreed to use sabres as the weapon.

10. There seems to be a hitch his end on this one, as his programme budget does not cover sabres, and he will have to get special clearance from John Birt at the head of the BBC to hire one. Even if he does, he will have to then use producer choice to get the best possible offer on temporary sabre use which means going round all the sabre-suppliers to the BBC for tenders in order to get the cheapest deal.

11. This process will involved three staff full-time for weeks and weeks, thus costing far more than just going out and buying a sabre.

12. I have begun to lose my patience on this one and I have accused the BBC of having a crazy sabre policy.

13. Much to my surprise, I have now been rung up by the Head Of Swordplay, BBC TV, who is incensed by my criticism of BBC sabre policy and has challenged me to a duel.

14. I have discovered from secret sources that the Head of Music Radio 3 and the Head Of Swordplay, BBC TV, do not know each other by sight, and it might be possible for me to arrange a duel at which they fight each other, each under the impression that they are fighting Miles Kington.

15. I will let you know if there are any more developments.

To GILL COLERIDGE
February 21, 2006

Dear Gill,

I thought I ought to recap on the minutes of our lunch so as to establish what we discussed and what we thought we should do about it.

The waitress asked us if we were ready to order yet. I said I wasn't.

So did you.

I asked her if they had had a busy night the previous night, it being Valentine's Day.

She said she had not been here, but had had a quiet evening with her girlfriend, and blushed. You said you might have the tuna.

I said I might have the smoked haddock.

You said, Go on, have a rib-eye steak, that's a real man's dish, Miles, go on, prove you're a man.

I ignored this and said that the last time I had been to the Electric, it had been a cinema. In fact, I had been to it just after it opened and had seen *Winchester '73* with James Stewart. This must have been in the mid-60s. The seating had been bought cheap from other cinemas, and there were big gaps in some rows.

You ignored this and said that you preferred to sit with your back to the wall, as sitting where I was you might catch sight of yourself in the overhead mirror, and there was nothing you hated quite like seeing yourself in the mirror. Going to have your hair cut was a nightmare for you, as you stared at yourself the whole time.

I thought of saying that I had to sit the whole lunch looking at you, and it wasn't too bad at all, really, but I thought better of it.

You said that it was difficult to hear people talk in the Electric, as it was all polished floors and metal tables, which were very reflective and did not absorb sound.

The waitress asked us if we were ready to order yet. We said we were.

You chose the tuna and I had the haddock.

You said you thought I was going to have the steak.

I said steak was for men who felt they had to prove themselves.

After that we talked about writing and things, but I'll deal with that in another letter when I can remember what it was we said.

love

————————

Fax to GILL COLERIDGE
May 7, 2006

Dear Gill,

I said I would write and tell you how the *Independent* Five Years of Simon Kelner Victory Parade went, and here I am.

Getting to the *Independent* was easy enough. Mark you, asking Simon Kelner was no help. When he rang me the other week, he asked me if I was coming and I said yes and I asked him how to get there, and, because he couldn't exactly say, "Well, you ask your chauffeur to take you there," he said. "Go to the end of the tube line and get the DLR." I asked him which tube line that was. "Denise!" I heard him shout, "which tube line is it that comes down here? And, by the way, what does DLR stand for?"

So I took a train from Bath to Paddington, and I went to Bond Street to see a painting show, and then got the Jubilee Line to somewhere way down beyond Canary Wharf and then got the DLR to South Quay, and then got out into the suburbs of Liverpool, or so it seemed, but a friendly passer-by, probably an illegal immigrant, pointed the way to the *Independent*. I got through the strict security check (I had to promise on the Bible not to assassinate Simon Kelner and to buy the *Indy* every day) and found myself on the first floor, meeting the subs who had only been a set of voices until now. So that's what Rob looks like! And Andrew! And Matthew! Well, well, well. And all the time you can sense Rob and Andrew and Matthew thinking, Hmm, Kington's not as funny to look at as we thought, and he's a lot older than us, and he's going to a party to which we haven't been invited, and which we wouldn't want to go to even if we had been invited, still, it would be nice to be asked . . .

And then I was whisked up to the fabulous fourth floor, where the editor's quarters are. His rooms are guarded by black body-guards wielding scimitars, his vanity is served by luscious half-clad Nubian maidens drifting around in ostrich feathers, and messengers arrive on horse back every ten minutes bearing invitations to lunch, which he refuses, or sells on to his minions. I was frisked and had my waiter's friend, my little penknife+corkscrew, taken away from me. "We cannot take any risks today of all days," murmured the bodyguards, as they gently beat me to a pulp.

The ceremony began with the arrival of famous ex-editors of the paper (Andreas Whittam Smith), famous ex-editors of other papers (Donald Trelford), famous Fleet Street figures (Donald Trelford and Andreas Whittam Smith), famous old sporting writers (Donald Trelford) and people who had once been film censor (Andreas W S). Yes, there were whole pairs of celebrities there! I also spotted Ken Clarke, played by Roy Hudd, and Peter Mandelson, looking grate-ful for the invitation. Janet Street-Porter came in, said: "Strewth! I've just remembered I'm not editor any more!" and went out again. Drinks were given out to anaesthetise the throng, and then a drum sounded and a voice said: "There will now be speeches in praise of our glorious leader! Anyone talking through them will be shot!" which seemed fair enough, so I stopped talking to Paul Vallely (just one of many people there whose hair had gone white since I last talked to them – who says the *Indy* doesn't change people?) and stood to attention under the marquee on the flat roof overlooking the glorious vista of old East West North India Docks, which once housed a bustling dock life and now was inhabited only by three half-sunk dredgers.

The first speech was by a man called Ivan Fallon. He was CEO. He said that in all the years he had lived, he had never worked for such a brilliant editor as Simon Kelner. Laughter. No, seriously, he hadn't. Everything about the paper had improved dramatically under the Great Leader, except perhaps the circulation and the advertising. A man called Terry got up and said it was tremendously exciting working with Simon, and to prove it, he would tell a story whose ending he forgot. He then read out a message from a man called Bernard in Australia which amused the people who knew who Bernard was, though not very much. Simon Kelner got up and said lots of people bought the paper for Fisk alone. Fisk blushed. Simon said he wanted to pay tribute to his PA, Jan, who was his office wife. Having Jan here and his wife at home meant that wherever he was, he was sure to get a bollocking. Laughter. No, but seriously. He wanted to pay tribute to lots of people, in the office and elsewhere. He then did so. People looked very impressed that the great leader knew the names of all these people, though from where I was standing I could see that he had them all written down. He then said that having shown how modest he was, and how relieved not to have got the bullet, and how much he was looking forward to the next five years, and how grateful he was to Tony O'Reilly for subsidising his every whim, we could go back to drinking.

I talked socially to quite a few people, like John Walsh, Paul Vallely, Mary Dejevsky, John Lichfield, Philip Hensher, Tom Sutcliffe, and enjoyed that, but didn't really talk business to anyone. What I thought was odd was that none of the editorial or management people talked to me. All the fellow journalists say the usual thing ("How do you do it, five days a week? And some of it quite good too?") but I thought at least one of the others, maybe Ian the deputy editor or someone, would come and introduce themselves. I tried myself, but they were always embedded in terrible conversations with terrible people, so I got back to talking to more writers, like Fisk and Yasmin Alibhai-Brown, who competed on various levels, like comparing the number of death threats they got, and the number of languages they spoke. ("I'm learning Farsi at the moment," said Fisk. "It's much more useful than you might think.")

Still, at least I achieved a presence, and established that they all think I'm a treasure, like a valued but out-of-the-way National Trust property. I realised retrospectively that one of the white haired gents was Brian MacArthur of *The Times*.

Perhaps I should have chatted him up . . .

Thanks for your call yesterday about the 49 ages of Life Class. I tell you what – as I was on the train, on a mobile, not taking notes, it would be nice if you could jot down as briefly as possible the gist of what you said so that I can write it on my wrist in biro before going into the exam hall.

I left *Independent* Towers at 9 p.m. I jumped into a taxi. It got me to Paddington in 30 minutes and I caught the 9.33 home. A miracle. Perhaps God was telling me to go home to the country and not come back just yet.

love

7

On Writing

In 2006, Miles wrote some advice for wannabe writers:

When people tell me that they want to be a writer, I slip them a tenner and say: "Do us a favour – there are too many of us already – just go and do something else instead, and here's a small inducement." If they keep the money and go away, but don't give up writing, and don't give the money back, I know they are born to be writers. That's the one lovely, pure, idealistic thing that writers really care about: money. What do writers talk about when two or three of them are gathered together? Well, yes, how bad all other writers are, but after that it's money.

(Constantine Fitzgibbon was once taken by Graham Greene to see André Gide in North Africa somewhere. He was terribly excited at the prospect of spending a day with two of the most famous writers in the world. But they talked about rights, and percentages, and royalties the whole time, and never mentioned literature once. The only question addressed by Gide to Fitzgibbon was: "Who is your agent in New York?" "I haven't got one," said Fitzgibbon. "Oh," said Gide, and did not say another thing to him. You may be wondering who Constantine Fitzgibbon was. Alas, in the 1950s he was once one of the most up and coming novelists. He is now forgotten. His wife, Theodora Fitzgibbon, is still remembered, because she wrote good cookery books.)

I remember years ago a young schoolboy wrote to all the famous novelists he could think of, from Greene to Somerset Maugham, asking them for their advice on how to write novels. He got at least eight very good replies. HE THEN SOLD THESE REPLIES TO A SUNDAY NEWSPAPER, which made a feature article out of them. That boy was never going to be a novelist, always a journalist. I have no idea what happened to him.

When I was on the staff of Punch, readers would send us

hundreds of pieces each week, thinking they could write as well as us. Maybe they could. But how could we use their stuff? THEN WE WOULD BE ADMITTING THAT THEY COULD WRITE AS WELL AS US. We used to divide the pieces up and share them out, and if any showed promise we would circulate them round the staff. They usually fell at the following hurdles.

1. Not funny.
2. Might have been funny at the time, but not when written down.
3. The writer thought that a funny story or funny incident was funny in itself, but it is the way it is written that makes the difference.
4. They could also be dismissed as "The day the washing machine broke down" or "This is a comic incident which happened to me in the war and all my friends have persuaded me to send it to Punch". Oh, false friends.
5. Too much like Alan Coren or P. G. Wodehouse or someone.
6. Not enough like Alan Coren or P. G. Wodehouse or someone.

The only pieces we accepted were quirky ones which we couldn't categorise.

Sometimes we would get a really nice piece which didn't fit in with Punch. An analysis of supermarket trolley behaviour perhaps. In fact, we did get that once. I wrote back and suggested that the writer should send it to a grocery magazine, which probably needed humour much more than Punch did. He wrote back later and said he had done so, and it had been accepted, and he had been paid much more than Punch could offer.

So there you are. The four golden rules of writing are:-

1. Don't send articles to Punch, which no longer exists.
2. Don't accept invitations to meet famous homosexual French writers in the Sahara. It's a long way to go to get a peppermint tea and talk about TV rights.
3. Get a good agent, or, if you can't get a good agent, take a good

agent hostage and force him/her to represent you at gunpoint, which might also make a good plot for a novel.

4. If all else fails, write a cookery book.

Oh, and 5, when you write something for a book called something like So You Wannabe A Writer, remember to copyright your contribution.

These series of hints to budding writers are copyright Miles Kington, in all parts of the known universe, in all formats, in all media, in all colours, in all languages, and if you reprint them without permission you will get a mysterious wasting disease for which there is no known cure. Except, perhaps, money.

_____

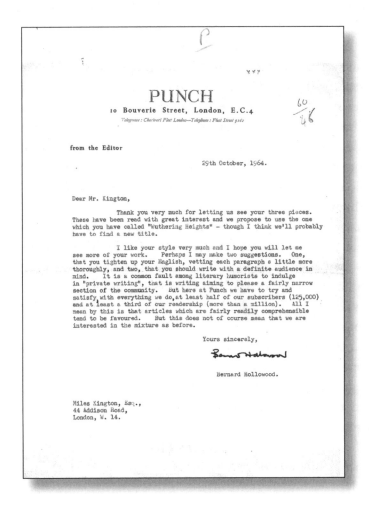

PUNCH
10 Bouverie Street, London, E.C.4
Telegrams : Charivari Fleet London—Telephone : Fleet Street 9161

60
46

from the Editor

29th October, 1964.

Dear Mr. Kington,

Thank you very much for letting us see your three pieces. These have been read with great interest and we propose to use the one which you have called "Wuthering Heights" – though I think we'll probably have to find a new title.

I like your style very much and I hope you will let me see more of your work. Perhaps I may make two suggestions. One, that you tighten up your English, vetting each paragraph a little more thoroughly, and two, that you should write with a definite audience in mind. It is a common fault among literary humorists to indulge in "private writing", that is writing aiming to please a fairly narrow section of the community. But here at Punch we have to try and satisfy with everything we do, at least half of our subscribers (125,000) and at least a third of our readership (more than a million). All I mean by this is that articles which are fairly readily comprehensible tend to be favoured. But this does not of course mean that we are interested in the mixture as before.

Yours sincerely,

Bernard Hollowood.

Miles Kington, Esq.,
44 Addison Road,
London, W. 14.

To PETER DICKINSON[1]
August 20, 1965

Dear Peter Dickinson,

As you say, the last few things I have sent you have not been quite as crammed with good things as you or I would like.

However I don't think this is necessarily because I am going through a stale period (although I may be) but is more on account of the way I try to write. Whenever I have tried to build a piece around a news item or something funny that happened to me, which seems to be the building plan of piece-writers today, the result has been quite colourless or indistinguishable from everyone else's or both.

I usually start from an odd phrase or interesting sentence and try to follow up the train of thought which it sets off. Any story or theme usually emerges from the association of ideas en route. This is a fairly risky procedure, and I have often stared at an interesting sentence for hours on end, only to decide that it is entirely devoid of interest. I have sometimes completed whole pieces and come to the same decision. But when the process works, I think it pays off. I would never have thought of the mixture of railways and poetry in "Poet on the foot-plate" if I had just sat down and searched for a subject; I was halfway through the piece before I knew what it was about.

What I am leading up to is that I am not sure with a lot of pieces whether they have come off or not, so I submit them just in case. When they come back, I am not surprised or very dismayed. It is worth having three or four dud pieces if the next one works. So I hope you do not feel I am in an awful decline if you have to reject stuff of mine.

As a matter of fact, I am working on a series of pieces at the moment slightly different from anything I have submitted, which I will send along when I have enough ready. They will amaze, delight and charm you and I will send a stamped addressed envelope for their return.

Diffidently I would like to suggest a theme for a series of pieces in *Punch*. I often wonder how far back the history of the humorous piece as a sort of genre goes. Books with titles like "A Short Guide to Western Literature" never include chapters on humorists unless they are humorous novelists or playwrights, but there must be a handful of worthy writers of short pieces who deserve to be remembered. People like Max Beerbohm, S.J. Perelman and Stephen Leacock are still read, if not by a very large audience, but there must be others just as good in danger of sinking into obscurity.

Two that I have just read for the first time are Ambrose Bierce and Alphonse Allais. Of course, it may be that in the glow of discovery I have not realised that both writers have a vast underground readership, but it may be not. Do you think it would be a good idea for *Punch* to print one piece each week by five or six such authors? I'm thinking for example of a pleasant Bierce piece which starts "Early one June morning in 1872 I murdered my father – an act which made a deep impression on me at the time." How well-known is he? Until a month ago he was a vague name to me.

As for Allais, I first heard of him about two months ago in a book by Roger Shattuck called *The Banquet Years*, which is about the avant-garde in Paris about 1800–1915. He seems to have been a sort of court jester to the artistic nobility; he wrote for avant-garde as well as derrier-garde weeklies. I have since bought a collection of his pieces in Livre de Poche edition, and many of them are pretty good and quite modern in flavour. It's a bit difficult to tell from the short preface but it sounds as if the collection has appeared, not in response to great demand, but in an effort to re-establish him.

I haven't checked thoroughly, but I have an idea that he has hardly been translated at all. Could it be any interest if I sent along renderings of a few of his pieces? It would be the first time that I had ever combined my French studies and my writing . . .

I seem to have got quite enthusiastic about my different suggestions. At least it would have one advantage over most *Punch* series – the writers would be out of copyright. Allais died in 1905. Bierce, according to my edition, "in 1913, disillusioned and weary, disappeared into Mexico after notifying friends, 'if you hear of my being stood up against a Mexican stone wall and being shot to rags, please know I think it is a pretty good way to depart this life'. While many legends persist, the story of his last days has never been told." This more or less puts both of them beyond the fifty year limit (it is fifty years for copyright, isn't it?).

There must be other writers of equal quality to make up the quota that you know of and I don't. Heine? Ring Lardner? It could be quite an interesting collection and even cause one or two readers to go off and hunt for more of their writings. He said diffidently.

I didn't really intend this letter to be so long, so I will cut it off here. I hope my next submissions will be more felicitous. I'll do my best anyway.

yours sincerely

––––––––––

When he was starting out, Miles received thoughtful and generous advice on his writing, particularly from Peter Dickinson at Punch. *When he became an established writer himself, he was equally liberal with his advice.*

To ALASDAIR RILEY[2]
October 27, 1976

Dear Alasdair,

Well, let me see, just <u>how</u> do you write a "Londoner's Diary" par? How about this?

When he flew into London today, bronzed happy Miles Kington looked spruce and fit despite his incredible 49-towns-in-3-days tour of West Dorset. 'Actually,' he confessed, 'there aren't 49 towns in West Dorset, only three, but I kept commuting between them. I was publicising the forthcoming book by Frank Muir, 'One Man and his Ego', and I must have signed at least half a dozen copies in Crewkerne alone. I suppose I should have been publicising my own forthcoming book, but somehow it seemed to me the Muir book had more chance of success.' He was immediately whisked away in a waiting car to answer a few questions at Hounslow Police Station.

Or even this.

Miles Kington, in addition to playing the bass in Instant Sunshine, writing funny articles for *Punch* and reviewing jazz for *The Times*, which proves he will do anything for money, has just launched into the field of French translation. Without a parachute.

Oh come on. Here we go for the last time.

Miles Kington writes humour for *Punch* and jazz reviews for *The Times* but his first book, out on Nov 4, isn't strictly by him at all. It is a collection of seventy pieces by French humorist Alphonse Allais, translated by Kington. Allais died over 70 years ago but has never appeared in English before, which may explain why most people haven't heard of him. Actually, says Kington, most people don't even seem to believe in him. When he did a radio talk on Allais three years ago, his friends assumed he'd made the whole thing up. His publishers required constant reassurance that Allais really existed. And the other day, when the *Telegraph Magazine* commissioned Kington to write a piece on Allais, they rang back later and asked him to cross his heart and hope to die and promise he wasn't making Allais up.

Well, is he making him up? "Certainly not," says Kington. "It's bad enough trying to write my own stuff let alone having to write someone else's as well. Though I did have a nasty moment last year when I visited Allais's birthplace to coincide with the 70th anniversary of his death and found no traces of the man at all. My God, I thought, perhaps I did make him up. Then to my great relief I met an aged man – 94 now – who had actually known Allais in his youth; the only man left alive who can remember him. Of course, you've only got my word for that . . ."

And now the question the whole world is asking: is there really such a person as Miles Kington? Certainly, said dashing, debonair, drunken Alasdair Riley today. I saw him as recently as last Friday, lying in a gutter in Fleet Street – at least, I saw someone wearing Kington's hat lying in a gutter in Fleet Street. I never knew him personally but I know several people personally who have borrowed his hat, or one like it. Also, Miles Kington writes most of my stuff in "Londoner's Diary" and that seems to clinch the matter.

Unless of course it's Alphonse Allais who writes it all. The whole thing is very mysterious. Waiter, another bottle of your excellent Beaujolais.

yours

Alphonse Allais
p.p. Miles Kington

To ANNE BAR DIN-WEISSMAN
June 9, 1982

Dear Anne,

Right. Thanks. To answer your one question (how can one be humorous every day) . . . I used to be humorous once a week when working at *Punch*. That was far harder. Every time the effort came round, the muscles were cold and stiff, and had to be cajoled into action. Once a day is easy – the juices are still flowing from the day before, and it has a roll-on effect. I don't know what a roll-on effect is, but that is what it has.

I once met an errant female literary lecturer who told me I was escaping from responsibility. Right! I say. I was lying, of course; I was just escaping from her.

yours sincerely

To JAMES WATSON[3]
October 29, 1983

Dear James,

Jesus, you mean you haven't been sending the novel to publishers all this time? This was your only copy? Idiot. Never trust friends.

I can only grovel briefly over taking so long – Christ knows why. Some sort of mental block. Don't know which.

Partly, I think, because the novel was so different from what I expected. You have a definite and undeniable comic talent which is here only incidentally on display, and what you have attempted is so far from . . .

I think you write very well and I didn't enjoy this at all.

I felt that what might have been a rather telling short story had got blown up somehow into a novel of flatulent significance. The people in the novel simply weren't worth the effort you had expended on them. In its own terms it worked quite well, but I found myself resisting the terms on which you had written it. I don't quite think like R Boston that you had written five different novels, but I can see why he thought that.

Start again.

I kept thinking that what I was reading was not so much a novel, more an attempt by the writer to expiate or explain away experiences of his own.

I thought certain sections – like the early relationship of father with baby, or the man's experiences in the bicycle firm – were very good, but not out of the same book.

I think it's far too late for anyone to be interested in homosexual school exploits.

I thought the final explanation of everything in terms of a kind of madness was very good, but far too late.

I was maddened by the writer's urge to comment on everything as it happened and to explain it psychologically. It was all too knowing and remote, so that everything ended up in a kind of cotton wool.

Above all, I sensed that it was all very important to you but could never quite crack why it should all be very important to us. If you were trying to tackle the problem of man's situation in a woman's world, or – well, I'm not sure what you thought you really were tackling.

I think you write very well, but I don't think this is it. You ought to write novels as good as your letters.

To MICHAEL LANGAN
September 4, 1985

Dear Mr Langan,

I can testify, as Mr Kington's secretary; that he is far too busy to answer letters, all of which I have to reply to. In fact, he is far too busy even to read them. In fact, though you probably won't believe this, he is far too busy even to write his own articles, all of which I have to write as well. What does Mr Kington do? You may well ask. I believe he spends most of his time writing Bernard Levin's articles, as of course Mr Levin is far too busy to write his own material.

I once asked Mr Kington how to get into journalism. "That's not the problem," he told me. "The problem is how to get out of journalism."

If I were you, I would write as much as possible and send it to as many places as possible, though not to Mr Kington, who is terribly busy, though not half as busy as I am.

yours sincerely

pp Miles Kington

Iris Volepenny, Secretary

PS I have to forge his signature as well.

To TONY BENNETT[4]
January 15, 1986

Dear Tony Bennett.

Little did I think on the first day I entered Fleet Street (actually was just passing through by taxi to my job at Stockbroker Towers in the City, yes, a millionaire at 21 and a pauper at 22, how did I manage it? Easy – I left the taxi outside the building and forgot it was there until a year later when an indignant driver said: ("Hey, mate, that's £1,000,002 on the clock, are you going to pay it, then?") I didn't give him much of a tip, I can tell you) that one day, simply by saying a nice thing about Knockabout Comics; it would lead to the offer of a job writing introductions to books. Just like Prince Philip. I expect you've tried Prince Philip already? Well, I don't mind being second choice.

I'd love to write an intro for either book, but jazz being my great love I'd go for Max Zillion if I had to make a choice. £150 is fine. I take it you've tried Alexei Sayle already? Well, I don't mind being third choice. But if you're publishing next month, haven't you left things a bit late? You publishers. You're almost as bad as authors. Talk about artists . . . Do you know the story about Phil May? Apparently he agreed to do the cover for some Christmas number of a magazine, but disappeared in November to go to ground in Margate, leaving no address behind. The editor got so distraught that in early December he went down to Margate and tramped the streets of that fair city with a sandwich board reading: "WHAT ABOUT THE CHRISTMAS ISSUE?"

l take it you've tried Nicholas Parsons already?

yours

———————

To MR LEDGARD
January 20, 1986

Dear Mr Ledgard,

Thanks for your nice letter about five years ago. I got into Fleet Street by writing lots of stuff and sending it to lots of places. It took ages and it was a very painful experience, but you eventually get there. Meeting well-known journalists for lunch doesn't help at all. I once inveigled Peter Simple into taking me out for a drink, and he never said a word, except "That's Patrick Skene Catling". A ginger-haired man came in and lurched drunkenly over me.

Fifteen years later I met Catling again and reminded him of this encounter. He was sick over me. So you see.

The first encounter, incidentally, took place at the Wig and Pen

Club. I thought it was a northern drinking club called the Wigan Pen Club. I was wrong.

yours

——————————

To RICHARD INGLEBY
February 18, 1986

Dear Richard Ingleby,

Thank you for your letter of Dec 15, and I write in return to give you advice on how to become a great magazine editor. Now, you may reasonably object that you never wrote to me in the first place to ask how to become a great magazine editor, and that is fair enough, but I am so used to writing back to people who have written to me, telling them how to become a great magazine editor, that I reckon I might do the same for you. Now, none of them either have written to ask me about being an editor – many of them simply write in to ask what brand of shampoo I use and why it has led to early baldness – but being an editor is what I tell them about and it is what I am going to tell you about.

First of all, you have to make up your mind whether you are going to be the editor of a great magazine or the great editor of the magazine. If you have decided the former, to be the editor of a great magazine, then my advice is, frankly, forget it. There has not been a great magazine for many years, not since the *Spectator* of Addison and Steele in the 17th century, and if you read the *Spectator* of those days you will find that it was terrible. No readers' competition, no Jeffrey Bernard, no advertising to speak of.

It is much easier to be the great editor of a magazine. The best way to start doing this is by throwing lots of parties. £200 should be enough to throw a good party, especially if lots of people bring their own drink, and that's far cheaper than actually starting a magazine. I know a man in New York who threw launch parties for his magazine for nearly ten years, without bringing out a single issue. In fact, he got to know so many important people that after a while it became quite unnecessary to start the magazine at all, and he threw a final party for its closing down before going on to become a judge on the Pulitzer Prize, after which he could make a handsome living from bribes. But I digress.

The second important thing is to get many famous writers for your magazine. This is harder, and in the case of Somerset Maugham, impossible. Nevertheless, it is necessary, if only to get the advertising in. What I always advise is to search out people <u>with the same name as famous writers</u>. Have a look through your local phone book; I am sure there are any amount of Graham Greenes and William Boyds and RS Thomases, who would be only too willing to stand in. I am not saying that William Boyd is a great writer, far from it, but he is printed by Penguin and that is the same thing these days. If you can write to an advertiser and say truthfully and confidently, we have Colin Wilson, Angus Wilson and AN Wilson writing for the next issue, they will come through with the cash and piles of it. Mark you, I am not suggesting that all your writers should be called Wilson, as even the thickest advertiser will say to himself, Ho ho young Ingleby has been going though the W's in the Durham phone book. But I am sure you get the point.

Third, and most important, the first issue always sells best. Therefore, only have a first issue. Keep changing the name of your magazine every time you bring it out. I notice you have chosen Rumblesoup as the name of your first issue. Not bad, even if it sounds like a deservedly forgotten Marx Brothers film. But for heaven's sake get the name changed next time round. Other possibilities are Simple Simon, Illustrated London Nudes and True Detective Confessions.

They are not good possibilities, but they are possibilities.

Finally, it seems to be important to have lots of pretty girls on your staff. I am not sure why this is, but all the famous magazines I visited had lots of pretty girls on the staff, and I expect there was a good reason for it. Perhaps they are there for the parties. I am not sure. One followed me home once, but I forgot to ask her about it.

If, on the other hand, you only wrote to ask what kind of shampoo I use, why, I am glad to tell you. It is Swarfega Oily Shampoo for Lemony hair. And I am pleased to report that I have never had any trouble with natural citrus deposits in my rapidly shrinking coiffure. I owe it all to Swarfega.

yours sincerely

PS I have written this letter because I knew I would never write you an article. Use it if you want to. Send me a copy if it ever comes out.

———————

To JULIAN TYNDALE-BISCOE
August 29, 1986

Dear Mr Tyndale-Biscoe,
    Go to university.
    Infiltrate a stringer for a national newspaper.
    Sell them stories about the scandalous goings on at university.
    Get a small job with them when you leave college. Rise inexorably to the top.
    When you are editor, you will be able to write at last what you have always wanted to write, but you probably won't be able to by then.
    Otherwise, just write and keep sending stuff. But send it to the right place. If you write a funny piece about caravans, don't send it to *Punch*. Send it to a caravan magazine.
    Etc.

yours

———————

To MELANIE McNUTT
April 18, 1987

Dear Melanie McNutt,
    As you heard, I have been away from Britain for most of the last two months in Burma and China, so this is really the first opportunity I have had to answer your letter about Sir Charles Hardie.

Now, knowing nothing about Hardie except what you tell me, my immediate reactions are that a ghost writer would not be a good or at least a normal solution to the problem of getting his book done. A ghost writer is almost always used when the subject of the book is incredibly famous or at least famous enough to sell a book, but cannot write to save himself. In Sir Charles's case it seems to be the other way round; he sounds accomplished enough to deal with writing his own story but not famous enough to sell the book.

I know that you said that he has sat on more boards than anyone else in history, but I have to temper your enthusiasm by saying that being a director on a board is not a guarantee of an exciting or even interesting life. It sounds to me as if your Sir Charles tells a lively story about his life and you think that it would make a good book, which does not always follow, but at least you could capitalise on his ability with an anecdote. It might be possible to arrange an interview with Sir Charles in a magazine or possibly a small profile of him on the radio – they are always looking for such things – and that in turn would interest a publisher, certainly much more than if you approached a publisher directly.

I'm afraid you have to put yourself in the position of a publisher, who is offered an unwritten book about an octogenarian business-man. His immediate reaction will be: why should I publish it? There are plenty of witty old men who have sat on boards . . . You have to intrigue the publisher somehow – offer him juicy secrets, reminis-cences about the great and famous, unknown insights into history or simply some incredibly good writing. It is a possible task, but I would not like to have to undertake it, and I am not sure you should either. If Hardie does not respond to urging to write a book, it may be that he has a good reason for this.

Anyway, enough of airy theorising. I am, as you surmise, a busy man, solely because I leave everything to the last minute, but the next time I am passing the V & A I shall make sure I drop in and see your ceramic kingdom and you as well, if you are there. I've never met anyone from Corsicans.

yours sincerely

To MME GOLASZEWSKI
May 21, 1988

Dear Mme Golaszewski,

I hope you won't be offended if I say that reading an analysis of the way I write is very confusing for me – I hardly recognise myself, because I see my writing in a totally different way from you. You analyse it from the outside; I build it from the inside. I don't use structural analysis much at all – any piece which I plan well in advance usually turns out worse than pieces which evolve as I write. Very often I start with a vague idea, an opening line and one joke, not knowing where I am going and that is the sort I enjoy best. It is often the one that turns out best too. But when I work it out in advance, it goes cold on the page; well-built but uninteresting, like, a dish which has been reheated too often.

It might be true to say that my main aim is to surprise the reader. But actually I think it is to surprise myself. My favourite music is jazz, and in a sense every piece is like a jazz solo on a barely stated theme.

In other words, I am the last person you should ask for advice on my writing. Especially when I cannot remember having written a piece – I could only just recall the two you sent me.

yours sincerely

To MISS RUBY SEATON
June 11, 1991

Dear Miss Seaton,

I am afraid the struggle for freelance writing is much the same at 84 as at 18, and you have to tickle people's fancies by telling them new things or making old ones seem new. Now, I'm going to take a tremendous liberty here and say that in my opinion although your piece is very affable, it really doesn't go far enough. Unless, for instance, we know how frail you are, the actual achievement of getting from here to here does not seem great. You say you did it alone. Actually, as the reader knows, you didn't; you had a lot of help from passers-by and strangers.

I'm going to take another liberty, by suggesting that you could use the same material in a much more interesting way, and that is by writing a piece which advised octogenarians on how to enlist sympathy and get assistance: "I travelled to Heathrow alone with lots of people – the full story" – that sort of thing. Even make it a sort of advice column, "Over 80? Can't do the 100 metres in 10 seconds any more? Here's how to get people to help you, without them realising . . ."

I fear that in its present form your piece is just too nice, but a bit helpless, to make it.

yours sincerely

———————

To HELEN KUNZEMANN
May 8, 1992

Dear Helen Kunzem~~xx~~n

(great typing, eh?) Thanks for the letter and enclosure, as they say, and heaven knows what made you write to me with a piece of writing so different from my stuff, but anyway. It's hard to tell from that what sort of a writer you would make but it's easy to spot that you are a good observer of the way people behave, including yourself, and that you listen well.

But, what you sent me was really a raw two sides of raw experience, the sort thing you get in a diary. Where writing starts is where you decide what you want to do with it. Does it become a story about men's ability to understand? Does it become a comic story about falling for an Englishman in a land of (supposedly) hot-blooded Latin lovers? (That appeals to me.) Does it need more dialogue between you and the man? These are the sorts of questions you should be teasing out. As it is, what you have written so far is too conversational to do well as prose style, (too many) stray thoughts in brackets, too many exclamation marks . . .

Incidentally, was it intentional that you mention in the "story" that you threw yourself at the guy's feet after only a week, this making it sound a bit spur of the moment rather than the passion of the lifetime?

I wouldn't give up teaching just yet. People write because they can't help it. And they know when it is time to give other things up.

yours

———————

To MARKUS MARKLOVE
December 17, 1993

Dear Markus MarkLove,

I have done as you asked and read your article, and my true and honest opinion of it is that, whatever its merits, it is not an article as the press understands the word "article". It is a clarion call for your own beliefs. These beliefs to me – and probably to lots of other people – seem to be a mixture of "green" and Christian beliefs which, however cogent they are, are not the sort of thing which newspapers often like to print, any more than they like to print extracts from the Liberal Democrat manifesto or the Bible. What you say is not "news". It is lobby material. If Jesus arrived today, what he would say would not be news either.

Whoever gave you my name obviously did not know very much about me, as I am neither a Christian nor a believer in any religion; so it is hardly likely that l would support your attempts to convert the world. I do not feel I can recommend you to anyone in the media world, partly because I do not know enough people in the media world, partly because I have not enough confidence in any religion to recommend it to anyone.

I return the material you delivered to me. I cannot even wish you luck, as I mistrust all religions and that includes yours.

yours sincerely

To MARGARET FORSTER
May, 1994

Dear Margaret,

I'm sorry that I should have rung up while Hunter was committing suicide over the end of his new book the other day, but if it is any help I have a few hints to offer to those finding difficulty with the last page of an oeuvre.

1. Pretend the word processor has cut the book off and there is nothing you can do about it by printing in capitals: SORRY MEMORY FULL COMPUTER RECOMMENDS YOU START NEXT BOOK

2. Somewhat surrealistically, segue into the reviews of the book actually at the end of your text. You can write these yourself of course, but sign them Anthony Burgess, etc.

3. Do some ads for other books, like they used to have in novels and biogs years ago.

4. Write a test paper on what the reader should know so far.

5. Make the last page an application form for a GOLD Mastercard.

6. Make the last line CONTINUED IN VOLUME 2.

7. Make the last line THIS PUBLISHER HAS JUST BEEN BOUGHT BY RUPERT MURDOCH AND I REFUSE TO WRITE A SINGLE WORD FOR HIM.

8. If all else fails, reprint the beginning of the book back to front and upside down.

love

––––––––––

To DAVID LOVEGRACE
March 26, 1998

Dear David Lovegrace,

I really am not in the business of delivering judgement on other people's writing – life is far too short, etc – but I have raced through your samples and I honestly find them hard to make head or tail of. I think this is because they are couched in legalese, and are making fun of things legal, and therefore I am inclined to think that if published at all, they should be published in a legal setting – solicitor's magazines etc – where they will be found funny.

If you do send them somewhere else, I would seriously advise you to a) make them legible, as people do not submit things in handwriting any more b) send return postage, as most people will be tempted to throw submissions away if not accompanied by SAE. I am made of softer stuff. But please don't send me any more. I can't say anything else.

   yours sincerely

8

Correspondents

Miles received an enormous number of letters from a wide and diverse readership, particularly in response to his newspaper columns, and while he didn't answer them all, he replied to an astonishing number, although it might take him a year or more to do so. Fan letters could be very intense, from requests for signed photographs and meetings to declarations of love, marital advice, stalking, anger and abuse, and occasionally the offer to help him find God.

To GARY N. GIBBON
September 27, 1977

Dear Gary,

Nice to get a fan letter. I have framed it and put it on the wall so that I can throw darts at it. Yesterday I scored two signatures and a treble address. However, I am in a bit of a quandary over your request for a signed photograph. The only one I have handy is not very good and anyway it would be a shame to rip it out of my passport. I suppose one of these days I shall have to have some more taken, but it's a bit embarrassing going along to a studio and paying for photographs of yourself. It isn't much better going along to Charing Cross Station and sitting in one of those little booths, because the wind whistles in under the curtains and undoes your carefully combed hair. I could at a pinch steal one from the holiday family album, but I don't really think you want a picture of me digging sandcastles.

So do you mind accepting a signed letter instead? I promise that the next time I come across some photographs of me, or even get photographed by the police when I am next arrested, I will send you one.

yours

To GARY N. GIBBON
January 19, 1978

Dear Gary N. Gibbon etc,

Not so fast. People can prove anything from a sample of hand-writing and I would not like you going round the landscape saying, "You can tell from Miles Kington's t's that he beats his wife and probably other people's wives as well", so you will have to make do with my typing and my signature. I have analysed your writing and it is fairly obvious from the way you form your words that you are having trouble with your spelling. So before it lands you in serious trouble, write out a thousand times:

{list}hallo
absence
received{list/}

I am glad you have enjoyed Instant Sunshine. With any luck we can put popular music back fifty years and promote a revival of dinner jackets; in fact, we are trying to get Moss Bros to sponsor us, but so far they have not answered except with a brief puzzling note to the effect that "These are not the trousers that were with the suit when you hired it".

I think that answers all your questions, especially as you did not ask any.

(signed in Mr Kington's absence by Magnus Magnusson, Des O'Connor and Kevin Keegan)

———————

To GARY N. GIBBON
May 4, 1979

Dear idiot child,

I have analysed your typewriting in your last letter and find that it is two thirds gin. Or maybe that was something else I analysed. When you get to my age, the grasp begins to go, you begin to repeat repeat yourself and the brain cells drop out increasingly fast. I try calling it dandruff but it doesn't fool me.

Distressing signs in your last letter of trying to emulate me. I implore you to model your prose style on someone better or at least richer than me. Jim Slater, for instance, author of the immortal "Tiggly Wiggly goes to Singapore and makes a cool £2m in the bond market".

I have calculated that if Thatcher's voice goes on dropping at an octave a month, she will be perceptible in mid-July only by very big dogs.

Now get back to that novel.

yours
father of ten

Memorandum to CYNDI FAIRCHILD
November, 1981

Dear Cyndi,

Here, as requested, is a piece of anonymous writing paper. Well, yes, I did once get a visitation from a female reader who descended on my doorstep, but I couldn't read her Christian name either so it never really came to anything.

Guinea pig tastes all right. I get one once a week from the local pet shop and roast it. They think I have now got a huge collection. I daren't tell them I'm just eating them. Hamster's OK, too. Stick insects are quite nice, browned in the oven as cocktail delicacies.

Llamas are terrible in every respect.

I once met Jilly Cooper. We fell in love on the spot but her husband was there as well. The next time we met she had forgotten all about it.

Love is a confidence trick played by nature to ensure that parents stay together till the children are grown up. It doesn't seem to be working very well at the moment. Because nature seems at a loss to think of anything else.

Well, of course I know exactly what makes men tick, but we men have a conspiracy never to let on, so sadly I can't enlighten you. All

I can say is that men seem much more attractive till you get to know them, which is why I fear we are doomed never to meet.

yours

———————

To ANGELA LOBB
June 21, 1983

Dear Mrs Lobb,

Thanks for your nice but agonised letter. Quite honestly, I have never been very happy with the position of my piece since I left the obituary page, especially mixed up with the concise crossword down there, as it made a peculiar shape when I cut it out, as well as for other reasons. So eventually I persuaded them to move it and I think it looks quite good where it is, especially as they've jettisoned that terrible photo of me. (I'm very good-looking from behind.) But this morning I had a letter from a bloke who thinks I am not so funny when my piece appears in one vertical slab. Honestly, what is a poor girl to do?

I'm glad I cheer you up, but I'm sorry you need cheering up.

I feel a touch weighed down myself, having had a spate of deaths recently. The only close one was my father, last November, but after that it was my aunt's companion, an old colleague from *Punch*, a cousin who played jazz piano and my favourite jazz pianist of all time (Earl Hines). I'm too young (41) to deal with all this already, but at least I'm getting used to it, so when I pop off myself I shall be far from upset. Wasn't it Woody Allen who said: I'm not afraid of dying, I just don't want to be there when it happens? Yes, must be.

Joking apart, I am sorry about your loss, but I have the British disease of not knowing what to say when people die. Keep taking the column . . .

yours sincerely

To ALASTAIR FORBES[1]
February 16, 1984

Dear Mr Forbes,

I'm afraid yours is the sort of postcard one tends to store up and reread rather than answer, as a reply would only spoil it. However, it would be equally churlish to go on doing that too long, so I am writing now to say that although it's nice to get cheering letters from readers, it's best of all to get letters from writers you admire. I have read a great deal of your stuff, mostly in the *Spectator*, and always been bemused by your knowledge of things that no-one has a right to know much about. (Assuming you are the same person.) I seem to remember one piece you wrote based loosely on some early North African tale-telling by Richard Hughes, which told me more about Morocco than I am ever likely to know again.

Nobody ever learns things from reading my pieces. The opposite, in fact. I spin an airy tale, or float a kite, or invent a fact, and sure enough sooner or later a reader tells me the truth. If I mention General Galtieri's medals, I get a letter from a Wing Co pointing out in fact that Argentine generals tend not to wear medals. If I say that William books are not published behind the Iron Curtain, I get a letter from Richmal Crompton's niece quoting from the Czech translation.

It is possible even to do this with cartoons. Francis Wilford-Smith, who draws as Smilby, is an avid collector of old blues records. Now, there is one blues record recorded in the 1930s of which <u>no</u> copy is known to exist, so one day, just for laughs, he put it into an otherwise straightforward sexy cartoon he was doing for *Playboy* – there on the floor, along with the couple, lay the record with the number. People wrote to him from all over the States about this rare record. Nobody wrote to him about the couple. Nice to know there are some things much more important than sex. They still haven't found the record, mark you, but he's made friends with a lot of boring blues collectors in the USA.

If I ever come to la Suisse, I shall come and meet you. First I will have to find out how to pronounce Oex. I still don't know if Jean Françaix sounded his x.

Well, as I said, thanks for the card. Think I'll break off there and read it again.

yours

————————

To CATHY POKIN
June 6, 1984

Dear Cathy,

You don't realise this, but you wrote to me on my birthday.

Amazing coincidence. Next time, send a small present. A diamond or piece of gold bullion would do.

Thanks for your letter, which came as a pleasant surprise – I didn't know you could receive BBC programmes <u>and</u> *Punch* in Chicago, which shows how much I know about Chicago. I was also heartened by the quality of your French shining through the Franglais; I've always believed that Americans were very bad linguists, even as bad as the British, so it's good to know that things are on the mend.

Most of my time these days is spent writing a daily humorous column for the *Times* (of London), which I don't suppose you get in Chicago – it's not always easy to get in London – and although the pay is bad, I do get a free groupie with the job. She's getting on in years, poor thing, about sixty-seven now, and far too frail to actually get to the office, so we only meet once a year for a glass of Coke and her reminiscences about "that young fellow Frank Sinatra" who apparently once broke her camera in a fracas. She still keeps the pieces under her pillow. Anyway, I'll get in touch as soon as she retires or kicks the bucket, and maybe we can talk about things then.

yours

To GRAHAM SPIERS
July 26, 1984

Dear Mr Spiers,

Thanks for your chatty and subtly nattering letter. Why can't people write more letters like that?

There was a programme on Radio 3 last night based on Maupassant's last months, as described by his valet Francois. Bit dreary, I thought, as they did go on about his syphilitic descent. Anyone can get syphilis, but only Guy de M could write those stories. I taped it, though, as I have a close friend who is the top venereologist at St Thomas's and he might well be interested in the diseased bits. He usually is. I had a blocked ear recently and he offered to look at it. Hardly your speciality, I said. Don't be so sure, he said. I had an Italian waiter last year who had a genital wart in his ear.

"Wow," I said. "How did it get there?"

"Alas," he said, "I cannot speak Italian so I had to refer him to a colleague and I never found out. I didn't eat Italian for six months, though."

How did I get on to all that? Very briefly, I took French and German all the way through to Oxford, though as I played so much jazz at Oxford I started there with a scholarship and ended up with only a Third. I have kept up the French ever since, mostly by reading rather than chatting and even once translated a whole book. A selection of pieces by Alphonse Allais who I secretly believe was an Englishman born in the wrong place.

My filing system is so rotten that I can't remember which piece (May 25) you liked so much. But thanks.

I have – and this is where you can stop reading, if you know what's good for you – contracted to do a book on prejudice round the world, and to this end I am collecting all contacts with foreign experience to plague them shortly with requests for knowledge about local angles. You know – what the different regions of France think of each other, etc. Would you mind if I pestered you one day? You sound like a kindred spirit, even if you read the *Guardian*. Give it up, man! Get the *Herald Tribune*, like me. The only American paper that thinks Americans are kinda dumb.

I'd love to know just how you use Franglais, my version, as a teaching tool. Is it just a question of "Now turn this into decent French" or something more subtle? I once came across a French book which tried to do the same thing in reverse, called "Sky, My Husband!" (Ciel, mon mari, ha ha) but I didn't reckon it much. Well, I wouldn't, would I?

You may be interested/aghast to know that Channel 4 are broadcasting ten ¼ hour programmes based on *Let's Parler Franglais*. A small TV company got a commission from their educational (!) department to do it, and asked all the famous people they could think of to act in a short sketch each. Result: people like Cliff Richard, Sacha Distel, Willy Rushton, Nicholas Parsons etc making a star-studded cast. The company went bankrupt last month, but fortunately Channel 4 already had the tapes. This all starts on Aug 6. The ones I've seen all work quite well, though I was convinced they wouldn't. This thing's getting out of hand.

You will also be delighted to know that everyone in England was dead pleased that France won the European Cup. And it wasn't just because the Germans lost.

yours sincerely

———————

To HORACE HARRIS
HM Prison, Maidstone
December 5, 1985

Dear Horace Harris,

It's a strange thing, but the only other letter I got about that piece was from a bloke in Wormwood Scrubs. Someone once told me a nice story about Richmal Crompton – the old lady who wrote all the William books. She went to give a speech at a prison in Kent, Maidstone for all I know, and before she got up to speak, the literary screw in charge said to the assembled men: "Now, has anyone here read a William book?" Every man Jack put his hand up. "Dear me," said Richmal Crompton, "I am responsible for a lot, aren't I?"

I have bad news: "The Moreover Book of Life's Laws" was

totally made up. But I have good news too. Penguin have just put out a collection of my *Times* stuff, which I enclose. I hope it goes down well. I hope it gets to you, come to that. Let me know if it doesn't.

Write again anyway, if you like.

yours sincerely

———————

To FATHER CHARLES DILKE
April 9, 1986

Dear Fr Dilke,

I have left your letter of Feb 19 unanswered until now for the quite good reason that there is nothing in it that really needed answering and for the even better reason that I had a lot of work to do. If you can call writing daily for *The Times* work. I actually went to *The Times* the other day, and a picket shouted at me, "Are you a scab?"

"If a scab is the healthy growth left after a wound has been formed, then yes, I am indeed," I replied with dignity from my armour-plated London cab.

The pickets then formed into two distinct groups, one arguing that my cab should be rolled over immediately and set fire to, the other pleading that anyone with my care for words should be cheered through the line, nem con. Luckily, most of them seemed to assume that Nemcon was some sort of print union they had not heard of, and I was allowed in. Later, I left by the little-known Thames exit from Fort Wapping and took a passing lighter back to Westminster. It sank as soon as I arrived. Tragic perhaps, but it turned out to be one of these new-fangled disposable lighters.

You must be a luminary of Brompton Oratory. This was a place that I always wanted to see because George Borrow, one of my erstwhile heroes, was apparently buried in Brompton Oratory. It was not until I arrived in London at the age of twenty and decided to go on a Borrow pilgrimage that I discovered he had actually been interred in Brompton Cemetery. I searched for many years there among the bracken and brambles until I found his grave next to that of Samuel Smiles, once famous for the Victorian concept of self-help, and now chiefly remarkable for a grave overgrown with hedge parsley. It is for this reason that I have never been inside Brompton Oratory. Architecturally I am told that it is magnificent, but that for wild flowers it is poorly provided.

I trust this letter answers none of the points you raise. I only wrote it because you write such a nice letter.

yours sincerely

———————

To ROBERT HARRIS
May 21, 1986

Dear Mr Harris,

Thank you very much for your suggestion for Mr Kington about meetings, and the possibility of an article on these events. Unfortunately, Mr Kington is in a meeting at the moment, so I have not been able to put your suggestion to him, but I will do so as soon as he is free and I am sure he will be very interested in it.

I ought to warn you perhaps that he often uses ideas sent to him by readers without attributing them to the donor, and indeed without paying them, so that if by any chance he does take advantage of it, I am afraid you will only know by reading his piece in *The Times*. I myself have often uttered fanciful ideas in his presence which I thought he did not even register, but lo and behold they have turned up in articles a few days later. He is that kind of man.

If you will excuse me, I can just see Mr Kington coming out of his meeting . . . I am sorry, but Mr Kington has just gone into another meeting. I am afraid he is like that.

yours sincerely
Deb Freebody, secretary to Miles Kington

To MRS P. JOHNSON
September 22, 1986

Dear Mrs Johnson,

No, no, you have completely missed my point. I find rabies, crashes and murders as terrible as you do. What I also object to (and what I was trying to attack in my article) was the habit of papers and TV of dwelling on these things in horrified fascination for a brief season, and then dropping them for the next fashionable horror. It is almost as if the papers long for some horror, and I'm afraid to say that it is almost as if the readers and viewers do too.

I was very struck by the comments of a Czech émigré to the US recently, who said that he was delighted to be away from the Communist media, which started every new bulletin with glowing propaganda. What he couldn't understand was why this was replaced in the West by rapes, crashes, disasters, murders etc, which all took pride of place at the top of the news list. I don't really fathom it either.

My approach to the subject, in my piece, was to use irony, which always takes the risk of backfiring. It certainly backfired with you. Believe me, I wasn't being callous; I was being upset by the callousness of the media in rubbing their hands over rabies, or whatever.

If you don't mind, I'll do what you did and drop a copy of my letter towards the editor, just reassure him that I am not a monster.

yours sincerely

To FELICITY GIVEN [2]
November 18, 1988

Dear Mrs Given,

Normally I wouldn't dream of getting in touch with any of my former places of education, but I was tickled by your request for old alternative magazines. While at Glenalmond I co-ran a magazine called *Quintet* which ran for two issues. The first was a bit dull, the second a beasty, and we made money on both – I can remember bicycling round Perth and Crieff on hot summery days when the tarmac came up in big black blisters and so did I, soft talking shops into giving us an ad and lots of money and all the artwork. One of my fellow writers, Alex Cockburn, is now a pretty big journalistic figure in the USA, and I am a columnist for the *Independent*, so it was not all wasted. On the other hand, a bloke called Tudor Barnard who wrote poetry became a professor of marine biology in Sweden, so you can never tell. And the bloke called Duncan Campbell, who took over when I left, is now a big wheel on *City Limits*. He is not the famous Duncan Campbell, but he would be if the other one didn't exist, if you see what I mean. And he also lives with Julie Christie, which is a distinction I never rose to. Mark you, I have always been totally unable to recognise Julie Christie in film, photo or (once in my own home) in the flesh, so it is just as well that I never aspired to live with her. I wouldn't know who she was. I wouldn't know I <u>was</u> living with her. She would come home in the evening and I would say: "Hello, who are you?"

Now the bad news. Since leaving my last home and arriving here, I have lost sight of the old mags. I am not even sure if I have a spare copy. But if I should find one, you can have it. If it's my very last one, I could at least photocopy it.

I also ran a jazz band while at Glenalmond, of which I have a recording. This would be about 1958–59. It was terrible, but quite good considering. The marine biologist was on alto, and Cockburn was on bass. Nobody was wasted, you see. Our proudest moment was getting up before the pipe band which traditionally played round all the dormitories on the last morning of term, very early, and going round before them playing rousing New Orleans music. I say, how the old memories come back. I wish they wouldn't. I am busy enough as it is.

yours sincerely

To BETTY JENNINGS
March 22, 1989

Dear Mrs Jennings,

Whenever people write to me saying No reply required, or No answer of course! I always reply immediately. It's the other letters, the urgent, important, cheque-requiring ones, which I never get round to, which explains why my affairs have sent three accountants crazy and bankrupted a small bank in North Wales.

Say what you like about the present regime, at least they did invent the YTS scheme, for which I am truly grateful, as all my columns are written by a cheap team of YTS people who live in my attic upstairs and whom I let out for a walk now and again if I am satisfied with their work. Very often they do not come back, such is the disloyalty of youth today, and then I have to hire more. But all my letters are written by myself, for which I pay myself a handsome fee.

God knows what I would do if I were a widow at 71, but I suspect I would probably go bicycling or something irresponsible like that, and then write about it. Pretty much what I do already . . . Thanks very much for writing. Praise to a writer is better than the finest malt whisky.

yours sincerely

———————

To ARIELLA BERGER
May 22, 1991

Dear Ariella Berger,

Hold on there. Steady. Slow down. If you did reread my piece, you would find that I had not in the least belittled Nazi war crimes. They were horrible, they are horrible. All genocide is horrible, and all cruelty is horrible. Unfortunately, it is still going. What I was suggesting was that the government was slightly aiming at the wrong target in going after a few aged Nazi war criminals (which can't, as some rabbis have pointed out, bring any dead Jewish people back again) when there are people alive here and now who are practising their own form of holocaust on their subject populations. To say that we have more chance of helping now than taking revenge for what happened 50 years ago is not to say what happened 50 years ago is unimportant. That is something you read into my piece. I don't think I wrote it.

I think you're half right about education. I think when people know the truth, it does sober them. But I think that people would not be deterred even by the full horrific facts. There's always going to be a part of humanity that actually approves of and quite enjoys inflicting cruelty on another part of humanity.

If you do see my piece again and still think I was saying what you said I was, show me the passage. But I'd be surprised beyond belief. I think you got hold of the wrong end of the stick in a big way. So far from being anti-semitic I am if anything prejudiced in favour of them. I even went on a visit to Belsen once, while in Germany. I didn't enjoy it much, believe me.

———————

To GEORGE D GRAY
July 8, 1992

Dear Mr Gray

What a great pleasure to be the recipient of your fan letter – I hope you stop writing them now, so that I can claim to be the only one you ever wrote to . . . Yes, it's odd, considering how much pleasure Mencken can give, how few people seem to find him. Another example is a French humorist called Alphonse Allais, who I consider to be a great man and who remains unknown. I once translated a whole bookful of his stuff. He is still unknown.

What you say about Mencken reminds me of what Richard Cobb wrote about another undervalued Frenchman, Raymond Queneau. I started reading Queneau's novels because they were funny, but Cobb said that if you talk to any Queneau-lover, you find you are often talking about a different writer. People value writers for what they themselves are looking for, and which tends to govern what they find. So, he said, I have heard Queneau described as 1) a master of linguistics 2) a funny man 3) a surrealist 4) a great stylist. Cobb himself said he valued Queneau above all as the chronicler of French suburban life and all the little details that involved, which is not surprising as Cobb himself was hooked on French bourgeois life. You can see how Mencken, too, would attract different people, for different reasons so I have had one letter from a man who sees Mencken only as a linguist and lexicographer, another from a man who values Mencken most of all as a music critic . . .

I shall be in Edinburgh in a month's time, oddly, performing in the Festival. I have been several times before, playing the double bass in a cabaret group called Instant Sunshine, but this time I am taking a great jump into the unknown and doing a tiny one-man show at the Pleasance Theatre which purports to guide people through the jungle of the fringe. It's on at 11.30 at night, when everyone including me should be home in bed . . . but if a space appears in my schedule, or the show folds with no audience, I may well come knocking on your door and paying my compliments. I wouldn't normally dream of saying such a thing, but anything seems possible at Festival time . . .

yours sincerely

———————

To BRENDAN GLACKEN[3]
February 1, 1994

Dear Brendan Glacken,

What a surprise and delight to get a letter from Dublin, a thing which has never happened to me before, even though I wrote thousands of fan letters to Flann O'Brien only to find that he had been dead for years.

The only humour festival I have ever been to, apart from the weekly *Punch* lunch, was one in India. It took place about ten years ago, and was a World Humour Congress at Hyderabad. I read about it in the *Herald Tribune* some months previously, and was so captivated by the sound of it that I contacted the Indian Embassy to find out more. They did not even know it was planned, and asked me to tell them when I found out more about it. It was postponed once, briefly, when Mrs Gandhi was shot, as they felt it would look bad to have a wacky humour festival two days after she had died, but eventually it was held and it was wonderful – I could talk about it all night, and probably have. But whether it became a regular affair, I couldn't tell you. I doubt it, somehow. It had started out as a projected meeting laid on by the local Urdu Poetry Society, which had just grown and grown. I imagine they said afterwards, Never again. Tell you what – why don't you ask the Indian Embassy . . . ?

I don't see the *Irish Times* normally. Tell me what day you are on. Tell me something else. I recently had to do a small programme for Radio 4 on what makes the Irish laugh and I found myself interviewing, on the phone, Brendan O'Carroll, who talked among other things about his daily radio soap, *Mrs Brown's Boys*. Is it as funny as he made it sound?

———————

To MARTIN GWYNNE
April 14, 1994

Dear Martin,

It was nice of you to try to save my soul. I fear you may have failed. I started to read your pamphlet, but I quickly spotted something about it which you may not have noticed, i.e. that it is completely unreadable except for a convert. It also seems to assume that what the Bible says is true, which seems to me so wildly unlikely that I refuse to take it seriously.

I didn't see the *Sunday Telegraph* feature in which I am mentioned. A man rang me up to ask my opinions about God or otherwise. I should know by now that one always gets misquoted, but I have no idea what he made me say, so I can't comment on it. All I can say is what I believe: that it seems mightily unlikely to me that any of the major religions of the earth contains a lot of truth, except subjectively. I also think that goodness is far too important a matter to leave in the hands of a church. And I agree with Lord Melbourne that religion is all very well, but it shouldn't be allowed to intrude into private life. I really cannot see any more reason why

I should read your pamphlet than why I should rush out and buy a book on astrology, which many people think is the clue to every-thing.

I see or hear from you once every fifteen years or so. At Oxford you were very obsessed by horse racing. In the Tube, once, you told me you were deeply into City finance. Now it is religion. Who knows what it will be next time?

As you can see, I am a deeply frivolous person. It is too late to change this. If I awake on Judgement Day and God is there with all his instruments of justice, I hope I have the charity to cry out: "By Gum, Martin Gwynne was right all along!" But – I fear the odds are long against.

    yours
till the next time . . .

_____

To PETER J. GROVE
December 6, 1994

Dear Mr Grove,

I should know better by now than to bandy word derivations with readers, as I usually end up worse off (but better educated). Actually, I did know the *Macbeth* quote about scotching the snake, which is interesting, as Shakespeare clearly meant it to mean "wound", not "kill", and yet nowadays people always mean "kill", as: in "scotching the rumour", "scotching the mutiny" and so on. I have had a postcard from a reader which reads in its entirety:-

> Miles, A scotch is a tapered wooden block used to stop point blades closing accidentally following a points failure, used with a locking point clip to secure the other side. Incidentally, if the Achille Lauro had only a hijack and one fire in 47 years, why was it "a doomed vessel, with a chequered history"? Pretty good, I'd have thought, yours, Rod Mackay, signalman, Ystrad Mynach . . .

Totally irrelevant, very nice to get, and hard to answer.

Anyway, I'm glad you wrote, as we clearly have at least two things in common. My dad was a brewer, at Border Breweries in Wrexham, and I damned near became one as well, until sanity or maybe insanity prevailed. So I do vaguely remember all this brewing stuff, as well as one term you didn't mention, which is wort. Richard Boston is an old mate of mine – I even wrote for *Vole* many years ago. The other link is that I think Alkan is one of the great men in music. I find his stuff quite dizzying. I heard the Hamelin recital the other night (with other people around, unfortunately) and the discussion as well, but my greatest Alkan memory is of once going to hear Ronald Smith give a concert of his music. Tell me more about the society. I managed to tape the first ten minutes of the Solo Concerto – hadn't heard it for a while – was knocked out all over again. But that Hamelin should be an Alkan fan, and a Monty Python fan, and that a dead parrot should be a link, is almost too silly to be true . . . thanks for writing. Maybe tell me more about Alkan after Christmas, because before Christmas all my mail will go into a coma.

yours sincerely

––––––––––

To STEPHEN MARINKER[4]
December 7, 1995

Dear Mr Marinker,

Thank you for your letter of 4th December, and you haven't heard the last of me. I was delighted to read the history of Baked Beans. It put a lot of things into perspective for me, as I certainly had not realised that all the ingredients of Baked Beans had to be imported from elsewhere. H. J. Heinz have kept it very quiet that Baked Beans are in fact a luxury foreign delicacy and not the essentially British thing that everyone thinks they are, but your secret is safe with me. I was interested to read that navy beans were first spotted in Peru, as Peru seems to be a source of many interesting food stuffs such as the potato and the guinea pig. Yes, I have eaten roast guinea pig and can testify that it is rather like a rich form of rabbit. If you look at the huge painting of the Last Supper in Cusco Cathedral, you will see that the dish of the day for Jesus and his chums was roast guinea pig. I cannot remember, I am sorry to say, if navy beans were on the menu.

The last time I saw navy beans mentioned before your letter arrived was in a wonderful book called something like *Elvis Presley – His Life and Cuisine*, which was written by a man called David Adler who has painstakingly researched everything that Elvis ate and almost everyone who cooked for him. As he was in the American Army for two years, he ate a lot of beans, and there is duly a recipe in the book for navy beans cooked army-style.

I hope this information is useful to you, but I doubt it.

    yours sincerely

To JEROME LAYTON
December 13, 1995

Dear Mr Layton,

You wrote to me two months back about the Edith Cavell monument. I have an interesting story to tell you about this monument. As you know, it was carved by Jacob Epstein, who was thought to be rather modern in his day and when the monument was first unveiled before a group of celebrities to reveal a statue which was not entirely like the original woman, a well known writer was heard to exclaim "My God, they shot the wrong woman!"

I am afraid you may find this a bit irreverent but I think it is very funny.

    yours sincerely

To JOHN KING
May 22, 1996

Dear Mr King,

Alas, I have to confess that there is no such thing (to my knowledge) as an English-language compendium of Albanian proverbs. I made them all up myself.[5] The thing is that when you write a daily humorous column such as I do, you occasionally stockpile strange almost meaningful one-liners which swim around on your word processor memory like guests at a party who don't seem to know anybody else there, and you start feeling sorry for them . . .

So I devised the idea of just putting them together as a collection of modern proverbs, and when I had to invent a home for them, I thought Albania was safe, as very few people know anything about the place. I myself know nothing, except a long and quite funny story about King Zog. I knew sooner or later someone would turn up and say, "You made all this up!!", but as I make everything up every day, I am not too upset.

Anyway, I envy you your first-hand experience of the place. I would have answered your letter sooner, except that I work at home and the *Independent* takes about a month to forward my mail.

Incidentally, did you ever come across the American book of proverbs compiled by Paul Dickson and entitled by him *Universal Rules* and later *New Universal Rules*? Good stuff . . . One I remember is as follows: – "A memorandum is never sent to inform the recipient, only to safeguard the sender."

yours sincerely

———————

To H. S. HUDSON
May 24, 1996

Dear Mr Hudson,

I long ago learnt that if you send out signed photos of yourself, you soon have none left and a large photographer's bill. That stage was reached a long time ago, and I now have nothing left of me save a few spare passport photos making me look like Carlos the Jackal, and some water colours of me done by Prince Charles. Well, not by Prince Charles, but at least by someone much better. Carlos the Jackal, actually. Still, at least you get a genuine signed letter from me, which is worth a lot more than my signed photo. On the other hand, anything is worth a lot more than my signed photo.

yours

———————

To TOM KINSEY
October 1, 1997

Dear Tom Kinsey,

The dog has just pulled my modem, which has slopped a mug of tea, which has gone over your card, which has caused the ink to run, so I have got to write to you NOW or else your address will go too out of focus to work. Hey, I like your painting on the card, even with tea on it. Have you ever thought of trying to get shown at the Portal Gallery in Grafton Street? They specialise in very good so-called naive art from Beryl Cook to . . . to . . . Lots of other artists, and your stuff looks like their kind of stuff. Mark you, I know nothing about art. When I like people, it usually dooms them. I was asked this week to do a piece for *Fourth Column* (Radio 4, Friday 11.25 p.m.) and part of it deals with how it is possible to get through life with no visual sense. I grew up in Wales, which may have something to do with it. Whenever I wanted to rile the Welsh, I used to say that the reason for their terrific musical talent was God's desire to compensate for their lack of visual talent.

"How do you mean?" they would say, as they pelted me thoughtfully with nutty slag.

"Well," I would say, "never was a country made so beautiful by God, and never was so little done to improve it by the inhabitants."

Then I would make for the hills. Very touchy, the Welsh.

That's why I love them. You can make fun of a Scot for years and he'll hardly notice it, but the Welsh lose their rag gratifyingly quickly.

Are you Welsh?
Oh, sorry.
I think it was Leslie Holmes.
Got any more cards of your oeuvre?

———————

To H. RICHARDS
March 18, 1999

Dear Mr Richards,

I was very touched to get your letter about my Millennium prayers, though I was somewhat alarmed when you said my religion pieces brought the best out in me. As a person who hovers regularly between Anglicanism, agnosticism and apathy, I find myself alarmed at being paid such a compliment, but I am sure you mean well.

It reminds me of the time at school when our very last essay before we left was on the subject of God. I wrote a long essay proving to my satisfaction if not God's that He did not exist, probably, and left before I got it marked and returned. The headmaster gave it to my younger brother next term, remarking, "Very nice essay, and showing amply that Miles is deeply religious deep down . . ." It was one of the first examples I had of how unfairly religious people can argue. The most recent example I had of how wonderfully subversive religious people can be was, of course, your letter.

yours sincerely

———————

To T. L. SMITH
March 23, 1999

Dear Mr Smith,

I have been passed a copy of the furious letter you wrote to the editor about my piece on Yehudi Menuhin and cricket, and I would like to say how much I enjoyed it. Of course, I am sad that when people are cross they write to the editor about it, and when they are happy they write to me, but you learn to live with that.

Normally, I wouldn't answer a letter like yours on the reasonable grounds that it wasn't addressed to me, but as you got so many things wrong in such a short time, I thought I should try to help you out of some of your misapprehensions.

I may be a jazz fan, but I love classical music too.

My piece was not a sneer at the tributes paid to Menuhin. It was not a sneer at all. It was a parody of the kind of letters written after the main obituary has been printed, of anyone.

You know the sort of thing . . . "Dear Sir, I am surprised that you did not mention the revered place that the late Queen Mother had among beer-mat collectors, as her collection of beer-mats was one of the finest ever amassed inside or outside the Royal Family . . . Wartime experiences . . . charity work . . . secret love of poetry . . ." These are the sorts of thing always being adduced.

Some time ago I decided it might be fun to write fake tributes after the death of really famous people, tracing their (fictional) love of cricket. This would only work if they were really unlikely to have any link with cricket, so on previous occasions I have done it with Frank Sinatra, and one of the Kray brothers, and Marlene Dietrich, and Enoch Powell, and Iris Murdoch and others, all of them involving quite separate flights of fancy. The fact that I thought it might be fun to tie in Menuhin with cricket as well does not make me a foe of classical music except in your foaming imagination.

I am not sure what other signs you have had that I am despicable. I believe you are wrong when you say that my use of cricket in obituary tributes is unoriginal. If you have any examples of either of these two, I shall be happy to learn them.

yours sincerely

From ANDREW MOTION
July 1, 1999

TWO PAGES FOR Miles Kington

Dear Mr Kington,

I was sincerely flattered by your column yesterday. But I know a gauntlet when I see one.

With best wishes
Andrew Motion

Passport Office Blues

The thing about the passport queue is this:
I stand about, half rotted-through by piss-
ing rain; my other half adrift; my kids
In tears, bored rigid, making stupid bids
To win my love back (not a hope of that) –
And think:
what is it this reminds me of? I know.
A summer holiday. Now I won't have to go.

To ANDREW MOTION
July 7, 1999

Dear Andrew Motion,

In my job I often invent characters whom my readers treat as real, so I have come to view my correspondents with a certain suspicion, just in case I'm having my leg pulled, which is exactly what I thought when I opened your letter. However, I thought your poem was much better than any fraud like me could make up, so I have now come firmly round to the opinion that you are the real thing. Probably.

Thanks very much . . .

It seems a shame to confine sight of it to me. Did you send a copy to the Letters at the *Independent*? Would you like me to slide it their way? If they knew I had it, they would be furious at my keeping it to myself . . . No, on reflection, I think I might keep it for my occasional round-up of reader's letters. Of course, they might not believe me even then, but think I had made it up. Recently I invented a man whose job was to do Neighbourhood Surveys. That is, when you moved into a new house and got all your surveys and law searches done, he also did a survey of your new neighbours to pinpoint potential troublemakers and nasties. The next day after I had used the piece in the paper I was rung up by the Canadian News Service (who had seen it on the Internet) wanting to know his phone number . . . What is truth? said jesting Pilate, and jesting was the right word.

The only time we have come close to contact before now was in a letter of Larkin's you printed in your excellent life, in which he complained of having to write some bloody piece for *Punch*, I had commissioned it from him.

    yours sincerely

———————

ROUND ROBIN LETTER
December 1999

As you can probably tell, this is a corporate-type letter from the Miles Kington Correspondence Customer Care Unit, and not quite a hand crafted and individually numbered production. This is because there were really quite a lot of you who wrote in about changed meanings, and if I answered you all individually, it would take me all night, and my wife would wonder where I was, and then I would be very tired at breakfast and fall asleep over the kippers, and she would get cross, and soon we'd start having arguments, and the cats would leave home, and then we'd have separate law-yers and after that it's all downhill. But as you probably saw, I quoted you in today's *Independent* (assuming today is Wednesday) so it was sort of worth writing to me. Thanks a lot anyway, and if you never write again, may I take this early opportunity of wishing you a very happy Christmas.

    yours sincerely

To ALEX LEWIS
November 16, 2000

Dear Mr Lewis,

Well, I think you're quite right. One journalist writing about another is pretty incestuous and boring. I hardly ever do it, though – you just happened to catch the one time when I thought I could make a point about people's writing styles not benefitting from contact with the Booker . . .

Actually, I think the worst thing about journalists, or at least about columnists, is the ceaseless parading of their opinions.

Where do they get so many opinions from? From thin air, I guess. Most of the columns you read, headed "Chlamydia Scott, Columnist Of The Year, writes about Siamese twins", come about not because Miss Scott is interested in Siamese twins but because some editor has rung her up and said, "Chlam, do us 1.000 words on Siamese whatsits will you?" And she does.

I once went to the *Times* library to look up some pieces of mine, and told the cuttings man what they were about. "Yours aren't under Subject, mate," he told me. "They're all in a big book marked Kington. Just you and Bernard Levin we do that for – don't put you under subject, just under your name."

"Why just me and Levin?"

"Because we can never work out what the fuck either of you is writing about."

I took it as a compliment.

yours sincerely

––––––––––

To JAMES HARRIS
October 8, 2001

Dear James Harris,

Many thanks for your long and lucid letter (qualities that don't always go together in the readers' letters racket, not that I get millions). There was a time when I kept in touch with the *New Yorker* – a long time – but we have drifted apart over the years. I think it was a mixture of reasons.

1. Leaving *Punch*, where they had a free copy.
2. Getting exasperated with some of the writing (I once struggled to the end of a long profile of the Bartók String Quartet, only to read the words "Concluded In The Next Issue").
3. Getting jealous of all the jazz I was missing in New York, carefully listed in the opening section.
4. Moving to Bath area, where I don't see it stocked anywhere.
5. Tina Brown.

Also, some of the lesser cartoons had a samey smartass quality about them, but you're right, the best ones are terrific. I liked your batch very much, even if I don't think that figure was as well drawn as you do. Do you remember a *Punch* cartoonist called Anton? Now SHE could draw tall elegant females. Apparently she was rather short and slightly bent herself, and compensated with all those visions of loveliness, all tall.

Well, perhaps I should give the *New Yorker* another try . . .

I have always liked Ludlow, even though I grew up near the wrong end of Shropshire – my father was based in Wrexham (cultural desert) and we knew the Overton–Oswestry–Ellesmere area quite well. I have even played in a group (Instant Sunshine) in the Ludlow Festival, in the big church. Not a great acoustic, as I remember. But show me a church with intimate cabaret acoustics . . .

I once quite by accident heard a talk about Ludlow and town planning, and how Ludlow was one of the very first places ever to be planned in advance, and the plots sold according to the architectural plan. Have I remembered right? The only other place I have come across such early planning was Notting Hill, where Mr Ladbroke in the 1840s got an architect to draw up a master plan before a single house had been built. And yes, I keep reading about Ludlow being the gastro-centre of the world outside London. I expect the chemists, GPs and gym owners are also thriving.

In answer to another question, no, I don't know those books on the *New Yorker*. I've read a couple, by Gill and Thurber, I think. I also remember Thurber and Perelman having a conversation about the *New Yorker*, and one saying, "Look, in the last resort it's only a magazine", and the other one hitting him in fury, but I can't remember which way round it was.

Good story, though. I met Brendan Gill once in New York and he took me to an ancient club where there was a very ancient man.

Gill (to ancient man): Tell the young Englishman about you and Mark Twain.

Ancient man: Well, young Englishman, I grew up in New York about 100 years ago, when there weren't many people here, just a few families like the Guggenheims and the Astors, and you could play in the middle of Sixth Avenue without danger. And one day my mother was walking along the road with me and she said to me: "Don't look now, but here comes Mark Twain." And I didn't look, and I never saw Mark Twain . . ."

yours sincerely

To FATHER SHARRATT
May 6, 2002

Dear Fr Sharratt,

All rejigging of newspapers is done to keep the blood circulation of the editor's ego going. At least, that's my theory. I can't think of any other good reason. I myself liked the former broadsheet format of the *Review*, even if everything seemed to need turning to Page 7 to finish off.

Still, whenever we say, "Oh, I liked the old format", we forget that once upon a time that was the new format, and when the old format wasn't old at all, but was just becoming the new new format, people (probably us) were saying, "Oh, I liked the old format best", and so on back through history.

Overheard in AD 70.

1st Man: What do you think of this New Testament, then?

2nd Man: It's horrible. I much prefer the Old Testament the way it was.

yours sincerely

———————

To TERRY HANCOCK
February 15, 2003

Dear Mr Hancock,

Thanks very much for your cheery note, and your slice of National Service life. Aden must have been stifling if you can remember conversations fifty years later.

I just missed National Service by about two years, and instead of meeting people in the army met them at Oxford. That was not quite the same thing, but still a good mix of people – the year I arrived there was a great influx of boys from King Edward VII Grammar School, Sheffield, who were not only very Yorkshire but all cleverer than me, which was alarming. I once asked one of the college servants (that's what they were called, I'm afraid) what the difference was between us and the National Service lot.

"They had a much higher standard of practical joke, sir," he said. "I remember one morning the Dean, who was rather unpopular, could not get out of his rooms at the top of his lodgings because barbed wire had been laid on all three floors of his staircase, in a fashion which could only be done by a commando, and only removed by a commando. And there was indeed an ex-commando in the college. We went to find him. Unfortunately, he had gone to London for the weekend . . ."

yours sincerely

To AVRIL JO MULCAHY
November 15, 2007

Dear Avril Jo Mulcahy,

I cannot believe that there is anyone in Britain alive today who finds the playground word "bum" upsetting. At least, I could not until I received your letter. Assuming you are not trying to pull my leg, I would venture to suggest that "butt", being American slang, is much more direct and in-your-face , as they say now, and that "posterior" is far too pompous and old-fashioned to be used any more.

No, madam, I cannot withdraw the word "bum". It is the mildest one I can think of, unless we are going to descend to words like "btm" and "behind". Perhaps you would prefer "buttocks". I wouldn't.

yours sincerely

9

Words

A love of words and of language governed Miles's writing. He had a natural aptitude for other languages and could speak German and French fluently by the time he left Oxford. Driven always by the desire to communicate, he then taught himself Spanish and Italian and attempted Portuguese, Burmese and Cantonese, enough to get by when in those countries. Franglais, created by him when at Punch, was not just "cod French" but carefully constructed, a fusion of English idioms and the structure of the French language. With regard to the English language, he was not a pedant but felt that accuracy had its place.

To GERALD LONG[1]
June 11, 1984

Dear Gerald Long,

I think it does you credit to get in touch with me after the last rather stuffy letter I sent you. I'm glad you did; I found your paper extremely interesting, probably because I agreed with almost everything you said even when I didn't quite follow it.

I see your distaste for the word Franglais has good grounds, but it is hard to know what to call it otherwise. Of course, what I call Franglais and what Étiemble calls Franglais are two quite different things. He's talking about French "corrupted" by Anglicisms; I'm talking about the somewhat artificial blend which I have tried to make into an amusing lingo. When other people write to me in their form of Franglais, it always differs radically from mine, and each from each other. But I will say this: I have tried as far as I can to observe French grammatical rules, agreements, genders, and so on, to introduce genuine French phrases, and to use a bit of slang here and there which may rub off on the reader.

I studied French as my major language at Oxford, so I have an affable nodding acquaintanceship with linguistic history, an affection for medieval French and a perpetual curiosity about words. Basically I find French much easier than Franglais and have several times had pieces returned by *Punch* with a note: "Yes, but you haven't included any English words." So I don't think we are too far apart in beliefs. If you like, I am trying to remove from the word Franglais the associations given it by Etiemble and giving it something more positive, if crude.

I sometimes think that the French defensiveness about their language mirrors our nervousness about American words. We tend to feel threatened by American slang, American technology, American jazz and showbiz talk, and to show the same blinkered desire to exclude it from our vision. So although we laugh at the French desire to search our linguistic baggage at the customs and confiscate foreign words, I think it's not entirely fitting for us to throw the first stone. I think also the British show a strange talent for being xenophobic and catholic at the same time. It happens with food: people blast off about filthy foreign cooking and yet the very same people are the first to go to a Chinese or Indian restaurant. We also refuse to learn foreign languages, and yet import their words with a will. For some reason, for instance, jazz fans in Britain always refer to themselves as aficionados, yet I don't think they even realise the word is Spanish and a bull-fighting term at that.

I've started rambling. I'd better stop. I hope you can spare that copy of your paper.

yours

———————

To ALAN CANNON[2]
December 5, 1985

Dear Mr Cannon,

Blimey, couldn't you have gone somewhere with a shorter address? Thanks for your learned letter, which had me thinking. Took me a few minutes to work out CACHOU. I think your idea of a dictionary with all possible combinations of letters is very good and quite crazy. As for the invention of new words . . . are there really any new words? They all seen to be chips of old words. My old teacher at school once told me that only one genuine new word had been created recently: gas. Later I discovered that he was wrong: quiz was also a new creation. The story goes that two gents in Dublin bet each other that one of them couldn't invent a new word and get it used. That night the man who had been betted went round Dublin writing "quiz" on every wall he could find. Next day, everyone was saying it: "Quiz? Quiz?? What's dis quiz den?" And it stuck.

I don't know if you're allowed to receive subversive literature from outside, but I'm taking the risk of enclosing a new paperback that Penguin are proposing to bankrupt themselves with. I hope you're out soon. If you can write letters like that, you should be all right.

There was a very good clue in *The Times* crossword the other day. "A pure NW Somerset resort." (6-5-4). Over to you.

Thanks for writing. Write again.

yours sincerely

To STANLEY BAXTER[3]
December 29, 1987

Dear Stanley Baxter,

As you can see from the date, my answer to you has got irretrievably mixed up with my thank you letters, and I would just like to say how grateful to you I am for the large bowl with the slight chip, it was just what I wanted. Moving now to any other business, I see that you have recently learnt that outwith is a Scottish word. This is worrying. Worrying for, you, mainly, because now you are going to say to yourself: I wonder how many of the other words which I had always thought were English are really Scottish? I wonder if I have been talking a broad kind of Scots ever since I got here 28 years ago? And nobody has understood a word I've said? . . . Which reminds me that Bill Forsyth, when first talking to Burt Lancaster about the latter's appearance in *Local Hero*, remained convinced afterwards that his quite strong Scots accent had remained impenetrable to Lancaster throughout.

Actually, I remember quite well being asked to try something for your Xmas Show. The reason I backed out was not that I didn't want to or wasn't flattered, but that from experience I've learnt painfully that being practised at one kind of humour (the written page) does not give you one scrap of qualification for writing another kind (spoken dialogue). SJ Perelman wrote the worst comic dialogue in the world, which is good in one way, because it means that I'm better than someone already, but it's still a long way to go. Tell you what though – if you're planning another show for next Christmas, I'll have a bash at starting something now. Even if it's only your thank you letters.

To STANLEY BAXTER
June 10, 1988

Dear Stanley,

I hardly knew Kenneth Williams at all, but I can remember him always talking about words and poetry – wish I had known him better. I dimly remember reading about you and him being mates from way back – was it in Peter Nichols's book, in the army days section? Think it was. I had a letter the other day from Geoff Nichols, jazz trumpeter and bandleader, who turned out to be Peter Nichols's brother. What a small world. Mark you, I have never met Peter, and as I was not able to comply with Geoff's desire for me to review his band, I may never meet him either. What a big world, after all.

If you ever do a Christmas special again, I had an idea once for a funny Christmas sketch lasting ten minutes and involving no dialogue at all, which started with Father Christmas trying to get down the chimney of a country house, and dislodging tiles, and ended up with ten Father Christmases sitting round, drinking tea, the whole house having been turned into a building site, surrounded by vans, holes in the ground etc . . . Well, it's funny in my mind.

When Kenneth died, someone quoted him on the radio as saying that he never wanted to lose sight of the early and gritty part of humour, as that was the real basis of all true English humour. If he was right, I had better get my act together, as I never made an earthy joke in my life. I tell you what worries me, though, more than that. The other day I was on the train just outside Reading. It had been there for ten minutes, quite immobile. The voice on the intercom suddenly came on and said: "We apologise for the delay. This is due to a lorry jammed under a bridge just ahead of us." What worried me was that I was the only person on the train who rushed to the window to have a look. Is there no curiosity any more?

Behave yourself, or you'll never be captain of England at cricket.

yours

———————

To ANN CARPENTER
February 3, 1997

Dear Ann Carpenter,

Thanks for your letter of support. It hadn't occurred to me to think that the pun disease has spread beyond cartoons, but of course you're right – it has attacked headlines everywhere.

Even the tabloids sport headings like "Queen Wins Yachtery!" (which is actually one of the better ones).

I suppose there is nothing new about it. When I worked at *Punch*, we used foolishly to delight in clever punning titles. I can even remember making them up before there was an article to pin them on – for years I hung on to "Naked as Nietzsche Intended" and "I Have Seen The Fuschsia And It Works" . . . I think I stuck the latter on to a Harry Secombe piece about gardening. He was not immune either. He called his only novel *Welsh Fargo*.

And the French humorist I once translated, Alphonse Allais, was nuts about puns – he used to invent Americans with names like Harry Covayre – and he was writing a hundred years ago . . .

Still, enough is enough. I will sign the pledge. I wish the cartoonists would. There was another one the other day, a punning cartoon, I mean, which showed a man standing up at a meeting of ALCOHOLICS SYNONYMOUS and saying, "I am a drinker, an inebriate a piss-artist, a wino . . ." Very clever. But funny?

Not often I reply by return to letters. It usually takes the *Independent* two months to send letters on to my workplace = home. Incidentally, I am sorry you referred me to last Thursday's paper. Hara-Cari, my foot.

yours sincerely

———————

To TREVOR GLOVER[4]
April 11, 1997

Dear Mr Glover,

Thanks for your letter. I am glad that someone else has memories of "shewn". Someone else wrote to tell me that George Bernard Shaw always wrote it as "shew", and for a moment I thought he meant it should be George Bernard Shew . . .

British Rail are (were) not just odd about spelling. They have vocabulary tics as well. I think the railways are the last people in the world to use words like "alight" and "tender" – take care when alighting, tendering the correct change etc. And they still invent words. "Station stop" is a new one. "The next station stop . . ." I used to think this was a stupid expression because the next station was also the next stop, but then someone pointed out to me that a train sails through many stations it doesn't stop at. I was once at Freshford station, our local village station, which is a request stop (no, I kid you not) and someone stuck their hand out to stop a train, and it stopped, though it was not meant to, simply because the driver was day-dreaming, and the guard leant out and shouted crossly: "We don't stop here!" and they went on again. (What an ill constructed sentence.)

The other day I was on Bath Spa station and spotted a poster urging us all to advertise on railways because the average "dwell time" on stations was seven minutes. Dwell time? Dwell time?

Incidentally, I recently had to review a new book by John Chilton called *Who's Who of British Jazz*, and the most off-beat entry I found mentioned Boosey and Hawkes. It was of Monia Liter, who I think was your erstwhile Head of Light Music. But it was his early years in Shanghai that caught the eye. "Played piano for silent films in Shanghai . . . Short stint with the Shanghai Symphony Orchestra . . ." How many of us can boast such a thing?

Thanks for writing.

yours etc

––––––––––

To MARTIN NEWELL
September 22, 1998

Dear Martin,

I would have answered your letter about rhyming slang years ago, but you only wrote it in June, so I'm only three months late. Good about the double rhyming . . . very good about the non-rhyming . . . I didn't realise my fancy was quite so behind reality. When you said about people inventing slang in Wivenhoe and then hearing it in the street years later, it reminded me of something I read by George Orwell in his journals. He wrote during the war that the most wonderfully lurid rumours kept circulating, but that, like jokes, nobody knew where they came from or who had started them. So he decided to start his own rumour (that beer was about to be rationed) and see how long it took to come back to him. To his chagrin, it never did. Which in turn reminds me of the experiment done by King James I. Apparently he wanted to find out what language children would grow up to speak if they had to devise one for themselves, so he arranged for two children to be brought up on an island by a deaf-mute nanny, so that he and his merry men could come back in ten years and find out how they communicated. The experiment went ahead, but James died meanwhile, and everyone else forgot about it, so they never went back to find out.

Yes, I have finally worked out a way of writing letters without ever having to make anything up or say anything about myself. Just get reminded of what other people have said.

The only answer I have to your Essex culture is a bit of West Country lore picked up in the local pub. The first time I went in there and asked after the Gents, a man pointed at a notice saying "Yertis". If you say it to yourself several times, in a local accent, it finally makes sense. Mark you, by that time you REALLY want to go to the loo.

How do you get on *Loose Ends* every week? Well done, anyway.

I watched the thing about Rosie Boycott the other day (with considerable lack of interest) for one reason and one only – to see what the place looked like.[5] I've never been there. I was once asked to lunch by Andrew Marr, and I refused, on the grounds that it would take me all day (and adding, sotto voce, that he'd be fired by then anyway).

So see you again one day, but not at the office probably. Sorry we didn't see each other at Bath Festival time. Are you back next year?

yours

———————

To BARRY QUINLAN
March 17, 1999

Dear Barry Quinlan,

I don't get many letters like yours, or, to put it another way, I've never had a letter quite like yours before, so thanks very much for taking the trouble to write. Of course, I would have answered sooner except that the letter has wended its weary way to Canary Wharf and back out to Wiltshire before it got to me – I don't ever go to the office, because I don't know where it is. I used to know where it was, but it moved. Then, before I could answer it, I had to leave it lying around for a while leaving it to mature and hoping people would read it by accident. (It worked. Four cleaning ladies have been and gone and resigned, saying they wouldn't work in a place where letters containing the F word were lying around.)

What made it even nicer was getting it from someone in Ireland, where they think more of words and language than they do here. For years I have worshipped at the shrine of Myles na Gopaleen, who was as funny as they ever come. Indeed, usually the only letters I get from Irish people come after I have borrowed the device which Myles used of the cliche expert. You know the format . . . ?

Q. Where will we carry on till?

A. We will carry on till the end.

Q. What kind of end will we carry on till?

A. The very end.

Q. I was thinking more of the flavour of the end.

A. Ah – to the bitter end!

Q. Good.

Whenever I use this format, I get furious Irish letters saying I have stolen the technique unacknowledged from Myles.

Which is only partly true, because HE stole it from an American called Frank Sullivan. When I tell them this, they never write back again. Of course, for all they know, I might be making up Frank Sullivan, though I'm not . . .

Along those lines, I had a friend at school called Alexander Cockburn (son of Claud, resident of Youghal, your neck of the woods) who used to make up weighty quotes from a historian called Kirschner, whom he had also made up, reckoning that examiners would not know this and give him the benefit of the doubt. He told me once, years later, that he had discovered there really was a historian called Kirschner.

Thanks again for the letter. As Ronnie Scott used to say, you have made a happy man very old.

––––––––––––

To PETER CALVIOU
July 23, 2002

Dear Mr Calviou,

I don't normally comment on the grammatical waywardness of

my fictional characters, as they should answer you directly, but it's an interesting point about the two nominative forms of the first person, which hadn't occurred to me before. I used to worry much more about grammar than I do now. It always set my teeth on edge to hear words used wrongly, or in the wrong order, or "like" when it should be "as", etc, but something happened to me that must happen to a lot of people. I met someone more pedantic than I was. He was David Taylor, on the staff of *Punch*, who would occasionally say, "Actually, Miles, it's 'fewer' not 'less'," or "Miles, I think you're confusing the usage of 'owing to' and 'due to' . . ."

This riled me so much (inwardly) that I started a gradual withdrawal from the Golan Heights of grammar. The last time I got hot under the collar was when I argued with a lady at a party that the genitive of Dickens was Dickens's and she swore it was Dickens'. She was a schoolteacher, and thus was free to spread faulty grammar. My only comfort was that her pupils probably would pay no attention.

I am afraid the Parceline joke is not new. I have made it up often myself. But it is still good. And thanks for writing.

————————

To THE REVD JOHN CAPERON
September 10, 2002

Dear Mr Caperon,

Thanks for the pamphlet on Dads and Sons. I have read it and am now a better father. My son read it and said, "Why wait till now? You could of been a better father from day one", so I clipped him round the ear-hole and I am now a worse father again.

The cruel thing about people writing "could of" is that it flies in the face of logic. When people put "due to" where perhaps they should have put "owing to", or use "less" for "fewer", it doesn't really matter, as the correctness is one of agreed usage rather than logic, but when people write "could of" instead of "could have" (which they only do because of the way they say "could've"), it actually messes up the way verbs work. It's like people clashing gears when driving.

I have noticed the distinction between "like" and "as" fade away too. I was told that you cannot say "Do like I say", only "Do as I say". Alas, no more. But if we spend all our time weeping into our mugs of tea over language change, we shall be sad people.

yours sincerely

To ED BARNETT

November 21, 2002

Dear Ed,

You must have blinked the other day when you were invaded by a small BBC team to listen to your words of wisdom on the past pluperfect, so you probably didn't realise that we were blinking as well – I hadn't really met the producer of the programme before that day, having been pitchforked into doing it at short notice. Listening to you reminded me that even if we learn the grammar of other languages – and I have done so with at least three in my life – we soon abandon any attempt to analyse our own language, or even to think about it analytically. After a while, we instinctively know what tense to use, even if we don't know what it's called. When we say, "If I were to come round tomorrow", we're actually using the subjunctive, but I bet not one in a thousand people in Britain would know that.

People are more and more starting to change the rules by saying "This is the worst thing that has happened to my husband and I", and instead of sympathising, all I want to do is say "my husband and me! It's the accusative, dummkopf!" But it's no use, as a) nobody knows what an accusative is b) the rules of the language are governed by what people do, not by what people want them to do, so eventually we have to hold up our hands and say, OK, the rules have changed.

Blimey, I didn't mean to say any of that. All I meant to say was that I was struck enough by meeting you that day to follow up my threat to hunt down the book by Donald MacIntosh I was talking about, and here it is. (I got it second-hand on the Internet for less than a fiver, so it's pointless even to think of paying me for it.) I thought that it was all about Cameroon. It's not; it's about other places in West Africa as well. But it might provide a good introduction, and although it's not bang up to date, it is at least written by someone living. Who knows – it may inspire you to write something yourself.

Well, good luck in the dark continent. I have no advice except to keep a diary, don't get Aids and write to your mum at least once a year.

yours sincerely

10

Friends

There are so many letters in this category that the selection has been determined by those that have that extra something that gives them an interest beyond the recipient. There remains in the archives a huge and wonderful collection of family letters that will have to wait for another publication, but included here are samples of the notes Miles would leave for family members.

To SPIKE MILLIGAN
September 19, 1981

Dear Spike,

My God, what kind of a shock is that to give a man at breakfast? I am busy torturing a sausage to death over a slow fire (brave to the end, he refused to admit whether he contained any meat or not) and then bang, through the letter box, an endorsement of my Churchill novel. That's the kind of letter that makes you pinch yourself and reread a dozen times, just in case. Then you tuck it in your socks to stop it going to your head.

What's so ironic is that without you I could never have written anything like that. *The Goons*, of course, but by 1960 I reckoned I was free of your influence, and then came along *Puckoon* and *The Bed Sitting Room* and *Oblomov*, but especially *Puckoon*, which was my favourite bedside reading for two years and replaced the Bible; in fact, I almost started a scheme for filling hotel bedrooms with a Gideon *Puckoon*. Then, in the 70s, *I Was Mussolini's Right-hand Chambermaid* etc, and a totally new way of looking at war. By 1980 I was again totally free of your influence and looking forward to a trouble-free decade, when along comes this letter. Bad cess to you, Sir.

Of course, to say I was influenced by you sounds academic. What

I really mean is that I stole your jokes, repainted them, put new numbers on them and restyled them, till I was convinced they were mine, and so they were in a manner of speaking, but it's still the old thing about little men standing on big men's shoulders. This is probably the only chance I'll ever get to say thanks for all the things you've unwittingly taught me, so I say it now.

I think you've misunderstood the Law Society and their policy to stop the jails being overcrowded. Yes, they've asked for shorter criminal sentences; but what they meant was sending only shorter criminals to jail. That way, they can get even more malefactors in the same space. Small claims courts, petty crime: all the same idea.

I don't have an office at *The Times*, so I didn't get my letter till Saturday, today, but it sustained me through one of the grimmest ordeals of my life. I had decided to bicycle along the canal at the other end of Ladbroke Grove as far as I could get, and pedalled the towpath through Ealing, Southall, West Drayton, Uxbridge and various strange back-of-civilisation places, alternatively green and gloom, until I got to the outskirts of Watford. It wasn't really grim at all, actually an eye-opening experience, but I had to battle with increasing rain and three punctures, so every now and again I said to myself Think of Spike's letter. Thus does a man sitting in the quiet warmth of 9 Orme Court find himself written into canal history.

Stop burbling, Kington. Go away, Milligan, and stop influencing me.

yours

———————

To HUNTER DAVIES
March 30, 1982

Dear Hunter,
    All I wanted to say was:
    – "Father's Day" is a classic and never gets any less classic.[1]
    – Anyone who can survive a piece by Tom Pocock and still seem

interesting has got to have something going for him. Will get your disused book.

– My Franglais piece next week is "Dans le Stamp Shop" and contains some heavy research.† I still have my 1951 Stanley Gibbons catalogue which dates to the year my interest in stamps. Its pages are crammed with unstuck in stamps.

Wonder if any are wondrously rare?

– Bought a 2nd hand book of yours from the library the other day. Very Happily Married Couple, etc. Lots of good stuff.

– The best wild flowers I ever saw were on a disused railway cutting near Harrogate.

– The best bike ride I've had for years was before Christmas, along the canal towpath from Ladbroke Grove to Watford. If your book goes well, I'll do one on Underused Canal Paths.

– Should I resign from *The Times*? Don't think so – it was hard enough getting in against Harold Evan's initial doubts. Basically, I'm a William Haley man anyway so I don't feel involved in this lot. Seeing my name on "Moreover" upsets me; it should be "From Our Humorous Correspondent".

yours

PS love to Margaret and all the fictional characters in your column.

To ANNIE MARYON-DAVIS[2]

March 31, 1983

Dear Annie,

Hey, I've just heard the news – Alan rang up and said, I've got a baby; at first I thought he said, Hi there, baby, so I was a bit frosty to begin with, as I hate familiarity – and I think you've been very clever. I mean I haven't heard the details or anything, like did you have to have acupuncture or do it all yourself or whatever is fashionable this year – but I was really thrilled anyway. In fact, maybe

---

† On pre-War Hungarian issues.

I'd rather not hear all the details as I'm pretty squeamish and faint at the sight of aspirin, so you can imagine what blood does to me. Mark you, being with three doctors has helped a lot and I can now talk about money and sex without feeling ill.

Jessica is a pretty name. I suppose you know it means "beautiful musician" in Spanish? Yes, I'm sure you knew that. Alan said you were trying to get away from Victorian names, which I think is pretty wise; I've met so many girls recently called Disraeli and Gladstone. Sophie helped give a party the other day and the other two girls involved were called – guess? Right. Emma and Polly.

My only news is that I have bought a new double bass. A friend of Caroline's in Bath buys and sells musical instruments and just happened to have a bass over Easter – the first he had had for six years – and just happened to ring up when I was in Bath and we whizzed over on Easter Monday and came away with this fine looking Hungarian beast. I didn't know it was Hungarian. He did.

"How do you know?" I said, very impressed. "It says on the label inside," he said.

When I told Alan about the new bass, he said: "Oh. I liked the old one." What kind of a parental remark is that? If someone told me they had had another child, I wouldn't say: "Oh. I liked your other ones better." Well, I'll get over it. We haven't decided what to call it yet. I'm thinking of a Victorian name, like a Very Variable or Rare Antique.

I suppose you know that Jessica in Welsh means "the church by the wood by the stream"? Yes, of course you do.

I know what you're going to ask. Can I get the announcement of the birth cheap in *The Times*? No, I'm afraid I can't. But I can get it in "Moreover" for free. Just let me know the wording, and the spelling of the following names . . .

Maryan . . . Davies . . . Lillyshall . . .

Jessica I can spell all right.

Is the ward named after the Professor Wrigley who invented chewing gum? If so, I'll lay in a stock for Jessica of this new grated carrot flavour gum. It's really good. But if you'd rather I put her down for Cheltenham Ladies School instead, just say so. As long as you don't ask me to be godfather. I'd feel very silly turning up to take her out of Cheltenham for the day and saying: "I'm her god-father." I'd much rather be her sugar daddy.

Did you know that in Turkish Jessica means "little earthquake"? Isn't language a wonderful thing?

———————

To MEGAN LLOYD GEORGE[3]
May, 1983

Dear Megan,

You never thought I'd write, did you? Go on, admit it, you didn't, did you? You thought I was just a pretty face and an ugly body, didn't you? I bet you said to everyone: Miles says he's going to write, but you know what these London people are like. Big shots. Show offs.

Well, I hope you're sorry now. Write out a hundred times: I have misjudged Miles Kington. He is not just a pretty face. He is swollen headed as well. And keep some grapes for me.

Would you like to hear all my news? Forget it. It would bore you stiff. Last night I went to a garden party committee meeting which lasted 1½ hours and that's how boring my news is. The only thing that came up of interest was something on the Notting Hill rapist. Although he seems to have stopped now, he was very active round here last year, with at least six victims and obviously a local as he knew the area so well.

There was a big police operation for weeks and weeks and although they caught no-one, he packed up his grotty little hobby. Well, now the rumour going round is that the rapist was a local policeman. Yep. Apparently his actions seemed to show an uncanny knowledge of where the police would be.

Makes you think, eh?

I thought of having a card printed for pushing round all the front doors in the neighbourhood: "24-HOUR RAPIST SERVICE. Just call our man, any time of day or night. Anything considered." And then give Notting Hill police station tel number. But then I thought it might be in poor taste, and also lead to my arrest.

I will now leave this subject, of which I have never had first-hand experience, and turn to something more important. How to behave in hospital. As it seems like you will spend the rest of your life in this hospital, or at least most of May, you'd better know the code. These are the three basic rules:

1. Steal other people's visitors.
2. Flirt with the doctor.
3. Have a white coat ready.

The first one hardly needs explaining. Other people's visitors are always more interesting than your own. Also, visitors find other patients more interesting. Many people go to visit a dear friend in hospital and discover when they get there, for the first time, that they have absolutely nothing to say to each other. The conversation goes like this.

Visitor: How are they treating you?
Patient: Fine. The nurses work so hard.
Visitor: How's the food?
Patient: It's all right. I refuse most of it.
Visitor: What are the other patients like?
Patient: Boring. One of them is dead, but the nurses have been too busy to notice.
Visitor: I've brought you a bottle of orange squash.
Patient: Great; that's the fifth I've had today.
Visitor: How are they treating you?
Patient: You've already asked me that.

The visitor has now been here a minute, there's another twenty-nine to go and he's already run out of conversation. He starts looking round at the other beds, desperate for something to say, and his eye falls on you. This is where you come in. You smile at him, wink, flutter your eyelids and blow a big kiss. It's fair to say that this will attract his attention. The next time he looks round, pat the bed, meaning: Come and sit here, sweetie. If he's worth anything at all, he'll come over and you can take it from there.

*

1. It saves a lot of time and bother if you arrange with the other patients in advance to swap visitors.

2. Flirting with the doctor. This is self-explanatory. Just murmur little remarks to him like: "I'd finish it all today, doctor. If it wasn't for you" or "I dreamt about you last night, doctor – you were behaving very unprofessionally" or "simply now let me examine you". If he brings round students with him, say in a loud voice: "I like the one in specs best!"

3. Always best to have a white coat handy so that you can walk round the hospital unmolested, pretending to be a staff member. Inspect other patients if you like, but only order operations for them if you're feeling really confident. It will also make it easier for you to smoke, if you smoke. If the worst comes to the worst, it's pretty easy to escape from a hospital in a white coat.

I'm going to be down in Bath at the weekend, and if we've absolutely nothing else to do, I suppose me and Caroline might force ourselves to come and see you. Don't be surprised if after a minute we go and talk to someone else. You'll probably be too busy chatting up doctors anyway.

The good weather seems to have gone away now. Pity. For a week I was sitting out in the sunshine, typing, and there's nothing much better than working at home, in the sunshine. I even got a small suntan and people said: You're looking so well! Funny thing is, you do feel better if you're brown. Quite illogical. If the NHS had any sense, it would give people suntan treatment instead of pills. OK, Megan, we've, uh, spotted this bad trouble you've got in your back. Yeah, bone trouble. So here's what we're going to do. We're going to get you brown all over. Yup. Here's an air ticket to the West Indies. Report to the doctor on Monday at the El Coco cocktail bar on the beach. Yes, the nice handsome one you keep flirting with. No, don't bother with a bathing-suit. They're very broad-minded there. Just take a white coat.

To JILLY COOPER
August 17, 1983

Dear Jilly,

Thanks for your letter. And thanks for your book as well, which is not as funny as mine but I think is much more valuable. I was accosted in a hotel the other day by a lady who wanted me to sign my piece in *The Times*. So, feeling bucked, I did so, whereupon she said that she had been at the lunch in Chichester and that I should have stayed for your speech which was absolutely hilarious. When are you giving it again? I'd like to be there. – Hope to see you soon.

To FRANCIS WILFORD-SMITH[4]
February 5, 1986

Dear Francis,

I have to say that my heart sank when I received the true looniness of the task that you set yourself in tabulating the first particle of the *Times* leaders. But dutifully I read your filed *Times* letter, and my spirits rose when I realised that you had penned another small masterpiece. I wager that the Letters Editor had not gone much beyond your opening remarks, a fate which meets most *Times* leaders probably. If you can wait until I bring out my Anthology of Forgotten Humour, or until we have done enough to warrant publishing the Smith–Kington letters, I am sure we can still get it in print. Your marshalling of the facts was masterly; you would make a great statesman, though a rotten politician.

Your dogged persistence reminded me of Douglas Hague.

He is an ageing industrial archaeologist who lives in Aberystwyth, where I was recently to take back my daughter Sophie to University, and whom I got to know at a time when I lived with Sally, my wife, who was a great camp-follower of archaeological outings, end of sentence. He now lives by himself in a small Welsh village called Llanafan – "You'll recognise my cottage. It's got flowers growing on it. No Welshman bothers with flowers." – where he pursues the following interests: Bardsey Island, pumping stations, drinking fountains, lighthouses, water-colour painting, old engines, Victorian architecture, the history of Aberystwyth ... I can't remember the other twenty.

He reverently came across an old manuscript account, 1700s or so, of how noblemen used to train dogs. He wrote an article about it. It was accepted nowhere. He became fanatical about getting it accepted. Eventually, after a year, he got it placed in an American magazine, having meanwhile become fairly expert on dog-training methods, despite the fact that he dislikes dogs.

Another example. He recently decided that he liked one of his drawings, of a sink, enough to get it turned into a tea cloth. He had a screen made and printed 1,000 cloths. He has sold 400 and is still out of pocket, but is now on to the next project.

His one big achievement, apart from saving half West Wales's industriana, is to have written a wonderful standard work on historic lighthouses. He wrote it with his life-long companion, Rosemary Christie (mother of Julie, the film star) who died recently and left him inconsolable. At least, he never appears sad, but talks about her the whole time.

The sink on the tea cloth, by the way, which is a wonderfully messy one, full of washing up and overflow, is Julie Christie's own sink. Anyone more worldly than him would have labelled it "Julie Christie's Sink" and cleaned up, but no.

If I ever got to know you well enough to give you a Christmas present, I think you know what you will get. A sink tea cloth. Every year.

I have just come across a new, to me, kind of music, klezmer music. It is apparently an old kind of Jewish or Yiddish music played in Eastern Europe at weddings, functions, pogroms etc. It has recently been revived by a US group called the Klezmorim who have done four LPs. Two on Arhoolie, two on Flying Fish. No-one had heard of the music, not even my Jewish friend, except Dobell's folk dept who dug it up effortlessly. It's weird and wonderful stuff – if you can imagine a blend of circus bands, silent film music, Kurt Weill, Charlestons, Arab music and *Fiddler on The Roof*, you're not far off. The leader of the group (who says nicely that Odesse was the New Orleans of Russia) claims it is the silent missing link between Prokofiev, Weill, early Artie Shaw and Gershwin.

I tell a lie. One of my Jewish friends had heard of it, a guy called Peter Walton who is a BBC TV producer, but what he really wants to do is be the ultimate quiz answerer, the great magpie mind (back to you and Douglas Hague again). The only time I got the better of him was when he asked me the following ridiculous question:-

"In the 1930s, the Duke of Windsor took a state trip across the Balkans on a railway train. What was the name of the engine driver?"

"You're not going to believe this," I made answer, "but I don't know."

"The King of Bulgaria!" he said gleefully. "He was a keen amateur driver."

"Hold on," I said. "That's his title. What was his name?"

Peter's brow darkened, and his orthodox Jewish beard grew thoughtful. He went away without a word. Years passed. We bumped into each other again.

"Hello," I said.

"Boris!" he shouted. "He was King Boris!"

You, of course, knew all about klezmer music, I bet. Tell me the truth.

And sorry about the typing.

love to all

————

To GEORGE MELLY
March 7, 1986

Dear George,

As you can see, this letter has been delivered by hand. Impressive, eh? But not half as impressive as the fact that I actually brought my typewriter to your doorstep to write the letter – yes, amazing but true, here I sit outside your house writing letters to you. Already three people have stopped to talk to me, and they have all said the same things: "Liked the book on Scottie Wilson, Mr Melly, and glad to see you've already started on the next one."

And now to business. I have a lovely and intelligent girlfriend who lives in Bath. But all is not sunshine in her life. As if to make up for her loveliness and intelligence the gods have decreed that she should work as a TV director for the BBC, poor thing. At the moment she is doing a film on battered wives/women in Bath and Bristol (a very dark subject) and asked me suddenly the other day if I knew any good Bessie Smith blues that would be apt as introductory music; something about cruel men.

My knowledge of Bessie Smith's songs is much worse than it should be (never listen to the words – you know what musicians are like) so I thought I'd turn to you. Funnily enough, I came across "Down-Hearted Blues" this morning, which has nearly the right sort of words. Sung by Mildred Bailey, with a quartet of Bunny Berigan, Johnny Hodges, Teddy Wilson and Grachan Monour. Stunning line-up, but quite the wrong voice for a blues.

What we need ideally is something like:-

All my life my man's mistreated me
So I'll tell my story to the BBC . . . .

Can you think of something strong but sorrowful with immediate impact?

A policeman has just stopped and said: "Here, don't you know it's unlawful to write in public places?"

"You've got it wrong," I told him. "It's unlawful to write on public places."

"You're all such smarty-pants, you blues singers," he said. "We've got our eye on you, Melly."

Sorry about that, George. Must go now.

yours

To JOANNA LUMLEY
May, 1986

Dear Jo,

I'm afraid that most of the civilised world is going to be crushed by news of your marriage, but I'm mega-delighted. It's your going to Wimbledon that depresses me.

Hey, that's really the best news in the world on all counts, except perhaps the fact that you're marrying a musician but we'll come to that in a moment. I could tell from your letter that you were three feet off the ground, and if you'll just pull in to the side of the road I intend to arrest you for unlawful flying in a metropolitan area. I fully intend to get married to Caroline as soon as we all get divorced, and now that I have your example of swift action before me I shall start getting galvanised. I think Caroline will be even more galvanised. "Hey, Miles, if Joanna Lumley can get married by next July, what about us? Come on, slow coach!" Blimey, here I am talking about me. I should be talking about you.

And what I want to say about you is that you are a lovely person, and the only one who ever had the courage to admit in print that you were scared of me, or something, and I have been in awe of you all the time, but I never had the courage to say so in print, so this will have to do. But the feeling of whirlwind happiness in your letter was quite intoxicating – I leapt out of bed and shouted: "That's terrific!" The postman, who delivers the mail to my bedside, came out of the kitchen where he had been making coffee for the two of us and said: "What's so terrific?" "Jo Lumley is getting married," I said.

"That's great," he said. "To a musician," I said. "Could be tricky," he said. "I'm coming to that in a moment," I said. "Good," he said, and went back into the kitchen.

Stephen Barlow, eh? Name rings a bell. Of course, he's not the only musician named Barlow. One of my fellow Instant Sunshiners is called David Barlow. There was a bloke called Jeremy Barlow, flautist, who married the daughter of my first *Punch* editor, Bernard Hollowood. There's a jazz musician called Dale Barlow. Perhaps there is a Music Academy for Barlow somewhere. My David Barlow has a father called Wilfred Barlow who is the prime mover in this country of the Alexander Technique. I once asked him to explain the Alexander Technique to me.

"Well," he said, "first you conquer all Greece, then you conquer all Persia, then you smash Turkey, then you sweep through India and then you die young."

Sounds much too time-consuming to me, so I've never bothered. Where was I? Oh yes about marrying, a musician. This can be dodgy, because of the way they listen to music. What you have to do is find out very early on whether he hums, or taps his feet or nods his head, or beats time on his knee and then you have to get used to it. Otherwise, musicians are great blokes.

I think your idea about the four of us getting together is great and I'll give you a ring by and by to fix something – Caroline has always wanted to meet you, and I'd like to meet Stephen, and it is far too long since you and I met, so whoopee. Caroline has spent most of her working life in the theatre, so you can talk drama, yawn yawn, while me and Stephen talk music, yawn yawn. But I also want to get down to Wimbledon, for a rather strange reason. I don't know if you ever frequented a strange delicatessen in Notting Hill, very near the Pizza Express, called Salik? Mr Salik was a cheery, small Polish Jewish man with a great twinkle who retired last year to his house in Wimbledon and I have always promised to go and see him, and I never have. He has a colourful history – spent two years in Siberia as a guest of the Russians, where he learnt to play the mandolin, then dropped into Arnhem with the Polish paratroops and was one of the few to get out, etc etc. So Wimbledon for me, now that I have two people to visit.

Of course, you know that musicians can be obsessional. I was once told a very good if sad story about a jazz musician, by a jazz musician. The musician came home very late one night, I mean very late, about 4 a.m., and his wife tore a strip off him. He mumbled some excuses, but they weren't good enough.

"I want the truth!" she shouted.

He lost his temper. "Well, if you really want to know, I've been in bed with another woman!"

She looked at him hostilely.

"You're lying to me. You've been having a blow with the lads and you're trying to cover up, aren't you?"

Yes, well. It depends how you tell them. I'm thinking of hiring Les Dawson or Frankie Howerd to tell it to me, and see if it really works.

Why is it that whenever I write or talk to you, I always ramble like a man in the desert? All I wanted to say was that I think it's terrific news. Being incredibly happy is a very good way of getting through a mid-life crisis.

To ISABEL MAYNARD
June 21, 1986

Dear Isabel,

This is ridiculous. I shall actually be in Bath before this letter gets to you. On the other hand, I shall be gone again by the time it arrives. On the third hand, I can't think of anything to say.

Yes, it's true. World-famous author Miles Kington ran his fingers through his last few remaining hairs, and whispered to himself: "So it has finally come to this. I am written out at last." He whispered it so faintly that he could not, in fact, make out a word he was saying. "My God," he shouted, "so it has come to this at last! I cannot even make myself heard!" That's better, he thought. At least I could hear most of that.

He looked again at the sheet of paper in front of him. Dear Isabel, it said. What a great beginning, he thought. I used to be able to write beginnings. His favourite beginning was "Bang! Bang! Bang! Bang! Four shots ripped into his groin and he was off on the most exciting adventure of his life." Unfortunately, it had been written by someone else. Another beginning he liked a lot was "in the beginning was the word, and the word was God." He had never been able to work out what that meant and had not, in fact, ever got further than that, though he had heard that the book contained lots of good stories, some of them true.

Dear Isabel. The world-famous megastar (but only in Bath)

thought of all the Isabels he had known. There was Loony Isabel, the demented opera singer he had befriended in the Gobi Desert (and who ran off with his bottle of brandy). There was Miss Isabel Carstairs, the cool librarian from Edinburgh, who had written to point out that his copy of *War and Peace* was now fifteen years overdue and he owed £689.35 in fines. There was also Isabel the wife of the peat farmer for whom he had worked for six long years to earn the money to pay off the library fines. By the sixth year they had still not dug any peat. "How long does it take for peat to mature?" he asked the farmer one day. The farmer thought about it. "About 45,000 years, I'd say," he said. He left the next day. He couldn't wait 45,000 years – the library fines would be enormous by then.

The Bath-famous writer cheered up slightly. He could see the bottom of the page coming. Hooray, he thought. (More exciting rubbish to come!)

He'd once known a penguin called Isabel. He'd been on a package holiday to the Falkland Islands and made friends with a BBC man making a film about penguins. The BBC man who was called Roger had introduced him one day to the main penguin. "This is Isobel," he said. "With an 'o'," he added. Kington had nodded at the penguin who, to his surprise, waddled over and shook him warmly by the flipper. There were 5,000 more penguins on the beach, looking like off-duty waiters or retired dance band musicians.

"How do you tell Isobel from the others?" he asked.

"I don't," said Roger. "They're all identical, as far as I'm concerned. But then they're all called Isobel as well. With an o."

5,000 o's. It was a lot.

"How do you explain this unusual fact?" said Kington, notepad at the ready.

"Nothing unusual about it," said Roger. "For instance, I know 5,000 other people at the BBC and they're all called Roger. With an o," he added.

Kington thought about this for a moment.

"Doesn't that create problems?"

"Of course, it does. That's why I've come out to the Falklands."

Yes, Kington had led a pretty exciting life. And now here he was, totally written out.

Dear Isabel, said the sheet of paper. With an a. Kington suddenly lost his temper and tore it up, then placed another sheet in his typewriter and carefully typed the words,

Dear Isabel,

When you get this letter, I shall be far away. I have decided to go to Australia and start a new life. yours, a world-weary author.

Seventy-two hours later the plane touched down in Melbourne and Miles Kington stepped out. It had been a ghastly flight. He had sat next to a kangaroo called Roger who had drunk far too many lagers and then tried to put the air stewardess in his pouch. But here he was at last in Australia, land of opportunity and opera singers. And nobody recognised him. It was wonderful.

"Excuse me," said a voice, "but don't I know you from Bath, England?"

Kington got straight back on the aircraft and didn't stop till he was sitting again in his little room, in London, England. There was a sheet of typewritten paper in his typewriter. It said "Dear Isabel". He groaned. It was going to be one of those days, he could tell.

———————

To ALEXEI SAYLE[5]
June 26, 1986

Dear Alexei Sayle,

Did you get a garbled message from me recently on your phone machine? If not, here is a transcript of it.

"Oh, hello, this is Miles Kington and a garbled phone message, er, right, the bleep has gone, so I'll start recording, er, just wanted to say that all your stuff in *Time Out* is bloody funny. I'm very jealous, er, that's it, really."

Also, I thought your novel was smashing. You want to knock off all this stand-up stuff and get down to writing. You have some great ideas.

Must go now. I'm on holiday in five minutes.

yours sincerely

To BASIL BOOTHROYD
September 8, 1986

Dear Colleague,

I am sure you are aware that sub-editors often trim away the best bits of pieces, so you will not be surprised to learn that what I originally wrote read as follows:-

"Many of the most famous song titles are in the form of questions, though I am sure that the more scholarly and well-informed of my readers will dispute this – I shall especially be surprised if this statement does not produce a well-argued letter from a certain B Boothroyd of Sussex."

As usual, they cut it down to the bare bones, so I was delighted to get your letter even so.

The Irish song title should of course have read "Who Wants to Gut Killarney?", but I didn't know what this meant and felt free to change it.

I am writing this in the picket line at Wapping, where from time to time I hurl screwed up pieces of paper with great ferocity and velocity at the castle walls. My fellow pickets would be chagrined to know that this is the only way I can now deliver my copy.

Nice to hear from you, Basil, and I am impressed to see that you have got one of those new-fangled processors that can deal with the sheet music of Glocca Morra. I had the great honour of visiting Glocca Morra recently, a small suburb of Denmark Street, where they still produce songs which rhyme girls' names with place-names. "I'm Sexy Ada from Old Granada", "I'm Lovely Lil, from Old Seville", and so on. Their 1986 hit, "I'm Dirty Norm from Benidorm" never quite took off, but you can't do it every time.

My favourite song title of all time was "Here Today and Out the Other". My girl-friend has a favourite soul singer called Booker Prize Jr. but I wonder if she's telling me the truth.

love

To BRYAN FORBES and NANETTE NEWMAN[6]
June 28, 1988

Dear Bryan and Nanette,

Well, you could have knocked me over with a ten pound hammer.
I am not used to receiving such letters early in the morning. I
screamed and fell swooning to the floor as I brought the morning
tea in. My wife thought it was the usual thing – another terrible
blackmail threat about my colourful past life – and by the time I
had come round had dealt with it swiftly. "I don't know who this
Forbes and Newman person is," she said. "but I have sent them a
large sum of money, and I fancy you won't be bothered again." So
if you get a cheque from this address, please return it.

My life has changed somewhat since we last met, which I think
was the time when Princess Margaret came to see you do your TV
show, Nanette. Did I ever tell you that I had a funny story prepared
that evening about bicycling in London, all about the time I ran
into the Earl of Snowdon? AND I COULDN'T USE IT BECAUSE
SHE WAS IN THE AUDIENCE? That was also the evening that I
was asked back to Kensington Palace for supper and I said no,
because I had a vital deadline to catch that night. It might have
changed my life socially, if I had said yes . . . Anyway, it's just that
last year I got divorced, got remarried, moved out of London,
arrived here, changed from the *Times* to *Independent*, had a baby
(next oldest child is 19) and lost a mother-in-law, the last two on
the same day. This year I'm lying down a lot.

I wish I thought the column was as good as you say. Now and
again I think "That was a definite goody", but most of the time I
have a vision of the golden column that was meant to be, fading
over the grey reality of the one I actually wrote.

I wouldn't have you rewrite one word of your letter, mark you.

yours

To ROY FISHER[7]
September 21, 1991

Dear Roy,

A couple of years ago my wife and I were taken to see a jazz jamboree at Dyrham Park in the open air, at which the most famous band but not the best was Kenny Ball's. I had an old mate playing piano in another group, Barney Bates, so I went backstage to say hello – not backstage so much as behind the stand on the gravelly terrace in front of the great house.

Barney said to my 2 yr old son, Adam, who was kicking around in the gravel: "Sonny, a fiver if you kick over Kenny Ball's pint. That's him over there." My son smiled as if he understood, which he didn't, and wandered off. Five minutes later came a loud shout: "Who the hell's been putting gravel in my beer?" It was Kenny Ball. It was my son. "Here, lad," said Barney, "here's a quid. You are a true music-lover."

I don't know why I brought it up, except that last night I had to see quarter of an hour of old Kenny at the local school, because we're playing there quite soon and I wanted to test the acoustics. Nobody should look like that. Most of Kenny Ball's band do – they all start sprouting those spivvy, second hand car moustaches, without which apparently you cannot sing raunchy yet meaningless lyrics into an unoffending mike.

Your tape with Mel Hill is lovely, but I don't want to write about that yet. I had a letter from Mel Hill, most of which was about playing in D Flat, which I'm still thinking about. What I'm writing about now is the anthology of jazz writing I'm working on, now nearing its deadline, for which I very much want to use your piece on bass players and their availability. I could get it via the BBC archives 'n' script 'n' transcript dept, but that's kinda time-consuming; so I thought first I would write and ask if you had it lying around and could get me a copy of it.

What's the magic word? Please.

A copy of it, please. That's better.

You can see I still have a young child. Unless, of course, you think there was another piece in that series which was better.

Or if you would rather send me a poem.

Personally, I do not intend at the moment to include any poetry. But I would quite like to include a note from one editor which says: "The inclusion of a Jack Kerouac poem in this volume does not imply any approval of it by the editors."

But I do have very warm memories of that piece, and it's exactly the kind of thing I think should go in. I keep cutting out rip-roaring stories by Barney Bigard about how mean Sidney Bechet was, or similar, and knowing in my heart of hearts it will not make the final cut.

We came to Buxton again this year, but it was very much in and out. Then a fortnight at Edinburgh, during which I amazed myself by seeing a jazzy harp player (Savourna Stevenson) and a jazzy bag-pipe player (Hamish Moore) and being knocked out by them both.

If I don't stop this letter soon, I can't start one which answers yours, at present wrapped round the tape with a rubber band.

    yours

———————

Fax to TERRY JONES[8]
from MILES KINGTON
on Valium

(It's a silly thing to say, but I don't think I've ever actually seen a Valium.)

July 8, 1992

Dear Mr Jones,

Thank you for agreeing to act on behalf of Boules International.[9] I enclose the entire correspondence I have had with the organisers so that you do not feel you are being left out of anything. What is missing from all this is the feeling of summer gaiety, the madcap excitement as you feel you might actually win a point, the delirious relief as you realise you are going to be knocked out by a team that takes things far more seriously than you do, the smell of barbecued quail wafting over the ancient square, the hoarse cries of the police as they beat back admirers, the incessant chanting of the hordes of Bath estate agents (PRICE REDUCED! PRICE REDUCED!), the gay abandon of a drink in one's hand (last year I was offered, and accepted, a large Pernod from an enchanting French girl who turned out to be on the other side – as one of my players said to me, "If you weren't the captain, you'd be dropped by now") . . .

I think it will be fun. What I am taking for granted so far is that a) you are coming to play b) you are bringing Alison with you, both of which would give me great pleasure and Caroline says aye to that. And what about if, on Saturday night, we all went to Home-wood Park, not a mile away, to dine and discuss tactics?

The more I think about Gilliam, the more I think, what a good idea. Would you like me to ring him, so he can sense over the phone what a splendid bloke I am and ask him to stay the night as well? With his partner etc? By the way, I never asked you about children and dependants, but that too is no problem.

If I have gone too far in my assumptions, let me know.

Incidentally, to play the game needs no great experience. The main assets are:

1. Luck
2. Tolerable spatial co-ordination (e.g. ability to get rolled up paper in litter bin)
3. The sort of competitiveness you always disclaim but secretly know you have
4. Willingness to have one practice session beforehand.
5. Glass of something in one hand.
6. Captain who has played before, so can be blamed for any loss of form or exit from con test.
7. The possession of enough boules.

5, 6 and 7 are already to hand, so I see no problem.

Incidentally, I have reread my exchange with Palin, and he is going to a wedding in Suffolk. Whether it is part of a programme is not clear.

The most enjoyable thing about last year's competition was that one or two French restaurants had practised like demons to win at their national game, and were all knocked out early on. The final was between an English and Chinese team. Much crying was done into the red wine that night.

Hey, I'm looking forward to this. I'll phone you tomorrow about Gilliam – if no go, I'll spend the rest of the week either getting someone agreeable to both, or wrecking Palin's wedding. Incidentally, D Addams (no, hold on, it's Adams) is now going out to the Montreux Jazz Festival first. Because it's in Switzerland, I guess, where they have no lorries.

Fax to TERRY JONES
July 9, 1992

Terry!

All problems solved. It suddenly occurred to me that I don't have to go to London for a boules player necessarily, so I have engaged the services of a man from Taunton, called PHIL HAMMOND.

Actually, Dr Phil Hammond. He is, apart from being a junior hospital doctor, a comedy veteran, as he is part of a funny duo called Struck Off and Die who were a bit of a hit at the Edinburgh Festival last year, and have done quite a lot of TV since. I have to admit a connection; Caroline has directed a lot of their TV and stage stuff, but as they all made a good job of it, I don't see why I shouldn't mention it. Not only that but Phil stood against William Waldegrave in the election, as a junior hospital doctor and got less votes than William Waldegrave. Not only that, but he plays boules a bit – I can distinctly remember playing with him on top of Carlton Hill last year, in Edinburgh.

I asked him if he had ever met you. He said, yes, once, here. You had, rather late at night, solemnly said to his girlfriend, "I have only loved two women in my life and you are one of them." Apparently you later said to Phil, "I have only ever loved two men in my life, and you are one of them."

I told him you had changed a lot. In the old days you were much more broad-minded, and you used to shout out "I love everybody!" and fall over. I need hardly say that this did not actually happen to my recollection.

Did I say that the rules allow flexible teams? That is, Alison and Caroline can also play their whack, if they can find male members ready to drop out.

I'm off to London today, but I'll ring you in the post-Hungarian Alison newsflash era to hear the latest . . .

To SOPHIE KINGTON
September 8, 1993

Dear Sophie

I got your recorded message on our strange device and thought you were owed an explanation of why I wasn't there to bid you farewell to Southwold. Well, it was like this, your honour. I was away in Scotland attending to me cousin Laurence's Highland Games in Blairgowrie – we went there last year and the rain and whisky fell in equal proportions, and the cousin said, Come back next year, see the sunshine. So we did, and it was. He spent a lot of his time harvesting barley, but we also had a chance to motor up to Edinburgh one night during the Festival and see – no, not Instant Sunshine, who I'm afraid have to do without me now, but to see a piper called Hamish Moore and a Scottish clarinettist called Dick Lee – just the two of them – play some wonderful sort of jazz/pipe/folk duo. It could have been even better if I wasn't driving and therefore sober.

The rain last year had kept all the sideshows away, but they were here this year at the Blair Highland Games in all their candy floss glory, including that old Scots favourite the bouncy castle (for in Scotland it should be the bouncy, decrepit, freezing cold, death-duty-watch beetle-ridden castle) on which Adam revealed that he was no true Scotsman, and that the kilt was actually safety-pinned to his shorts underneath. They asked after you and said, when were you going to come up and see them with this nice new boyfriend we kept telling them about . . . anyway, I rang Tom this morning to see if he was a) around b) in possession of yr S'wold address, and the following conversation took place.

Me: Tom!
Tom: Hi, Dad. What time is it?
Dad: Coming up to 9 a.m.
Tom: Hmm. What day is it?
Dad: Hold on, I'll ask . . . Wednesday.
Tom: Hmm. Better get up. Bye.
Dad: No, hold on! What's the Southwold address and why aren't you there?
Tom: I slightly messed it up this year by not getting time off. What's the weather like?
Dad: It's raining a bit, it's Wednesday and it's about 9 a.m.
Tom: Hmm. Maybe it's a good thing I didn't go after all.
Dad: What's their address?
Tom: Whose?
(Skip the next 5 minutes . . .)
Tom: So I should think "next to the Sailors' Reading Room" will get there. Tell Sophie if you write to her that I was up.
Dad: Sure.
Tom: SILENCE
Dad: Hey, don't go back to sleep!
Tom: Cool it! . . .

The other day I taped a tourist programme on the Philippines, one of those "Rough Guide to . . ." type programmes, thinking you might be interested. Might you be interested? Tell Mum thanks for her info on the railways and daffodils and tell Paul (both actually, lots of best wishes, and if you happen to come back via the craft market where ten years ago I bought some silly slippers with sheep-swool inside, get me some more). We had a nice time going up to Scotland, staying at a pub in Kirkby Lonsdale en route overnight, and a rotten time coming back, doing the whole 470 miles in the day. Might one see you on Adam's birthday, Sep 18, a Saturday. I think we have hired a bouncy castle, so you can have as many free goes as you like. That's all. Oh, no, something else. Overheard on radio, a country and western song title: "My Wife Ran Off with My Best Friend, And Now I Really Miss Him" . . .

To MELVYN BRAGG
April 15, 1994

Dear Melvyn,

My false eye lashes fell into my soup with surprise when l heard my case come up for discussion on *Start the Week*. No, I don't take soup early on Monday mornings – I had, as I often do, taped the programme for later listening, and so I didn't hear me being talked about till Tuesday or Wednesday. After getting over the initial shock of joy and horror at realising that anyone up there reads me, I buckled down to the job of working out the question someone had posed on the programme: Is Miles Kington sad at not having a bigger public profile and not being born fifteen years later? After falling asleep several times at the enormity of the idea, I concluded that I wasn't sad at all.

Actually, I faced this problem years ago. In the early 1960s, after leaving Oxford, I wrote with Terry Jones for a while, and just as we were starting to get somewhere, he said he'd rather go off and write with someone called Michael Palin. That was fine by me, as I would rather write printed humour, and he and Palin were performers as I never would be. So even then I saw my friends wave good-bye and go off and become Monty Python, while I went to join *Punch* in its declining years. I suppose this means that if I wanted a bigger public pose, I didn't have to be born later – Palin and Jones were already doing it in my generation. And there have been times when I have deliberately turned down the chance to go public – I was offered the Barry Norman *Film '81* slot, and I was even offered the chance to go round the world in 80 days before Michael was, but both times I said no because I actually prefer to write and not be recognised.

The more serious question is why I have never got down to the job of being a serious artist, with novels, plays, etc. This was answered satisfactorily for me years ago by SJ. Perelman in a wonderful interview in the *Paris Review* (there was another equally good one in the same issue by Evelyn Waugh) when the interviewer asked if he was ever going to write a proper book. Perelman replied, as near as I can remember in these words:-

"It may surprise you to know that for several decades now I have been approached by studious interviewees with foreheads as big as cantaloupe melons who want to know when I am going to knock off this frivolous stuff I'm doing and get down to the big novel I am longing to write, and that I have always told them the same thing, viz. that I am quite happy working on the tiny scale which I enjoy, and that although in America, where size is all, and where the muralist is prized every time above the miniaturist, my work is given scant regard, I think it has its own value."

I feel exactly the same way. The only flaw in the argument is that as I reread Perelman, he doesn't stand up to revisiting. So I would rather substitute the names of Myles na Gopaleen or Alphonse Allais, both writers of short pieces who seem terrific years later.

Mark you, I only have thoughts like this every ten years. Most of the time I just enjoy having ideas and seeing if they work. One of John Dankworth's arrangers, a man called Lindop, said that a classical composer had once said to him: "I envy you deeply. You write a piece one day and hear it played the same week. I write a piece and hear it maybe in a year when I've forgotten about it." I'd rather be with Lindop on the whole.

Melvyn, can I ask you a favour? I desperately regret missing your *South Bank Show* on Jean-Claude Carrière, one of my great heroes, and as far as I can tell from TV-HQ it would cost hundreds of pounds to get a copy. Is there any chance you have a spare copy I could view? Or that you can tell me who I should get in touch with using your magic name to acquire one? I first came across Carrière's name years ago when he edited an anthology called *Humour 1900* which taught me a lot about French humour. About all there is to know, actually. Which isn't a great deal.

yours from the sticks

To JOANNA LUMLEY
May 24, 1996

Dear Jo,

This is a belated response to yours of, um, March 27th, in which you claim rather incredibly to have found a perfect hill in Dumfriesshire which has a spring of water at the top. I thought the whole point of water was that it ran downhill.

Still, I expect you know what you're doing. It does sound an amazing place. I hope you have got it ready for the day when we drive past to Edinburgh to the Festival. I thought that by leaving Instant Sunshine I had guaranteed never having to appear on the Fringe again, but Caroline uses me vicariously to achieve various subterranean theatrical ambitions, and has persuaded me to do a two-man show with another bloke called "The Death of Tchaikovsky – A Sherlock Holmes mystery". The whole point of this is, as you and Stephen probably know, that Tchaikovsky's death in October 1893 is still a mystery.

Cholera? That's what they said. Suicide, because of a homosexual scandal? That's what many people now think . . .

What people have not realised till now is that Sherlock Holmes himself was dead at the time – or at least was thought dead after his disappearance in the Reichenbach Falls. In fact, it later turned out, he was travelling incognito through Europe, solving crimes here and there, and seeing far-off places – so why could he not have been in St Petersburg when Tchaikovsky died?

After all, Tchaikovsky had been in England only six months previously, to get a Cambridge music degree (honorary, I hasten to add) so it is quite possible that . . .

Enough. It gets a lot sillier before it gets sensible again. I had lunch with Anthony Holden the other day, a man who in his time has been:-

1) Author of a best-selling book on Prince Charles
2) My boss at *The Times*
3) Member of the British poker team – he has just come back

from Las Vegas $6,000 better off, after the world champion-
ships
4) Newly disillusioned with the monarchy
5) Author of a life of Tchaikovsky

And it was about Pyotr Ilyich that I went to talk to him. He was
quite taken with the Holmes idea, and pressed dozens of
Tchaikovsky books on me, which wasn't quite the point, as I never
find that information helps very much . . .

Where was I? Right. Scotland. Now, a change of subject.

They have revived *Call My Bluff* as a daytime TV programme,
and I was lured up to Pebble Mill to do one. Different personnel
entirely. If they ask you, think twice. They try to do a dozen programmes per day, and whereas in the old days *Call My Bluff* was
like a gentle ladies' and gents' club, this one is like the changing
room at the municipal baths.

Where was I? Oh, yes – thanks for thinking of me about the jazz
books. I've got the old Humphrey Lyttelton one, but not the blues
one, and I shall hang on to both. Thanks ever so – I never turn a
book away from this door.

Now to business. I have been offered a berth in this year's boules
match again, and you are my first choice – any chance that you
and Stephen can make it on July 14th, the Sunday, the actual
Bastille Day? It would be wonderful if you could. I am asking
you partly because everyone else would think it wonderful too, but
even more than that because you played rather well and competi-
tively last time. Let me know so on, so that I can put it in my diary.
I have had the damn thing all year and haven't written anything in
it yet.

Finally – you are a stylist and will appreciate this – I was in Terminal 2 at Heathrow recently, in the gents' loo, and half-listening to
a pair of men who had just come in, English, workers, mates, one
black, one white. They both started washing their hands at the same
time and both leapt back because the water was boiling. They
cursed and flapped their hands, and then the white guy said to his
mate: "I'd have thought you'd have been all right with your skin."

The black guy looked at him reproachfully and said:- "I'm only a heathen, not a rhino."

Wasn't that beautiful?

love

To CAROLINE and ADAM KINGTON

Dear Caroline and Adam,

After I took my late book back to the library, I went to the Book Fair, but there was no Book Fair. I got the day wrong. It's tomorrow. So I cycled home instead, and let me tell you – it's bloody cold out on the bike today, and you can't bicycle fast to get warm because there are all these PEOPLE out for a walk with their families and dogs, and if you go fast you RUN THEM OVER.

"Excuse me?"

"Yes?"

"Is this yours?"

"That old handbag? I don't think so."

"Actually, it's not an old handbag. It's a small dog. Well, it used to be a small dog. I just ran over it . . ."

"My God! That was our dog."

"Oh dear . . . I'm sorry . . ."

"Mother! This man has just run over our dog . . . Mother! Mother? Where has she got to?"

"Well, I'm afraid I've run over her as well . . ."

"GET THAT BICYCLIST!"

But that's the whole point of having a bicycle. A quick get away . . .

Oh. You've just come back.

To JOHN CLEESE
December, 1996

Dear John,

I have racked my brains and cannot think of anything I have written about animals that would do for a live audience. I once did a lawyer's advice column on animal rights (Can a dog leave everything in its will to an old folk's home? etc) and if I come across it I will fax it to you.

I also keep thinking of the legendary South Korean saying, "A dog is not just for Christmas, it is also for lunch", but this may not please Americans.

However, I have a train of thought you may care to work on. Years ago on American TV I saw an animal psychiatrist. His job was to talk animals through crises. When married couples split up, their pets have identity crises, and it was his job (this is all odd to us English) to talk the pet through the split, help it to identify with the partner he was staying with, which must have been tough if the dog or cat preferred the other one . . .

So far so good. But there is a new trend in the USA, towards the idea of animals that can communicate. There was recently a film called *Congo* in which a gorilla is taught by Americans to speak, and when they start talking to her they find she wants to go back to the jungle so they take her back, etc etc. (Thus becoming the only Hollywood film in history in which one of the characters is allowed to say she would rather leave America and go and live somewhere else.) Well, when you have talking animals, you're going to have something else new: animals going on shows like Oprah Winfrey and airing their personal problems. Loads of problems, like loss of weight in summer ("Does it suit me? Will my mate go off me?") and identity problems (Stick insect: "I have the body of a stick insect, but I feel like a holly tree. I am trapped inside the body of something I do not feel I am!"), and even worse forced marriages (Panda: "Suddenly, one day, I am told to marry this thing, this overweight panda. I have never been on a date! And suddenly I have to get married! They are surprised we do not have children! Well, what do you expect when neither of us has ever done it or knows what to do! Also, she has very bad breath. And only speaks Russian. Yes, I've got problems all right . . .") and legal problems (Dog: "I am going to sue my master for watching too much TV and going for too few walks. We are looking at $13m . . .")

A thought.

Caroline thinks you sound tired too.

I once wrote a Cold War piece in which the Americans decided that the world might be blown up by nuclear arms and taken over by ants, so they were training an all-American ant to take over, just in case. Little did they know that the Russians were working on an all-conquering Leninist ant-eater . . . Bit dated now, though.

Sorry to be so little help. Call our counselling hot line any time you like.

To STEVE VOLK[10]
Early February, 1997

Dear Steve,

This is to say thank you for reading Tom's script and to apologise for nagging you about it, however subtly I thought I was doing it. It is also in case he never writes back to thank you. He is a good boy but badly brought up. I blame the government, personally.

Still, you are very honoured, because he has never asked me to read his script. In fact I think he specifically asked me not to.

This is what father-son relationships are all about.

In return I undertake to

a) read any script any son of yours ever writes

b) get an extra standby haggis for Saturday

c) let you drink as much whisky as you like

d) let you declaim as much Burns poetry as you like

e) provide financial backing for any scheme dreamt up by your friend Binkie up to the value of £1.50.

Big thrill next week – I have been invited to the premiere of *Fierce Creatures*, the new John Cleese film. Never been to a film premiere before. Never again. There is a party afterwards at the Natural

History Museum. Maybe this time I won't take my bicycle. I once bicycled through London in a dinner jacket to go to a dinner. Doesn't matter if you get oil on black clothes. Incidentally, talking of oil, I had an odd session with my dentist in Widcombe yesterday. He was on crutches. Not a skiing accident but after an operation to shorten one leg. He had had one leg longer by three centimetres than the other since childhood and finally had taken the decision to get a bit of bone chopped out. The very idea makes my willy go funny, as Geoffrey Dickinson used to say. I am afraid it would take too long to explain who he was.

What was that about oil? Oh yes – the dentist told me that he was now so used to wearing those protective gloves which stop him catching or spreading AIDS that he now uses them for all dirty household tasks, like oil changes and clearing drains and weeding etc. Great idea, I said. I'll sell you some, he said. So I now have a box of 100 very thin gloves for £6. Can't think what to wear them for.

Has Pat seen the new sculpture by Igor Ustinov? I hope she does soon. I don't know what to think about it until I hear what she thinks.

Thank you for reading this letter. Let me know what you think of it before I go to America.

your old chum

———————

To BARRY TOOK
February 11, 1998

Dear Barry,

Saw your face in the local paper the other day. The caption read "Famed ex-Air Force trumpeter Barry 'Quick-How-Many-Sharps-In-The-Key-Of-A-Are-There?' Took will be coming to Bath soon to chair a charity evening in aid of something or other", and I remember saying to the wife as I read it, "Look, Barry's coming to Bath," and she said, "Barry's coming to bath what?" and immediately we were off again on one of our interminable wrangles.

But that is not what I am writing to you about.

Very recently I saw you on a tribute to Kenny Everett on the culture channel, delivering a verdict so profound that I couldn't quite make out what you meant.

Nor is that what I am writing to you about.

This is it.

Recently I have been presenting a series of 6 half-hour TV programmes for BBC Wales and seen only in Wales, on eccentric Welsh aristocratic families (they weren't that eccentric – most of them refused to admit they were Welsh, which shows great good sense) and the executive producer, who is called Simon Heaven, poor chap, said the next series he was planning was a social history of rugby.

"You ought to get in a bit of that great comic sketch," I said, "where they portrayed the spread of rugby, with the public schoolboys trying to describe the game to each other . . ."

"Which one is that?" he said.

"Oh," I said, with faltering memory, "when one of the boys says, 'look, you two bend over and put your arms round each other and I'll put my head between your bottoms . . .' and it goes on like that and he is more or less lynched on the spot as a pervert . . ."

"Who did that sketch?" he said. "I'd love to have it. I must have it!"

But I can't remember who did it. But if anyone can, you can.

Can't you?

If the rugby thing means anything to you, let me know.

Caroline sends lots of love to you and Lynn and so do I.

To SHERIDAN MORLEY
September 30, 1999

Dear Sheridan,

Directing *The Three Redgraves*? That's one Chekhov play I've never heard of. I shall make a special effort to come.

Incidentally, I hear you're interested in unknown Noël Coward plays so I started writing one once. Judging from the enclosed, do you think it's worth persevering with?

I went to the first night of *Emma* at the Tricycle, stood next to Michael Billington in the gents at the interval. Gosh, he's older and chubbier than twenty years ago.

"So, what do you think of *Emma*?" I asked.

"Not sure yet," he said, so glibly that I realised he always said this. "Tell you one thing, though. They say that masturbation is the English vice. I think it's adaptation."

He may be right about adaptation, but I think he's wrong about masturbation. Isn't it flagellation?

I was utterly amazed to see the aged Larry Adler in the audience.

"What are you doing here?" I gasped at the interval, when I wasn't peeing next to Billington.

"God knows," he said. "Victor Lownes brought me. Is that the interval or can I go home now?"

Emma is worth seeing, despite what Larry Adler may tell you, or Billington, come to that.

love and kisses

———————

To MAEVE BINCHY
November 2, 1999

Dear Maeve Binchy,

Oh, thanks very much. I was meant to be working this morning and now I've spent most of it reading your book. It has left me feeling immensely cheered up and very ill. I have also made my will again, three times. Now I'll have to work a lot this afternoon.

It's always nice to get a cheery postcard about a piece but especially from a fellow writer, if I can call both of us that. I was actually feeling a bit down at the time because I have been invited to a party in London tonight (launch of several new books by Craig Brown) and can't go, as I had promised to accompany the wife to some dreary charity do in Bath (she had promised to please a friend), and every time I miss a jolly boozy party in London full of famous people, I think I will never be invited to one again and people will forget I exist and I will become a non-person collecting gum boots in the country. People always say that women have to be twice as good to be as good, but there are other categories this applies to as well, and I sometimes think that people who never go to London are a separate category. And then I think what a load of codswallop this is, and cheer up instantly.

I'll take a rain check on the drink, but if we ever work in the same office together, I'll claim it instantly. Incidentally, do you know why it's called "taking a rain check"? It never occurred to me until I went to a baseball game once, in New York, and noticed that the ticket for the game had a tear-off section promising readmission on another day if the game were rained off and it was called a rain check.

I started limping last year, but I was put in touch with a lovely osteopath who has cleared it up by hurting my ankles a lot. Better than having your hip replaced. On the other hand, I'll never get a book out of it . . .

yours and all that

Email to ADAM KINGTON
November 14, 2000

Dear Adam,

I am writing and sending this at about midday on Tuesday November 14th, and I thought I would send just a simple message to begin with to make sure I am getting through to you all right.

The simple message is as follows:-

"Can you lend me a million pounds? All right, a hundred pounds, then? All right, 10p, then?"

That was the only message I could think of, apart from "If your tattoos are missing, please let your newsagent know."

Every time I look at the word "tattoos", I think it looks wrongly spelt. Shouldn't it be "tattooes", with an -e added, like "potatoes" or "tomatoes"?

No, "tattooes" looks wrong too.

Perhaps you would care to look it up in a dictionary for me. There will be a small reward.

Let me know if you get this and I will send you a longer and more interesting one.

love,
Dad

To DOTTI IRVING[11]
March 12, 2001

Dear Dotti,

Yes, I've changed my phone message.

God bless you for reminding me.

I dictated a new phone message greeting this morning.

It now says: "You have reached the right number for Miles Kington. If you wish to offer him work, press One. If you wish to pay him money, press Two. If he owes you money, this is the wrong number for Miles Kington and we have never heard of him. If you are a high-powered public relations agency trying to get coverage for National Poetry Day, aw' wi' ye. If you want a mini-cab, I'll be there in ten minutes . . ."

It goes on in a similar vein for a while, then runs out of space. I believe I'm right in saying I am the first person ever to run out of tape while recording a brief greeting message.

To put it another way, we are splendiferously delighted that you can make the w/e of April 12, and the whole weekend has been pencilled in for you in the diary, then decorated with pen tracings and finally coloured gaily in 4 different shades. Splendid! I said to Caroline, "Hey – we should look out a few art galleries and museums and theatres and cinemas they can visit!" and she said, "I don't think that's quite the weekend they're looking for – that's just what they're getting away from," so now we have earmarked a few badger setts and rabbit warrens you might wish to look down.

Adam says, does this mean he has to go on a course to Wales as well? I said of course it did.

love

PS Was it you that voted Bill Bryson the most popular writer on Britain of all time? I believe it was. It has been said before and it will be again, but time and time again it turns out to be the foreign writers who have the sharpest eye for a country. Think of Tocqueville. Think of Bernard Shaw. Think of Peter Mayle. Oh, no, don't think of Peter Mayle. That ruins the whole case. Did I read somewhere that Bryson is coming back to the UK to reside? Now, why is he doing that?

To SEBASTIAN FAULKS
May 9, 2001

Dear Sebastian,

I have been meaning to get back in touch with you for years, but was finally prompted to do so by hearing you on "Start The Weeks" With Paxman, talking about "On Green Dolphin Street" (which has always been one of my favourite tunes and one of my favourite jazz titles).

It was specifically when you said you had dreamt you were in a jazz club in New York in 1959 etc etc. In 1959 I had just left school at Christmas and had nine months to fill in before taking up my place at Oxford. I hung around the old home doing nothing until, thank God, my dad finally kicked me out of the house and made me go and stay with an aunt in the West Indies. I finally drifted up via Greyhound bus from Miami to New York, where I stayed for three months working and going to as many jazz clubs as possible. Admittedly, this was 1960, but still I was there and if you ever write a novel with the same setting again, I can prove an awfully useful source of research. It was still possible then to cross the Atlantic by scheduled liner, and I came back on the *SS Bremen*, the North German Lloyd Line. My God, seems like another era . . .

Things were just warming up in 1960 for the American election, with Kennedy standing for the first time. Also the first time a Catholic had ever stood and people seriously wondered if a Papist could ever be elected. I can remember in a loo in a jazz club seeing the graffiti "Mao Tse Tung For President!", under which someone else had written: "Good man, but think of the religion problem . . ."

Odd coincidence. I met you through Mike James. Mike James played the trumpet. You dreamt you were playing the trumpet. Probably means nothing, but . . .

I used to live at No 51, Ladbroke Grove, in the garden flat, and I am trying to work out where 35 is. Somewhere in Pyjama Row, I think. That is the elegant row of houses down towards the police station where A Sampson lived (lives). I had always heard that the houses were painted different colours for free to feature in a paint advertisement, and dubbed mockingly Pyjama Row because of the striped effect.

Look – although hidden away in the country, I am having a party in London this Saturday in an attempt to lure out my old London friends, and I would be delighted if you and your wife were free to come. (See enclosed. Actually, you probably have seen enclosed already . . .) Even if not, it would be nice to meet again – it was through you I got on to the *Independent* in the first place, and I am now ready to consult you about my next career move.

    yours

Email to JOHN CLEESE
May 17, 2001

Dear John,

What a great big surprise to get greetings from the other side of the world, and many thanks for the e-pop-up card. Every now and again I group my family round the computer screen to turn on the magic display again, and see the words "We are attempting to make contact with this Website – do not go away!" come up again. How we cheer. But by and by we get the little film, and it does not fail to make me a popular man. My son Adam is very impressed that I have met you. One day he hopes to meet you too. I would advise against this, as your aura will then fade quickly. He knows Terry Jones quite well by now, and is consequently terribly unimpressed by him.

Business. If you haven't changed your mind, then Caroline and I would love to establish dinner with you on Wed June 27, with or without Hutches, but preferably with. I'll have my dinner agent draw up a dinner contract and send it to your dinner agent for ratification. End of business.

I was shocked and made miserable by the news of Douglas Adams's death. I knew him well enough to want to know him a lot more. Alas, too late. When I hear of the deaths of people I like but didn't talk to enough, I immediately start talking far too much to other people who are still alive, which alarms them more than somewhat ... Adams was the first person I ever heard use the expression "e-mail", years and years ago. I asked him to explain. He did. I didn't like the sound of it at all. I think I was right, actually, but it's too late to do anything about it now.

My birthday party in London was, as far as I could make out, good fun. Nobody left for two days, which is always a good sign. Sarah Hutchinson was there for the first day, or so looking herself. My favourite cousin from Scotland turned up, sporting a foot-long beard and the clan kilt. You would like him; he is a genuine eccentric and lives in a castle near Blairgowrie. I once went with him to get an Indian takeaway in Blairgowrie, and found there were two Indian takeaways in Blairgowrie.

"Oh, well," I said, "at least the two Indian families are company for each other."

"I doubt it," he said. "They're not on speaking terms."

"Why not?"

"Sectarian differences."

"Really?"

"Aye. One family is Dundee Indian and the other is Glasgow Indian."

Isn't prejudice a wonderful thing?

It's raining here. Tomorrow Caroline is taking me on a surprise weekend to Amsterdam. Never been there. If you have advice about museums, now is the time.

love

To RICHARD INGRAMS
October 4, 2001

Dear Richard,

As the secretary of our meeting at The Star today, it is my duty to bring you the minutes of our lunch, which were as follows.

1. Whether to have the spicy fish cakes or something else. The result of voting was one for, one against. Mr Kington went for the stuffed chicken.

2. A discussion of Jane Ellison's novels. It was decided to keep an eye open for her second one, which dealt with Norman Balon and Jeff Bernard, though not under those names. There was a brief discussion of whether it was a good idea to be a professor of journalism, but it died for lack of interest.

3. A wide-ranging discussion on Alex Cockburn. It was decided inter alia that a) it was a bad thing to try to write like your father b) one should not let one's wives near Alex Cockburn.

4. Whether to pour millions of pounds into Bill Davies's new magazine, *The Malingerer*. It was felt not.

5. A brief discussion of Ingrams's new role as musical accompanist to Ian Hislop on the Clive Conway concert circuit. Mr Kington said he could not comment until he had heard the duo. Mr Ingrams said it was all right. Mr Kington said he would say that, wouldn't he? Mr Ingrams said that Mandy

Rice-Davies had said that first. Mr Kington said he had been in a musical group called Instant Sunshine for twenty years and wild horses wouldn't etc. Also he knew many music critics but none called Mandy.

6. There was a brief discussion of Richard Boston. Also Larry Adler. Also Richard Cobb. All were felt to be good things.

7. Mr Ingrams proposed the motion that Tina Brown was not as wonderfully glamorous as the late Bron Waugh had seemed to think, and that if she had been any good as a journalist, she would have picked up on a story about Richard Crossman which Mr Ingrams was still prepared to sell for good money. Passed nem con.

8. Mr Kington rambled on for a while about how easy it was to find out of print and long-lost books on the Internet. He said he had recently located a first edition of *Beachcomber*, in the days when it was written by D B Wyndham Lewis. Mr Ingrams said be blowed to that, what he wanted was a copy of Mr J B Morton's only children's book, *The Death of the Dragon*. Mr Kington said he would look into it.

When he got home, Mr Kington looked it up on the Internet and found there was one and one only copy available at a bookshop not a mile from *The Oldie*'s offices, namely Ulysses at 40 Museum St, see attached document, though he doubts Mr Ingrams will do anything about it.

There being nothing else of moment, the lunch broke up at shortly after coffee at about 2.30.

yours sincerely

———————

To WALLY FAWKES[12]
June 24, 2004

Dear Wally,

I have a correspondent in Guildford called Peter L Kelly who occasionally sends me cuttings which he thinks will interest me, and sometimes they do, especially as the last one was a full page spread from the *Ham and High* about your 80th, which makes you months and months younger than Leslie Phillips.

And it gives me an incentive at the raw age of 63 to write to add my tributes to the great man. Though I haven't seen you for years, I always felt it was a privilege and pleasure to have known you, no, I really mean it, although as I write the words I feel vaguely sick at my sentiments. So I'll put it another way.

Hi – how're you doing?

I still play a bit. I have drifted into a local trad/mainstream band with two good clarinettists in it (they do a mean duet version of "Old Stack O'Lee Blues") so all is not lost, and I still listen a lot. At the recent Bath Festival they had two wonderful clarinet players from Italy, both performing in a duo with an accordionist. One was called Gianluigi Trovesi and the other was called Gabriele Mirabassi. This information may be useful to you one day, e.g. if you are in a pub quiz and there is a question like: "Name at least two Italian clarinettists who normally perform with accordionists . . ." Otherwise it may not.

Last week I dreamt twice about Geoffrey Dickinson, who was alive and well in my dreams. Odd, that. And I heard recently that Bill Hewison was no longer among us. Nor Larry. Last time I saw Larry was at the Arnold Roth show, and I said to Larry: "Roth really can draw, can't he?" and Larry shook his shaggy locks at me, and said: "Not my type, old son. Never liked that kind of drawing. Get in there, do the joke and get out, that's my motto. Don't mess around."

Still, most of the time I don't dwell on mortality. I enjoy life too much. Bicycling, that's what keeps you young, though it also kills you unfortunately. Do you remember Ronnie Scott's adage? "The secret of staying young is mixing with older people." Hmmmmm.

Happy birthday, Wally. Many more.

your rural chum

II
Yes, No, Thanks

The pleasure that Miles took in writing letters is nowhere better exemplified than in his "thank you" letters, and, as he became increasingly well known, in those he wrote declining the many requests that came his way. Even when writing letters that, quite frankly, did not need to be written, his creativity and sense of fun flowed irrepressibly.

To FRANK MUIR
April 3, 1978

Dear Frank,

What I was about to say when you so coolly interrupted me was how knocked out by your cluster of relations and near-family I was, and how sorry I am to use expressions like "knocked out by" when there are perfectly good phrases like "bowled over" or "narrowly pushed into touch". In fact, the get-together after the show was like a very good party and I am sorry that it stopped before it had started. Not helped by the BBC's running out of wine. I think in future when the Beeb invites guests to shows it should add to the invitation that old student addition: "Bring a bottle."

I was very flattered by Jamie knowing about my Alphonse Allais and I am nursing a private project now whereby if I send him a copy, in ten years' time he may be able to do for Allais what he did for Satie. A film shot in Corsica, say. I don't think Allais ever did go to Corsica; though he did once go to Venice and reported back that the most striking thing about the great city was the overwhelming absence of the smell of horse dung.

I have made a firm resolution this time not to abandon entirely the stock of free learning lavished on us by Peter Moore, so I am adopting the word "turny" which – how could anyone forget? is applied to staggering sheep. I shall now go through life searching for someone at a party who knows what it means.

What I really set out to say was how much I enjoyed the show and how much, as usual, I appreciate your great kindness. No kidding.

Must go now and try out girder and joist on Coren.

———————

To PAMELA GOSSAGE[1]
March 15, 1982

Dear Pamela Gossage,

I am perfectly willing to write a profile of Gyles Brandreth for a flat fee of, say, £20,000. I can't think of any lesser sum that could possibly interest me in such a project. I've got to be honest. Even £20,000 wouldn't make it very interesting.

But thanks for your letter. I thought it was very funny.

yours sincerely

———————

To J. L. CARR
August 17, 1983

Dear Mr Carr,

Thank you for the *Dictionary of Astonishing British Animals*. I always like your dictionaries and this one is no exception, even though I am always doubtful about 10 percent of the entries in any of your anthologies. If possible I will try and mention it in *The Times*, but as I have also been sent a *Dictionary of Modern Philosophical Thought* running to about a thousand pages at the same time, you may have to share the same space with someone else.

I still think you are the greatest living English novelist.

yours sincerely

To EDWARD VILLIERS
August 18, 1983

Dear Mr Villiers,

I am afraid I won't be able to fit a visit to the Burke Society into my Christmas shopping programme, which is already well behind schedule.

To be quite candid, I don't think many prospective speakers are going to receive a scruffy xeroxed letter with their name typed in and then say to themselves: "This is the speaking engagement I have always dreamt of." What they're going to say is: "If he can't be bothered to write personally, I can't be bothered to speak personally."

Don't get me wrong. I don't want to seem heavy. But elementary psychology helps, you know. That's why I put typing mistakes in.[2] Looks personal. Like a badly tied bow-tie.

    yours sincerely

———————

To MR GALLINER[3]
June 11, 1984

Dear Mr Galliner,

Sorry about the belated reply. I have been trying to work out an answer. I think it is that you ought to have an original idea instead of half-copying someone else's. Englisch, or whatever, is not an entirely new idea, and it has yet to work properly. You might make it work, but I would not like to try or indeed be associated with the attempt. There's far more to this bastard language business than just writing a bastard language.

When you say you want to write sketches based on my ideas, I don't know what you mean, I don't like the sound of it. Remember, too, that many more people here have a smattering of French than of German.

This isn't a very good reply, but I hope you catch the tone of disapproval that permeates it.

    yours sincerely

To DAVID WALBANK[4]
August 1, 1985

Dear Mr Walbank,

I am now 44. At this late age, it is slowly being borne in upon me that any evening described as "funny" is likely to be an occasion of torture for all except professional comedians, showbiz clergymen, undergraduates who have recently left and who wished they hadn't, politicians in opposition and ambitious feminists.

I have further learnt that the kind of undergraduate who gets on committees is normally the last kind of undergraduate one would wish to meet socially.

I have also learnt that the funniest kind of speech at the Cambridge Union is the one which makes fun of the librarian and refers in a familiar style to any female member of the Union committee.

Finally, I have learnt that parking in Cambridge is exceedingly difficult except for those privileged members of society who have been put down for a parking space at birth.

For all these reasons, I am reluctantly driven to reject your invitation to speak at the Cambridge Union, as I am disqualified on all counts. You are welcome to read out this letter at the "funny" debate to explain my absence, even if you read it in a sarcastic tone of voice.

By the way, has it never occurred to the Cambridge Union that the only debate at which any self-respecting humorist would appear is a "serious" debate? What is the point of trying to oppose the Rev David Johnson when it is so much more fun opposing Michael Heseltine?

In my absence at the pre-debate dinner, I would like my mushrooms provençale to be sent to Ethiopia.

yours sincerely

To SIR ALASTAIR BURNET
October 26, 1986

Dear Sir Alastair,

It was very kind of you to take a moment off from your royal duties to drop me a line, and I fully accept your implicit invitation to cover your next tour. I do not share the general view of the British press that these things are best done by accompanying the touring party. And I much prefer to stay at home to write about foreign happenings, so I doubt that we shall ever meet.

I would have no idea how to write anything for *News at Ten*. Indeed, I had no idea that anything was written – I always imagined that you made it up as you went along. That's why I gave up watching TV news. "Pah," I exclaimed, throwing the cat at the screen. "I could make up better than that." "So could I," said the cat.

After the break: the cat does the TV criticism. Meanwhile I must clean the filthy typewriter.

yours sincerely

To BEL and JONATHAN DIMBLEBY
Autumn, 1986

Dear Bel and Jonathan,

Well, my goodness, if a bomb had fallen on the old place last night, the literary and media world would have been an empty place this morning; so glittering a gathering I have not seen since ... since ... well, I have to be honest, since last Wednesday's *Private Eye* outing, but that was different, they were all bitching about each other (to their faces, what's more), whereas everyone last night seemed really nice. I have to admit it. I enjoyed every moment of it. Especially David's speech which did for thrust-and-parry fencing what Tommy Cooper did for conjuring.

Another thing. If a bomb had fallen last night, it would have been quite a test for the *Independent*'s obituary department. Have you read, by the way, that the *Times* obit dept is getting tough?

Saying that people are raving old queens, or not to be trusted, etc? I have just been asked by them to do a piece on Humphrey Lyttelton, in case he suddenly swallows his trumpet, and I am in a dilemma now. Will they only accept the piece if I say, "Humphrey Lyttelton was a boring old Etonian who couldn't hold his drink and left illegitimate sons wherever he played"? It's a problem.

Caroline has gone off filming in the West Country for two days, so when I say that she joins me in saying thanks, it's a diplomatic fiction, but I think I'll get away with it.

She is filming at a school in Yeovil where all the heating and lighting is controlled by computer. This means that if the computer thinks there's nobody there, because it's so quiet, it switches the lights off. This means that during exams, when it's very quiet, a man is employed for no other purpose than to walk round the exam room clapping his hands every three or four minutes to keep the lights on. This is true.

I think you all did magnificently last night. Roll on your fiftieth birthday. So to speak.

———————

To PAUL WOOD[5]
July 1, 1987

Dear Mr Wood,

I wouldn't be unhappy to take part in a debate with you, especially in the company or opposition of Ian Hislop, but I really couldn't face debating a motion about humour. In my experience, the last thing a humorist wants to talk about is humour. Not only is it rather like taking work home from the office, it is also unutterably dull and pompous, because it is the one thing you can never be funny about. In the same sort of way, I find it extremely difficult to write a piece based on some funny news item. It's much easier to write a funny piece about death or disaster or the Arts Council.

I suppose that's why you quite often find so-called funny debates based on motions such as proverbs – This houses thinks you should look before you leap – because it provides a bare canvas on which a speaker can trace something interesting. Why not think up a few new proverbs? My favourite, done by *Mad* magazine years ago, was "Fools rush in and get the best seats".

Anyway, with an interesting motion, I'll play ball. But not with this one. I mean, who actually cares whether humour should be malicious or not?

yours sincerely

To STAFF AT PAN MACMILLAN[6]
post October 13, 1989

To Gail Lynch, Zarina Parmiter and all the other nice people at Pan,

Nobody ever sent me a bottle on publication day before. Somebody once threw one at me, but you know what ex-wives are like.

And it wasn't even my ex-wife.

It was the ex-wife of the man behind me.

"I'm so sorry," she said, coming over to inspect the damage, "I was aiming at the man behind you."

To cut a long story short, we went off to have a drink together and some time later got married. Strange, eh? Now she throws bottles at me in the privacy of our own home. She still has a bad aim though, and never hits me. In fact not so long ago she hit the plumber, which is a silly thing to do because you should never upset a plumber – they're far too valuable to annoy.

To cut a long story short, she did apologise to the plumber and they went off to have a drink together, and now she's moved in with him.

Funny thing, life.

I spend most of my time now, down the bottle bank, getting rid of the old glass round the house.

Where was I? Oh yes, thanks for the bottle. I was very touched.

To TERRY and ALISON JONES
September 25, 1990

Dear Terry and Alison,

Yes, it's a thank you letter. Yes, it's a thank you letter for throwing open your hospitality to us not so very long ago. Yes, it's one of those letters that starts, "Dear Terry and Alison, Thanks very much for having us to stay . . ." and you both look at each other and say, You wouldn't expect Miles to write conventional boring thank you letters like this, would you?

Poor old chap. He's cracking up.

Well, you're wrong! That wasn't a thank you letter. That was just warming up. This is the thank you letter.

Dear Terry and Alison,

I wonder if you have come across Percy, my pet bed bug, whom I must have left behind when staying with you? He looks a bit like this *. He was in bed with us the night we came to stay (oh, thanks for that, by the way) and we must have left him behind. I say <u>he</u>, but actually it was a she, and she was pregnant. Did you know that bed bugs can have over 4 million babies a week? Amazing, isn't it? So, of course, if you find one, it may be one of Percy's children. Anyway, Caroline is writing separately to say thanks and to ask if you've come across Bengy, her pet head louse.

One day we'll get you down here, see if we don't.

love

————————

To PETER STRINGFELLOW[7]
February 5, 1996

Dear Peter Stringfellow.

I am very touched that Larry (and you) should want me to be on the guest list at his 82nd birthday, but alas, I am buried so very deep in the country here that I only get to London about once a year, and when I do, I am usually in bed or back home by 8 p.m.

When I lived in London, I never slept at all (except at the office where I worked) and my erstwhile job as the *Times* jazz reviewer took me to Ronnie Scott's Club a lot of the time, where it is impossible to sleep at all as there is no room there to eat or drink, let alone sleep. Then one day I started going to sleep in jazz concerts and I knew my youth was over, so I moved out of London and came to this sleepy village in Wiltshire, where the fortnightly Womens Institute market is as exciting as it gets.

I will give you an example of how sleepy it is down here. In London, all phone boxes are filled with cards from lovely young girls called "New girl in from Brazil" or "Spanking Sue". In this village the phone box has only ever had one card put up, and that was from a guy who said he would deliver logs free. They're very good logs, incidentally, but on the other hand it's very difficult to meet new girls from Brazil down here. Of course, there are compensations; I believe it's very hard to get free delivery of logs in London. Swings and roundabouts.

So if I came to your party, it would disturb the tenor of my sleepy life for years on end. It's all right for Larry, but some of us are trying to grow old gracefully. Or, at least, peacefully.

Tell you what. I haven't got Larry's current address. I'd like to send him a card. Can you let me have his address? Have a great party.

To IAN LINDSAY
September 26, 1996

Dear Ian Lindsay,

I feel that your perseverance deserves some sort of response, although I am only writing back to say that I am the last sort of OG who is ever likely to turn up at an Old Glenalmond dinner. I tried attending a dinner of my old Oxford college once, and found it such a dreadful experience that I swore never again. I couldn't make out which was worse – meeting all these people I couldn't remember or meeting all these people I could remember.

I did actually receive two separate reminders about the OG Dinner. One was addressed to my father, W B N Kington, who has been dead for some time. Yes, you are certainly persevering . . .

Incidentally, I wonder if they have old boys' reunions in the next world . . . ?

yours sincerely

To GENEVIEVE FOX[8]
December 1, 1996

Dear Genevieve Fox,

I like the sound of your "Sons and Mothers" feature very much.

Unfortunately it is one I would rather read than contribute to, out of respect for my mother's memory.

My late mother was a very special sort of person. Not only was she a fine mother to me, but also, more unusually, a circus performer and worked for most of the time that I knew her as "Brigid, the Bearded Lady". So bearded was she that often I introduced her to people as my father.

"In that case," they would say, "who is the mild and meek-mannered man walking behind you?"

"That is my mother," I would say. "She changed sex shortly after I was born and became the man he had always wanted to be, but to me she will always be my mother."

Although my mother was bearded, her chief glory was her tattoos, which had been given her by an artist who had trained abroad but had never quite made it as a painter. He had always intended to be a landscape painter, which probably explains why most of the tattoos were scenes of Switzerland, and I can remember from an early age looking longingly upon my mother's unclothed form and conceiving an intense desire to go to Switzerland. This was granted when I was about ten, when all three of us went to the Alps for a fortnight, and saw at first-hand all the scenes familiar to us from my mother's tattoos. When my father thereafter talked to people glowingly about our Swiss trip he would often illustrate his remarks by reference to her tattoos, which she would obediently demonstrate, as other people might use slides or (these days) a video recording, but out of deference to her modesty he never referred to our morning in Zurich cathedral, as the corresponding tattoo was in an indelicate place.

It was only much later that I discovered my mother's dreadful secret, and that by a complete accident. I came in her bathroom one day thinking it to be empty and found an attractive-looking middle-aged lady there.

"Who are you?" I cried.

"Do you not recognise your mother?"

"Mother! But – where is your beard?"

"Lying on the chair behind you."

So it was for the first time that I learnt that my mother was not truly bearded and that she had always worn a false one.

Things were never quite the same. Of the truth about her tattoos I will not even speak. But shortly before she died, she asked me to swear that I would never reveal the truth about her beard, even in my autobiography.

"There are many people in many places with fond memories of Brigid, the Bearded Lady," she said. "I would not wish them to be disillusioned. I shall carry my secret to the grave. And my beard, too, please." I hope you understand if I am reluctant to contribute.

To JOHN CLEESE
February 11, 1997

Dear John,

Over the past month or two I have received from you

a) a phone call from California making you sound more tired than anyone should ever be without actually falling asleep

b) an invitation to the premiere of *Fierce Creatures*

c) a box of rather nice wine

and now I am writing to say thank you for all of them although I suppose I could have waited a bit longer to see if I was going to get anything else. I came to the film (which is I think the only film premiere I have ever been to) and thought lots of it was very funny, and some of it not, and though I have scratched my head I cannot make out why, nor how I would have made the film any differently. I also enjoyed the two singing Mexican waiters at the beginning, but perhaps you missed that bit. I have only seen one review of the film so far, in *Venue*, which is the Bristol equivalent of *Time Out* (= millions of reviews in impossibly small print) and in case you didn't see it, they liked it a lot.

I would have come to the party afterwards but had to get a train home, being one of these boring people who don't have overnight pieds-à-terre in London. If I had seen you there, I would have bid you beware of a forthcoming message from a man called Peter Boizot. Do you know of him? All his life he has espoused minority tastes. One of them is jazz. Another is field hockey. Another is his native town of Peterborough. Another is the Liberal Democrat party. Another is pizzas. Of course, pizzas are big business now, but when he started the Pizza Express thing thirty years ago, they were hardly known. Much to his surprise it bloomed and made him into a very rich man, thus allowing him to sponsor and patronise his other tastes, e.g. putting on jazz at the Pizza Expresses, endowing hockey teams, putting money into Peterborough Football Club etc . . . And the last time I saw him, which was just before the *Fierce Creatures* premiere, he said to me musingly, as he sat in his head office at Kettners, "So you're going to see John Cleese, are you? Now he might be rather a good person to contact as a Lib Dem man before the election . . ."

I'm not sure if he and I are still on speaking terms as last Saturday my home team Wrexham knocked Peterborough out of the Cup, but if he ever gets in touch, don't say you weren't warned.

I am sure my fax to you in New York was no use, but I wasn't sure what you wanted. On the other hand, I was pretty sure you didn't know what you wanted either. Meanwhile, in advance of the election I leave you with this thought from H L Mencken.

"Under democracy, one party always devotes its chief energies to trying to prove that the other party is unfit to rule – and both commonly succeed and are right."

To ANDREW ROBINSON[9]
July 19, 1997

Dear Mr Robinson,

Thank you for your or rather for Jonathan Boone's letter. But I wonder if either of you realises just how unrealistic a letter it is. You are asking a writer to travel 100 miles or more, stay overnight in a strange place with strange people and then talk for 12 minutes to more complete strangers at an ungodly hour before travelling 100 miles back again. You might get 12 minutes of interesting chat out of it. I wonder if you have considered what on earth the writer might get out of it. Unless he has an unusual sense of curiosity about Eton, I cannot think of any motive which would make a sensible writer do such a thing.

(I have done my share of talking at schools and universities, but in every case it was because it was nearby, or a fascinating prospect, or a favour repaid, or well-paid. No, I tell a lie – schools never offer money.)

I think Boone was making a joke when he suggested that my visit might boost the *Independent*'s circulation. I have to say that I work for the *Independent* as a freelance and although I want to see it succeed, I can never see myself going out on unpaid circulation-boosting missions.

So this letter is, I am afraid, to say no. It is also to wonder out loud why you thought I might say yes.

yours sincerely

———————

To PAUL BRETT[10]
October 22, 1997

Dear Mr Brett,

You keep writing to me saying that I have won a TOP CASH AWARD and wondering why I haven't got back to you. Well, I'll tell you. Shortly before my mother died, she made me promise to do three things: never to eat in a Little Chef, never to help old ladies cross the road ("They will only want to be helped back later, and then they'll want to come and stay with you, and then they'll try to take over," she said) and never to accept free gifts. I promised. Later, I wondered if by "free gifts" she meant large cash blandishments or simply free CDs and lipstick samples stuck to the front of magazines, but it was too late to ask her by then.

I did once attend a spiritualist séance where the medium got in touch with my mum, and I was about to ask her what kind of free gifts she meant, when the medium said: "Hold on – your mother has thought of a couple of other things she doesn't want you to do either", so I asked her to lose contact immediately before she could tell me.

I hope you understand.

yours sincerely

––––––––––

To THE RT HON SIR EDWARD HEATH
December 3, 1997

Dear Sir Edward,
Thank you for the invitation to speak in far-off Bexley, but I am afraid that a combination of distance, time, business and a dislike of public speaking will not permit me to accept it.

yours sincerely

––––––––––

To LIMPLEY STOKE FETE COMMITTEE
May, 1998

Dear Fete Committee,
I know it is unusual for anyone to resign from a committee before he has attended a single meeting, but I feel I am doing the right thing in withdrawing from the activities of the Limpley Stoke Fete Committee.

Actually, I am not even sure if I ever did join. All I can remember is being approached by Gordon Burton late on the evening of the salsa night and being asked if I would like to join. Under the influence of fiery alcohol I vaguely remember saying Yes. I cannot think why I said yes, as I have spent the second half of my life getting out of organisations and committees which I rashly joined in the first half of my life; I have never regretted any of these resignations, and nor has any of the committees I have resigned from.

I would not go so far as to say that I said Yes to Gordon Burton simply in order to resign at the first opportunity, but I know I am doing the right thing. I am not a good organising person and I am a very bad membership and meeting person. You may have noticed that I have not attended a single meeting so far. That is how good I am. I am afraid I will not be attending any more than I have attended already. But I would like to take this opportunity of saying how nice it would have been working with you, if I had ever done so.

yours sincerely

To DOT PERYER[11]
August 4, 1998

Dear Dot,

I am afraid I am unable to grant your request for a letter of tribute to Ralph Oswick, as in many ways the man has blighted my life ever since I moved to Bath in 1987.

Perhaps I can explain.

When I lived in Notting Hill prior to 1987, I was one of many writers residing in that very fashionable area and found that it was almost impossible to stand out in the crowd of writers and artists longing for fame and recognition. John Cleese lived round the corner, and Harold Pinter up the hill, and I once saw Barry Norman there, though it turned out he was lost. By moving to Bath, I thought I could make a belated bid for fame, or, failing that, at least get my photograph in the *Bath Chronicle*.

I was horrorstruck to find that the *Chronicle* had no interest in putting photos of creative artists in the paper unless they were members of the Natural Theatre Company, preferably including Ralph Oswick. Week after week, almost day after day, a picture of actors from this provincial group would be featured on the front even if it had no connection with the main news story, if the *Bath Chronicle* can ever be said to have a main news story. By the time I had settled in the Bath area, got married, had a child and located the nearest aromatherapist, I had seen Mr Oswick's photo in the paper some 270 times, sometimes in his own right, more often dressed up as a "comic turn".

I once had the pleasure of meeting the *Chronicle*'s editor, if it can be said to have an editor, and he told me that the Natural Theatre Company was the proudest achievement of the City of Bath.

"Really?" I said. "Including the rugby team? And the Roman Baths?"

"Certainly," he said. "I cannot see our rugby team surviving the change to professionalism. And the Roman Baths, like so many things in Bath, are only half-completed and do not work properly. But the Naturals are a great institution everywhere in the world except London, where they know nothing. Go anywhere. Go to Hamburg. Ask them about 'alte Ralphi aus Bath'."

It seems hard to believe, but less than a year after this conversation I was indeed in the fair city of Hamburg and had repaired to the Reeperbahn in search of the company of some local young person. What was my surprise when my eye fell upon the local theatre, called I think the St Pauli, and spotted a large sign proclaiming the arrival of the Bath Natural Theatre Co in a production of *Scarlatti's Birthday*.

"Ach, ja, der alte Ralphi!" was the response when I inquired about the production. They were there for a run of three weeks. A quick calculation told me that if I returned to Bath straightaway, I could spend nearly a month in the place without Oswick being around, and I did, but it was only a brief respite.

Since then my life has been a series of ups and downs. I am glad to say that Mr Oswick is often away on long trips with his "street theatre" company, winning prizes for his work in Tokyo and Rio de

Janeiro, due to the unremitting energy, artistry and invention of that comic troupe. That may well be so. What chiefly delights me is that when he is away winning prizes he is not in Bath, even though he has often had his photo in the *Bath Chronicle* while he was actually in Costa Rica, which does not say much for the news values of the *Bath Chronicle*, if such they have.

On the other hand, I have encountered him when I least expected him. For instance, I have been engaged in a series of Radio 4 programmes with Edward Enfield called *Double Vision*, for which we engaged the services of a local dignitary called Lady Margaret Oswick. Not only did she turn out to be the best thing on the programme, which is unforgivable, but she also turned out to be have more in common with Mr Ralph Oswick than the mere name would suggest.

Enough. I think I have come to terms with the man's success by now. (I may say that I have now had my photograph in the *Bath Chronicle*, pictured playing boules in Queen Square. It was not what I left Notting Hill to achieve, but never mind – I do not think Mr Oswick has ever achieved this. Go on, ask him! If he says he has, he lies.)

And now I receive a letter asking me to endorse him for some award or other! Well, I am not a jealous man. If nobody better can be found, I am sure he is the right man for the prize. I am sure he has a circle of faithful friends who will say no ill of him. My only dread is that, if Ralph Oswick does get this prize, they will put a photo of him receiving it on the front of the *Bath Chronicle*.

Never mind. I shall probably be back in Notting Hill by then.

———————

To HUGO TAGHOLM
September 24, 1998

Miles Kington belatedly thanks the *NEW STATESMAN* for its kind invitation to a party on Sunday but regrets that he has never been to a party conference and doesn't think he ought to start now, as there is a remote chance that he might enjoy and catch the habit.

To RICHARD INGRAMS
September 7, 1999

Dear Richard,

Just to say thanks for the lunch the other day in the *Oldie* basement, which I much enjoyed – everyone there seemed to be good
value and I would like to have sat next to all of them. Unfortunately, your seating plan made no allowance for this.

It's also very nice for me to get out of my rural rut. I shall be
sitting down to lunch here in West Wiltshire in an hour or two, and
my only company will be my wife, and we shall sit in the sunshine
having a Tuscan type picnic on the terrace of our garden with the
birds gambolling round our feet and the distant sound of what is
either thunder in Somerset or the army practising being gunners on
Salisbury Plain, and who would want to do that when he could be
dashing out into D'Arblay Street for a rushed sandwich and beaker
of warm coffee?

At the moment I am engaged in shifting books round the house,
after we had the painters in, and am putting the biographical stuff
upstairs, which means nothing to you, except that every book I pick
up to put on a new shelf, I start reading in an attempt to convince
myself that we don't really need it, which is fatal, because then I
just go on reading it.

The last book I got down was a two-volume collection of the
letters of Charles Kirkpatrick Sharpe, which I didn't even know I
had got – Sharpe turns out to be an antique man of letters in Edinburgh, contemporary of Walter Scott. I opened it at random. A
letter to Walter Scott, saying that he had reserved him a space in his
front window overlooking the place where Burke was due to be
executed next week, but he had better come early or he would give
it to someone else. Fascinating. I might hang on to it a bit longer
. . . And thus it is that one can never get rid of books.

Two things I wanted to say before I bring this drivel to a close.
One was that it would be nice if, at those *Oldie* lunches, you could
somehow do a brief introduction to everyone. The woman next to
you in the dress modelled on the pattern of a Liberty pocket diary
had left and gone home before I even realised it was P D James.

God knows what I would have said if I had known it was she. But I would have thought of something, even if only "What's it like to be on the verge of being abolished, Lady James?" (Talking of which, I wonder how pleased George Robertson felt at being handed a rather emasculated peerage . . .)

The other thing was that you said in an idle moment you might pass on your copy of Tina Brown's *Talk* magazine if no-one else needed it. I'd still like to see it, if it's going . . . I was going to pick up a copy of the *Erotic Review* of which I saw stacks in the place, but then I thought it was probably too late for me to get worked up about things, at my age. Did you ever hear George Melly being interviewed about sex? It was when he had turned 67, and the interviewer asked him what changes he had noticed at this advanced age. "Oh," he said, "For one thing, I've lost my sex drive." "Good heavens!" said the (female) interviewer. "What's that like?" "It's like being unchained from a lunatic," said George, and laughed a huge wheezy laugh. Excellent remark. I wonder if it was original. I certainly intend to use it myself.

Thanks again. See you. Roger, over and out.

yours

———————

To LIZ and ALAN BOOTY[12]
Easter, 2001

Dear Liz and Alan,

This is a note of some brevity but stunning sincerity to say thanks for the other evening, which was much fun – I very much liked the Jenkinses, John and, hold on, I've forgotten her name, no, Steph, that's it. I found myself chattering away to John like two houses on fire, which probably means we share a common taste for pedantry and the overgrown footpaths of literature.

I hope you got away to London the next morning, fresh as a daisy. I haven't been doing anything much except trying to be entertaining to Adam during his hols. He insisted that I take him and a friend ten-pin bowling to Melksham this afternoon. Which wasn't bad fun, actually. At one point, trying to make out how many more points I could score, I asked him how many skittles there were altogether, and he said in the insufferable way he can manage sometimes: "Has it ever occurred to you why it's called ten-pin bowling, Dad?"

No, he didn't. He called me "Miles". He's recently started calling me "Miles". I find it slightly worrying. Caroline says, as a magistrate, it's perfectly legal and I can't take out an injunction to force him to call me "daddy darling", so another strange landmark has been passed. I never called my father "Bill". Perhaps I could get Adam to call me "Bill". At least it would be a compromise.

See you. Thanks again.

love

───────────

To JENNY and LAURENCE BLAIR OLIPHANT[13]
June 11, 2001

Dear Jenny & Laurence,

You are number 267 on my thank you letter list, which explains why you haven't heard from me before. Actually, I haven't done Nos 1–266 yet, so you are highly privileged to get this hand-crafted, artist-fashioned, individually wrought heritage type thank you letter at all. And I haven't even sunk my tasting lips into the Super Famous Grouse yet, so I can't report back on its qualities, but it's only a matter of time.

Meanwhile, it was WONDERFUL to see you out of the hills and backwoods and in the sinful city. Thanks ever so much for making the effort – it brightened my old age considerably, and it's going to need brightening if they don't open up a few more footpaths soon.

Did I tell you that after the party in Soho, I dropped in on Pete King at Ronnie Scott's to ask him why he hadn't popped round to the party, as I had sent him an invite. He was absolutely mortified – "Oh God, Miles, was it tonight!?!? Oh bugger me, I really wanted to come and wish you Happy Birthday – tell you what, go downstairs to the bar there and have a drink on the house," so me and

Caroline and Isabel and Isabel's boyfriend Elliot went below and had a bottle of Ronnie Scott's house wine, and believe me, Ronnie Scott's house wine is all you'd expect it to be, i.e. not that nice. We shared this downstairs bar with four disreputable Americans who turned out to be the visiting group, the Bob Berg Quartet, who we didn't actually hear playing but who I remember as being rather unrelenting and uncomfortable, and drank up and left after being hugged to death by the big black doorman whose name I can't even remember, but who always remembers me (Monty – says Caroline – what a memory she has – she will have to be my walking database from now on), and then Isabel took us off to a very trendy and expensive cocktail bar which I disliked but where the caipirinhas were very good. (I'd forgotten about these drinks – very good Brazilian mixture of lime juice, rum, sugar and something else.)

(We went to Amsterdam the next weekend, and asked around if there was any American jazz in town. Yes, we were told – the Bob Berg Quartet. I gave it a miss.)

If I told you all this at Simpsons, forgive me. No other news except that we went to some jazz at the Bath Festival, none of which was as good as your Dundee stuff from the sound of it. There was a rather good wild quartet from Hungary called the Mikhail Dresky Qtet, also a solo pianist from Hungary who looked like Lenin (furious and hairy) and played like Liszt on speed in a jazz club. Ten minutes would have done me. We also heard David Murray (American virtuoso) and Louis Sclavis (French ditto) duetting, unaccompanied, on bass clarinets, which was riveting but not endlessly so. Fifteen minutes would have done me. In fact, the best music I have heard recently was in our back yard when Caroline drew me out one night, and said: "Sssh – listen, it's a nightingale!", and it was, assuming she was telling the truth.

We'll be in touch nearer the time of the great games. Till then, loads of love and – oh, can you do me a favour? Slip the enclosed across the road to Hetty and Reg. I wasn't sure of this address and postcode. I tried looking it up on the Royal Mail website, but although they help with most addresses, not this one.

Ta ra

To HOLLY and FAY PANTER[14]
June 12, 2001

Dear Holly and Fay,

You know that terrible moment after Christmas when your mother and father say: "You really ought to write some thank you letters, you know?", and you say: "Why do I have to write some thank you letters," and they say: "BECAUSE YOU'LL NEVER GET ANY MORE PRESENTS IF YOU DON'T, THAT'S WHY"?

Well, that moment has come to me, after my birthday in May, and Caroline is saying to me: "Have you written your thank you letters yet?", and I say: "Well, I haven't quite finished them yet," and she says: "Have you started them yet?", and I say: "Oh yes, I have nearly started them", and she says: "WELL, GET ON WITH IT, BECAUSE IF YOU DON'T WRITE YOUR THANK YOU LETTERS, THEN I WON'T GET ANY PRESENTS FOR MY NEXT BIRTHDAY!"

But that is not why I am writing to say thank you for the birdseed. I am writing on behalf of all the birds who are going to get the birdseed next winter. I can't give it to them yet, of course, because you're not meant to feed birds in the summer, but round about next November, when it gets cold and the snow covers the sunflower seedheads, there will be a tap tap tapping at my window and a crowd of pathetic birds will be standing outside saying: "Come on, buster, get that birdseed out here, we know ya got it! And hurry up, otherwise you might find your windows busted!" and then your birdseed will come in very useful to save my life.

We had a nightingale in the garden the other night. I had never seen one close to before. It doesn't look like much but it can sure sing. How do I know it was a nightingale? Because Caroline told me so. She is the ace bird spotter in this family. I am better at spotting trains than she is. Unfortunately, she has not the slightest interest in trains, and is never impressed.

Adam sends lots of love. Well, he doesn't actually – he is too busy watching a video. It's called *U-571*. It's all about submarine warfare. He has seen it before. It's a reward for finishing his school exams today. But Caroline sends her love. Well, no, she doesn't actually. She doesn't know I am writing to you. So she is cooking instead.

Still lots of love from me and Berry.

———————

To ANNIE and ALAN MARYON-DAVIS
October 4, 2001

Dear Annie and Al,

> It's National Poetry Day today,
> And so I send this letter to say
> How nice it was in your abode
> At No. 4, Sibella Road . . .

No, stop it! That way madness lies. But I did relish seeing you again, and Caroline said to me when I got home, "You were lucky – I envied you", which says it all.

I think I enjoyed lunch with Richard Ingrams. He took me to a tiny ex-caff called The Star which was decorated like a working class cafe but had trendy dishes like "spicy tuna fish cakes in its own jus" or "goujons-de quelque chose", and we all sat with our elbows in because the next table was so close, and the young waitress was stunningly pretty, and I think maybe that's why Richard goes there, because although she was so pretty he never looked at her once and I always think that's a give-away, don't you, girls?

The other high spot of my day was going into a phone box in Covent Garden just after coming out of Charing Cross tube and watching one of the street artists as he started his stint. A tall black guy, who just did control tricks with a football, like flipping it from his foot on to the top of his head, where it stayed stationary, and then rolling it to the back of his neck where it stayed stationary again, and then taking his shirt off while it stayed there. I was mesmerised. My phone bill had gone over £10 before I could drag myself away. Also, in Covent Garden, I went into a trendy coffee bar for elevenses, and as I had nothing to read I popped next door and bought the magazine published there. It was *The Lady*. It has opened my eyes to real life.

> It's time to stop writing to my host
> As I must go and catch the post
> But please believe me when I say
> That it was jolly nice to stay.
> Now it's your turn to stay down here
> – I'll send an invite, have no fear!

Love to all. And thanks for the hospitality. Incidentally, did I tell you that I had a dream while sleeping at your place, which had credits at the end? Just as I woke, the dream faded and there was definitely a scrolling up of writing which was either the production credits of the dream OR a trailer. You know, "The Following Dreams Will Be Coming Soon to This Empty Noddle . . ."

––––––––––––

To CAROLE STONE[15]
May 24, 2002

Dear Carole,

How very nice to hear from you after all these years. I have watched your rise to fame and, I hope, fortune, as one watches a new comet rise above the roofs of Trowbridge. I say Trowbridge, because I can't see anywhere else from here. In fact, I have not had such a thrilling letter since I once got one asking me to become a founder member of Groucho's. "It will never happen", I said to myself and refused. Now I am older and wiser and have no influential friends at all, and here comes your letter. God is giving me a last chance to get back into society. Unfortunately, I also live very far from London and hardly ever go there, and when I do go there, I spend all my time planning ways to get back, which is why I shall never be famous and never cut a dash in the world and never be asked to appear on *Any Questions* again. I was once a member of the Garrick Club and worked out after five years that I had had one lunch there and it had cost me £5,000. And I was living in London at the time! So I resigned.

I think you probably get the drift of my response which is that it is loony for me to belong to ANYTHING in London. When you are open and up and running, and terribly successful, you will see a pale face pressed against the window pane looking in at all the jollity, thin and envious. It will be me. Send a footman out with a sandwich. Oh, and get in touch if you ever open a branch in Trowbridge.

Caroline sends lots of love.

To JENNY ABRAMSKY[16]
May 30, 2002

Dear Jenny Abramsky,

I am writing to say thank you for inviting me to your party last night at Spencer House – being domiciled in West Wilts I don't see nearly enough of my old London mates any more, and parties like that are a wonderful chance to meet them again, as well as people I have always wanted to meet and people I ought to meet, and give them eight seconds each.

I was glad to have been there, as it seemed to go really well, the kind of party that leaves a very nice taste in the mouth.

Unfortunately, I have often found in the past that as time passes you only remember the nice taste and not a single detail about the party, and then the taste itself passes from memory, so I have occasionally found it a useful exercise the day afterwards to write down a representative sample of what people said, to trap the memories before they fade.

Here, for your interest, is some of what passed through my ears last night. And about all that I can remember.

Jenny Abramsky:-

"I am very glad you came! Do look around the house. It's amazing."

Playwright called Sheila:-

"You don't know me, but we have a very good mutual friend in Joy Melville. I think you worked at *Punch* together. She said you were very good at office cricket."

Deborah Moggach:-

"Was I on *Saturday Review* the other day? Yes, I think perhaps I was."

Barry Cryer:-

"A lot of people confused me with Barry Took, I was never quite sure why. The day after Tooky died, my wife got a lot of comforting phone calls from people who were reassuringly sad I'd gone."

Brian Hayes:-

"Doing a talk show every day is easy. Doing one a week is very hard work."

Roger McGough:-

"I was sitting in the bath one Saturday morning when I switched on *Loose Ends* and heard Ned say, 'And we also have Roger McGough doing some of his poetry, if he gets here in time', which came as a shock to me, as I knew I wasn't on the programme."

Simon Elmes:- (to Roger McGough)

"I'm amazed we've never worked together."

Roger McGough:-

"It turned out there was a new young poet who had called himself Roger the Goth. It wasn't me at all. For days afterwards people stopped me in the street and said they had heard me on *Loose Ends*. You could tell from their voice that they thought I had changed, probably for the worse, but didn't like to say so."

Simon Elmes:-

"Hold on! I've just remembered! We have met before! We once had a very merry lunch with Anna Howells!"

Roger McGough:-

"I don't remember that."

Steve Punt:-

"Hello. I'm Steve Punt."

Hugh Dennis:-

"I'm Hugh Dennis."

Lucy Armitage:-

"Miles! Hello!"

Me:-

"Hello, um . . ."

Lucy Armitage:-

"You remember! I produce the *News Quiz*! You came and did it for us at Wells! You wrote me a nice letter afterwards! And now you've forgotten who I am!"

Me:-

"Oh." (Thinks: I'll never be on the *News Quiz* again. So much for networking . . .)

A comedian who has asked to remain anonymous:-

"You think that Radio 4 plans everything years in advance, but it isn't true. Not so long ago, I was asked to get a series ready at four weeks' notice. I sometimes worry about them . . ."

Sean Rafferty:-

"Miles, do you know Donald McLeod?"

Me:-

"No, I don't – hello. Do you really know all that stuff you tell us on Radio 3?"

Donald McLeod:-

"Not a thing."

Waitress:-

"They're little mushroom risottos. I don't know what the dip is."

Barry Cryer:-

"If I ever get round to doing a video of myself for my own funeral, to speak to my friends from beyond the grave, I shall say 'I know you're all going to the bar after my funeral, but remember this – I shall be having a drink somewhere else with Eric Morecambe!'"

David Stafford:-

"Hi, Miles – we haven't seen each other since we used to do *Booked!* together. I still think that was the cleverest book programme that Radio 4 ever did."

Geoffrey Smith:-

"Hi!"

Me:-

"Was that a jazz group I heard playing indoors just now?"

Geoffrey Smith:-

"Yes. They're rather good. In fact, I thought it was a record to begin with."

Tony Gardner:-

"Miles! Hi! How old's Adam now! Fourteen? God, I don't believe it. Incidentally, I don't practise medicine any more – I'm a full-time luvvy – so if you are going to fall ill here at the party, don't look to me for help."

Me:- (to Simon Elmes)

"I have recently drifted into a sporadic correspondence with René Cutforth's widow, Sheila Cutforth. I really thought Rene was a wonderful broadcaster."

Simon Elmes:-

"I once got incredibly drunk with René Cutforth. He took me out at 4.30 one afternoon to his club, and we finished two bottles between us."

Me:-

"Of wine?"

Simon Elmes:-

"No. Whisky."

Mervyn Stutter:-

"Miles! Nice jacket."

Russell Davies:-

"I can't stay long. I can't drink much. I have to stay sober enough to go and do a gig with Clive James – he's reviving some of his old long poems and I'm doing them on stage with him tonight . . ."

Unknown person:- (at about 8.30).

"The invitation said the party was from 6.30–8.30, but they're going to have a job getting them out of here."

Me:-

"I've got to go, anyway. I've got to get the 9.30 train to Bath."

Taxi Driver:-

"Paddington Station? OK, sir . . ."

You may think it is a bit overlong for a thank you letter from a stranger, but I thought you'd like an impression of the party from someone who wasn't hosting it. Anyway, one day I am going to find my copy of that and be glad I wrote it. The one thing I am sorry about is that I never got to meet you, and I never followed your advice to look round the house. Some other time, I hope.

yours sincerely

———————

To CATRIONA and RICHARD TYSON[17]
September 29, 2003

Dear Catriona and Richard,

It's October coming up on Wednesday. No need to panic. Just thought you ought to know. Meanwhile, jolly nice to see you at the O+6d (pathetic attempt to do Moon and Sixpence in text style) and many thanks for the wonderful clematis plant, which is still alive.

Richard: "Is the fool writing just to say thanks for the pot plant? If he thinks I'm going to write and say thanks for a couple of plastic cocktail glasses, he's got another think coming."

Catriona (soothingly): "I'm sure there's another reason, dear. Maybe Caroline has told him to get on with his book and this is a displacement activity."

Got it in one, Catriona! Tell you what, though. To show you how seriously I take my autobiography, I'm going to make you an offer which I have made to no other client. I'm going to make a list of chapter headings from this book on my early life, and you can order a copy of any one you want in full.

Here goes.

CHAPTER FOUR

During a bitter argument with my parents, I use the ultimate weapon in family quarrels: I reveal to them that they are adopted. They are unmoved, and reveal that I am a selfish, ungrateful, tiresome child. This comes as a shock to me, as I had no idea of my real identity.

CHAPTER SEVEN

I start collecting railway engine numbers. The first one I collect is a GWR number, 4051. However, I am discovered in the engine shed as dark falls and am forced to replace it.

Disillusioned, I give up collecting train numbers and start collecting my brother's toys instead.

CHAPTER EIGHT

My father, who has a mania for passing on information, in case the accumulated knowledge of one generation is lost by the next, shows me how to chew chewing gum. Distracted by a passing hay wain, I fail to pay attention, and it is not till the age of twenty-one that I properly master the art of gum chewing.

CHAPTER THIRTEEN

After great pressure from my mother to tell me the facts of life, my father takes me aside one day and briefly sketches how matter was created in the Big Bang, how the primeval building blocks of the universe came from simple chemical reactions and how the moon was formed.

CHAPTER FOURTEEN

Learning by accident that my father has not acquainted me with the facts of life to which she was referring, she indignantly tells him to tell me about the birds and bees, or else. An hour later, I know as much as I need to know about the mating habits of birds and bees, which is to stand me in good stead in a pub quiz in May 1999 (see Chapter Ninety-Three).

CHAPTER SEVENTEEN

During a routine medical examination, the doctor asks me what club I support. "None," I tell him. "Football is boring." The doctor tells my parents he thinks I am homosexual and sends me for further tests. Nothing is found. I promise the doctor in future to say, "Chelsea". This is to cause me to be beaten up in 1991 (see Chapter Eighty-Six).

I'll be in touch shortly about theatre plans.

12
Fun

These letters, written for fun, defy any other categorisation.

To THE EDITOR, *THE TIMES*
December 14, 1979

Forgery at Royal Academy?

Sir,

I am pleased to see that one of the paintings in the Post-Impressionism exhibition is by the little-known French humorous writer Alphonse Allais, for if he is obscure as a writer he is even more obscure as a painter. The painting is one of his best being a white rectangle entitled "Anaemic Girls Going to their First Communion in a Snow Storm". (Not his absolute best, though, which I think is his black rectangle called "Negroes fighting in a Cave at Night".) As these paintings date from the early 1880s they may even be the first abstracts ever painted.

Unfortunately, the white painting at the RA, which is labelled a Modern Reconstruction has been hung – or rather pinned – in the upright or portrait position. I have always understood that he painted the picture in the landscape or wide-and-a-bit-shallow shape. That at least is how all his pictures are reproduced in his collected works, edited by the French school François Caradec. This means one of two things; either the modern reconstruction has been displayed 90° out of true (not 180°, as I believe is normal with modern paintings) or it is based on a forgery. Either way, I think the Royal Academy owes the public an explanation, or at least should indulge in some hasty repinning.

yours faithfully

To THE EDITOR, *THE TIMES*
December 29, 1979

Sir,

I am sorry that there has been no reaction from the Royal Academy about the all-white painting by Alphonse Allais in the Post-Expressionism show, entitled "Anaemic Girls going to their First Communion in a Snowstorm". I suggested (Dec 14) that it was displayed 90° out of true; Mr R Norton, while disputing this (Dec 29), affirms that it is a vital 17 millimetres short. But perhaps the RA's inactivity is a blessing in disguise, as it gives them a chance to examine an even more serious possibility – that the picture is hung back to front, with the painting facing the wall and the back facing the audience. I must urge the RA to examine the far side in case it proves whiter than this side, as indeed it may be by now.

This doubt would never have arisen, of course, if the RA had had the sense to display another Allais painting of a different colour, for instance his all-red rectangle entitled "Apoplectic Cardinals Harvesting Tomatoes by the Red Sea", as the back and front of this masterpiece are clearly distinguishable.

yours faithfully

———————

To SHEILA MACNAMARA[1]

Dear Sheila Macnamara,

As I failed to mention the exact nature of the loss of my virginity in the piece I wrote for you recently, I feel I ought to make amends now by revealing that it took place in the course of a rugby match when I was 18, unlikely as it may seem.

I was sent away in my teens to a boys' school in an uninhabited part of Scotland, so rugby opponents were few and far between. In order to bolster the fixture list we were forced to play against several of the girls' boarding schools in the area, and I happened to be chosen to play for the 2nd XV on the day we were playing St Margaret's Academy in Perthshire. St Margaret's had a fierce reputation for scrumming and tackling, but I wasn't quite prepared for the fierceness of the forward battle for possession. Sometimes they battled for possession of the ball, sometimes for bigger gain. At one point I heard one of their bigger forwards say: "I rather like the one with the eyebrows that meet in the middle – let's get him!" Thereafter I was subject to some of the most intimate indignities you could imagine, but as it all took place in the privacy of the scrum, nobody ever suspected a thing. I wasn't quite sure at the time what was happening, except that it was all very pleasurable, but when their scrum-half said to me at the end of the game, "No longer a virgin, eh, laddy!", it confirmed certain suspicions I had already entertained.

Curiously enough, some of my eyebrows fell out the day after the match, and they never met in the middle again. I played rugby quite often again, but, nothing remotely as interesting ever happened to me thereafter.

yours

———————

To TOM KINGTON[2]
October 12, 1986

Dear Tom,

Yes, this is your very own bit of personalised mail. Not like those wonderful things your father keeps getting through the post – all those bills, and reminders to write articles, and unsolicited free samples of drugs, and magazines about bicycles, and love letters from dotty women in Wales – which make you so jealous, but your very own letter. Yes, now you can make him jealous. Just open this letter at breakfast and read it slowly, making comments like:-

"My God, she hasn't really, has she?"

"Must have been a wild party. Three dead, eh?"

"Who would want to set fire to the old school?"

"That's a drug I've never tried."

"Esmeralda, eh? Wow."

It will make him wild with curiosity. Of course, he won't ask you outright what's in the letter, but later, when you're not around he will sneak into your room and have a look at the mysterious letter. But you've exchanged it for something quite different! Ingenious, eh?

Well, Tom, if you would like a letter like this to arrive every day, just get in touch with us. We are a new firm of letter-makers. We have already had several letters read out on *Points of View*, and last week on two days <u>all</u> the letters in the *Times* were written by us, plus Bernard Levin's article. It's a comparatively cheap service, too, though we do provide extras such as:-

    perfumed envelopes
    exploding envelopes
    mysterious female knickers
       at a price.

Don't tell your father, but all those letters from dotty women in Wales were written by us. We were asked to do it by a Mrs Maynard, who wanted to see if he would tell her about them. So you see, our service, which can start any time, really works.

Just get in touch. And let's see the colour of your money, stranger.

To MORRIS PHILIPSON[3]
February 5, 1987

Dear Morris,

Well, my recollections of our lunch together at the Berkeley Hotel are certainly different from yours. As I remember, you were in the grip of a fierce, claret-coloured hangover, and asked the waiter if he could recommend a quiet soup. Our discussion largely centred on whether man would ever find a good cure for a hangover, and if I was destined to be that man, so after we parted I have spent a good deal of time doing research into hangover cures.

I have certainly come up with some interesting material, involving none other than the unlikely figure of Al Capone. It isn't generally known, but during Prohibition days it wasn't just alcohol that was forbidden; hangover cures were forbidden as well. Hangover cures do not contain alcohol, of course, except for the very violent ones, but the reasoning behind the ban went as follows.

1. A hangover cure can only cure a hangover.
2. A hangover can only be brought on by alcohol.
3. Therefore the use of a hangover cure proves the intake of alcohol.
4. Therefore, as a hangover cure always accompanies an illegal act, hangover cures must be made illegal.

Various attempts were made to circumvent the anti-hangover cure law. Some lawyers maintained that the cure was quite ineffective anyway, others maintained that it could cure other things beside hangovers, or simply be taken as a pleasant drink in its own right, which was ridiculous as no hangover cure is pleasant. If it was, it wouldn't be a hangover cure.

But it was one of Al Capone's mob who first saw the most interesting implication of all this. Ordinary hangover cures were designed to cure hangovers caused by ordinary drink. However, during Prohibition people weren't drinking ordinary drink – they were drinking moonshine, and getting moonshine-based hangovers. Therefore what they needed, he reasoned, was a morphine hangover cure, which they could produce themselves and make a huge, illegal profit out of. Just as moonshine was chemically different from ordinary alcohol, so the hangover cure would be quite different as well.

The man in charge of the project was called Lucky "Legs" Lugano, about whom we know nothing except that he was a cousin of Capone's gun-maker. He led a team of bootleg chemists such as Leggy "Luck" Lugano and "Lucey" Legs Lugano, about whom we know nothing except that they were pseudonyms or made up by the newspapers, in an effort to distil moonshine hangover cures from herbs imported from Sicily. Much in the same way as German scientists were still trying to find the secret of nuclear fission when the war ended (and have not yet succeeded to this very day, it might be noted), Capone's hangover cure team were still hard at work when Prohibition ended without ever having found a really effective cure. The results were locked up in a secret vault in Chicago and were opened recently, but are believed to have evaporated as the vault was actually being opened.

It seems from what little evidence we have that the mission to find a moonshine hangover cure suffered from one great disadvantage; the team did not delegate any of its work and preferred to do all its testing alone. And as all the testing had to be done on people with hangovers, this meant that the team was drunk almost all the time, and a drunk team is not an effective team. Consider this scrap of dialogue from one research session . . .

Lucky:	I feel terrible. Jeez, I feel terrible.
Miss Stefani:	Shall I put that in the minutes, sir?
Lucky:	Just don't put anything in the minutes, right? Just shut up.
Legs:	What happened last night?
Luck:	We drank a pint of sherry, a pint of gin and a pint of beer.
Legs:	We did? What did we do that for?
Luck:	You remember. For research. Into . . .
Legs:	Into what?
Luck:	I don't remember.
Lucky:	I remember! Now I remember! Into a cure for hangovers!
All:	That's right!
Legs:	That's just great – we can actually cure this hangover we've got with the cure we've got!
Miss Stefani:	No, you can't.
All:	Why not?
Miss Stefani:	Because you drank all the cure last night as well. You linked arms and danced round the room, singing: "Let's take the cure now, let's take the cure now!" You then drank it all and went to bed.
Legs:	We didn't do anything stupid whilst we were drunk, did we, Miss Stefani?

Miss Stefani: You got in the car and drove around for a while, shooting up innocent passers-by.

Legs: But we didn't do anything stupid?

Miss Stefani: No, sir.

Lucky: Jeez, I feel terrible.

The rest of the transcript gets a bit technical after that, with the three men telling Miss Stefani in some detail what will happen to her and her parents back in Sicily if she ever tells anyone about all this.

As far as I can make out, the history of research into hangovers is caused by a conjunction of over 1,000 different chemical agents which can combine in many different ways to produce that familiar feeling of unease and nausea. (Research is also proceeding to whether "unease" is a genuine anagram of "nausea", or just a result of illiteracy among scientists.) Current thinking is that every hangover is slightly different, rather in the same way as all snowflakes are slightly different, and as no cure has ever been found for snowflakes, we fear that much the same is true of hangovers. What we have here is a case of a lot of scientists spending a lot of money on a project which they know they cannot win, and having a damned good time meanwhile. Here is a sample of recent research . . .

Dr Lugano: I feel terrible. Jeez, I feel terrible.

Dr Winkler: So, you shouldn't drink.

Dr Lugano: Drink? Who's drinking? Just because I have a hangover doesn't mean I have been drinking.

Dr Winkler: It does usually. What's your excuse?

Dr Lugano: It's hereditary.

Dr Winkler: Oh, come on! You expect a Nobel Prize-winner to believe that?

Dr Lugano: You're a Nobel Prize-winner?

Dr Winkler: No, but we could ring one up and ask him.

Dr Lugano: I've never told anyone this before, but my father was a hangover research specialist with Al Capone, and he had so many hangovers that I inherited them.

Dr Winkler: You know what? I think I will ring up a Nobel
        Prize-winner: and ask him if it's possible.

Dr Lugano: You don't know any.

Dr Winkler: Yes, I do. My father was a very important scientist
        during the war, in Germany. He met lots of people.

Dr Lugano: What was he working on?

Dr Winkler: Well, everyone thought it was a secret mission to
        discover nuclear explosives. In fact, it was a secret
        mission to discover a secret hangover cure.

Dr Lugano: No kidding! Did they ever find one?

Dr Winkler: Certainly not in time to win the War. I once asked
        my father if they ever found a cure and he said he
        couldn't remember but they sure had a great time.

Dr Lugano: Perhaps it would be best if none of this went down
        in the minutes, Miss Stefani.

Miss Stefani: That's all right, sir. I learnt tact from my mother.

The general feeling I'm afraid, is that hangovers are here to stay.
However, I have instituted a hopeful line of research myself which I
think could provide a breakthrough. The line of reasoning goes like
this. More numbers, please.

1. People feel dreadful after they have been drinking.
2. The normal reaction is to take steps to feel less dreadful.
3. These steps always feel, or lead directly to the next hangover.
4. Therefore, <u>why not take advantage of feeling dreadful?</u>

This is not as it sounds. We all perform certain functions best
when we are in a physical or psychological state for it. For instance,
a man who is feeling physically active and vital is likely to do well
in a sprint race, but not so well if he is called upon to stand in line
at a bank. A man who has the patience to conduct psychoanalysis
is not likely to do well if called upon to partake in a sprint race, and
so on. What we have to do, then, is find the functions which are
best performed when one is in the grip of a terminal hangover. For
instance, sitting still and groaning are best done during a hangover.

What involves sitting still and groaning? What involves staring into space, self-pity, twitching and going different colours?

Well, not as many things as we'd like but enough, enough.

Here is a list of some twenty.

1. Acting in any play by Samuel Beckett.
2. Opening letters from the tax people.
3. Watching TV videos of programmes you are not looking forward to watching.
4. Reading any book by Thomas Hardy.
5. Listening to a close relative on the telephone, in the sort of conversation where you are not called upon to do anything but make occasional, encouraging noises.
6. Offering yourself as a hostage in a siege.
7. Listening to anything by Stockhausen.
8. Tackling a crossword you can't do when you're feeling well.
9. Getting out your passport to see if your passport photo still looks worse than you.
10. Giving up smoking.
11. Ringing up telephone numbers you have written down without any name attached, and finally having the courage to find out if they are important or not.
12. Trying on the clothes which have been at the back of your cupboard for twelve years.

Well, that's some twenty ideas (some twenty is a phrase that we scientists use for twelve. "We scientists" is a phrase that high paid lobby groups use to describe themselves which offer some hope to those about to embark on a hangover). If you want to know more about this fascinating subject, just write to Hangovers for a Free World, CIA, Washington and we will get in touch.

Letter to follow.

yours

To CAROLINE KINGTON[4]

May 31, 1987

Hello darling,

  you don't know me but this geeser kingston what you're getting
married to, he's already married, and I don't mind telling you this,
as this bloke kingston what you're marrying, well, e's ruined my life
and now i intend to ruin his, my story is simple I am a barmaid
called Bertha, I wasn't always a barmaid called Bertha I used to be
a barmaid called Jan, but that's another story, Jan Morris, actually,
then that writer geezer called James Morris went and changed his
bleeding name to Jan, and I had to change mine; but that's another
story, anyway I first saw this bloke kingston in 1973 in the old dog
and truffle in mayfair, know the pub? it's mock tudor outside and
mock-cheerful inside, there's a snug and a lounge but no saloon
because the landlord didn't encourage people who couldn't afford
saloon prices 'e was a funny bloke the landlord, 'e 'ad a pet wart on
his left cheek which used to be able to tell the weather, honest, if it
wobbled it was going to rain and if it didn't it was going to be fine,
but one day his wart ran off with a carbuncle from Streatham, still
that's another story, where was I, oh yes, I was just getting ready for
the evening session one day, polishing glasses, because I can't see
very well when they're dirty, just my little joke, when all of a
sudden this bloke walks in and my knees trembled he was that
good-looking, 'e reminded me of that film star, what's his name,
vincent price, and he just looked at me and said: Are you ready to
come to the ends of the earth with me? Well, I said, I'm on duty
tonight but it's my day off, I could come then, is it far? Not very far,
he said. I measure all distances from Brisbane in Australia. Coo, I
said, because I can't measure anything from anywhere. Where's the
end of the world from Brisbane, then? I said. Right here in the Dog
an Truffle he said. I should have known then that he was a cheap-
skate, but you never learn, do you?

  Well, you certainly don't if you're going to marry this bloke
Kingston, he and I had an off and on relationship for years, sometimes I was off him, and sometimes I couldn't stand him, but there's
something about some men, isn't there? They're sort of irresistible

aren't they? This bloke wasn't but anyway. He had a trick of pulling at his ear which really used to annoy me. Don't pull it, I used to scream or it'll come off. The next night he was idly pulling at it – and it did come off! I nearly fainted. He slapped it on the bar, cool as a cucumber, and, said: Ever wonder where the old expression "lend me your ears" come from. Well, now you know. Course, it was a false ear, he was full of tricks like that, I remember one night he pulled off his head and put it on the bar, saying, I've lost my head over you, you little rascal, Dora, I was a barmaid called Dora at the time I had to keep changing my name so that the guvnor could avoid national insurance, something like that, but that's another story, I remember one night he said, Come on, girl, we're going to do the rounds, and he took me out and did we do the rounds? No, we had a round trip on the Circle Line. I wouldn't have minded so much, but he only bought two platform tickets, anyway if I were you I would have nothing to do with this bloke Steve Kingston, he's a rotter. No, Steve. Oh, different bloke, is it? Oops, my mistake. In that case all the best and I hope you're very happy, love Kim the barmaid, why kingston? Well, it's a long story . . .

for and on behalf of Miles Kington

———————

To BARRY TOOK
November 20, 1998

Dear Mr Took,

We understand that you have asked for a fax to be sent to you on behalf of Mr Kington of Limpley Stoke.

Before we can expedite this matter, we have to know what kind of fax you would prefer to receive.

We can offer the following alternatives.

1. The worrying fax.

This is a fax which says, EIGHT MORE PAGES TO FOLLOW, and then does not produce them.

2. The condolence fax.

This says: "Hi! The Samaritans here! We were having a bit of a flat morning, nothing much doing, so we thought we'd fax around and see if anyone needed, like, a chat about things. We were a bit lonely, actually, so PLEASE give us a ring . . ."

3. The junk fax.

This offers you a chance to buy Chinese sailing boats at very reasonable prices.

4. The lady's fax.

This is a fax on pink paper with the most heavenly scent of Cardinal Sin, the new smell from Yves St Laurent.

5. The laddish fax.

This is a fax which jumps out of the machine and head butts you. But only ironically.

6. The New Left fax.

Halfway through your reading this, the phone goes and it's Alastair Campbell, and he says: "I think what this fax is REALLY getting at is this . . ."

Don't forget. Dec 18th. Details will follow as sure as eggs is full of salmonella. Or is it listeria? Tell the wife, I haven't forgotten. She will know what I mean.

If she doesn't know what I mean, tell her I've forgotten too.

To CATHRYN CRANSTON
September 16, 2002

Cathryn Cranston
Publisher, Harvard Business Review,
International Offices
Tower House,
Sovereign Park,
Lathkill St
Market Harborough,
Leicestershire

LE16 9EF
United Kingdom

Dear Ms Cranston,

I think I have isolated the reasons for your under-achievement in business.

Your address is too long. Yes, it's as simple as that.

People who want to be Leaders and Get Ahead in Business don't have time for long addresses. Up to 40% of workforce time can be spent just typing it out, or checking the spelling. And think of all your potential customers who never reply to you because they can't be bothered.

Think of the real leaders of this world. George W Bush, for instance. His full address is George W Bush, The White House, Washington DC.

Think of the Pope (The Vatican, Nr Italy) or Fidel Castro (Havana, Cuba).

No wonder they are world leaders.

Please get in touch with me again when you have streamlined and rationalised your address. Then perhaps we can do business.

yours sincerely

———————

To GAVYN DAVIES
March 8, 2004

Dear Gavyn Davies,

I was going through some unanswered correspondence when I came across a letter written by you to me on Dec 16, announcing Mark Byford's appointment. I never quite knew why you had written to me at *The Independent* to tell me this, nor whether you wanted an answer, and as things have taken many dramatic turns since then, I do not suppose any answer of mine would have been sufficient.

I should have written back in due course to say how sorry I was that you and Greg Dyke had had to walk the plank.

However, as I have now written a piece for the *Independent* tomorrow detailing my bid to become the next Chairman of the BBC, I thought it was only fair that I did write to tell you in turn of what I was up to. If you have any hints on how to become Chairman, please let me know. They will remain my secret.

In case you are a *Guardian* reader, I enclose a copy of my piece.

yours sincerely

———————

To BEVIS NATHAN
May 19, 2004

Dear Bevis Nathan,

I know you wanted a careful résumé of my condition since my last visit, so here it is.

Day 1. Practise new exercise, getting up on to stair and down again, using good foot to get up and bad foot to get down.

Day 2. Good foot is now bad foot, and vice versa. Start again, reversing feet.

Day 3. Both feet feel quite good. Forget which is bad foot.

Day 4. Decide to pretend right leg is good leg. Do exercise for five minutes, then slip off bottom step of staircase, and hurt myself. Limping badly.

Day 5. Solicitor who lives across the road from me says I might have a case for malpractice here, being recommended wrong exercise by osteopath, etc. Say I couldn't possibly sue my osteopath. Solicitor says there might be a lot of money in it. Say, Oh, all right then.

Day 6. Solicitor phones from his office to say that, just to get all the facts straight, he was doing this exercise in his office as a demonstration and he too slipped and fell heavily against desk. He now has bruised ribs etc. He is thinking seriously of suing. "You can't sue my osteopath as well!" I say. "Not him," he says. "I'm thinking of suing you."

Can a solicitor sue his own client?

Day 7. Getting more complicated. The solicitor went to the

doctor and told him he had been injured while doing an exercise. "Oh?" said the doctor. "What exercise?" The solicitor showed him. The doctor tried it, and fell heavily. The solicitor made the mistake of laughing. The doctor is now suing the solicitor.

Day 8. I have decided to withdraw my case against my osteopath, in case anyone in court gets injured while trying out the exercise during the trial. This means that although there are still cases going forward, neither of them is against the osteopath. In fact, the osteopath will never get to know of all the damage he has caused unless I write to him and tell him.

Day 9. I write to him and tell him.

yours sincerely

13
Last Years

By the end of January 2007, Miles was losing weight and clearly unwell. There was no reduction in his work or letter writing however, and when he was finally diagnosed with cancer in late June, he decided to write another book, How Shall I Tell the Dog, *which was published after his death. His illness he made light of, telling only his closest friends. His last column appeared in* The Independent *on January 30, 2008, the day he died.*

To JOANNA LUMLEY
February 9, 2007

Dear Jo,

I don't know if you spotted the coincidence, but you and I both had pieces in the *Independent* on the same day, both on the subject of cruelty to turkeys.

Not only that, but both pieces were identical, word for word. I am therefore instructing my legal team to sue you for millions of pounds on the grounds of plagiarism, mental cruelty, and locking me up in a small, desperately untidy room to make me write my pieces . . .

Fantasy takes over again. Actually, it is quite a heart-warming thought to think that there might be a body called the RSPCW. The Royal Society for the Prevention of Cruelty to Writers . . .

"The door with some difficulty was broken down. The investigators broke through into the inner space, then recoiled with a gasp of horror. The conditions were as bad as anything they had ever seen. The carpet was entirely hidden in paper, an ashtray gave off the lethal fumes of a smouldering cigarette, several unfinished mugs told their hideous story of caffeine overload, and at the desk the writer himself seemed unaware of their entrance.

'Poor devil,' said one. 'It may be too late. He showed no auditory or visual reaction to our arrival.'

'How can a writer do this to himself?' said the other.

It was then that the writer looked up and registered their presence. He looked at them for a moment.

'If you're from the Inland Revenue,' he said, 'you can piss off. I am skint.'

'Poor fellow,' said the first one. 'He's hallucinating . . .'

'Come on,' said the other. 'We've got to get him out of here and into the fresh air. I wonder if he can walk unaided. Or has he lost the use of his legs?'

'I don't usually lose the use of my legs till about ten at night,' said the writer. 'Where were you thinking of taking me . . . ?' etc etc etc etc."

Mmmmmm . . . I think we have the makings of a piece here.

Thank you, Jo. Tricky ground we are on here, of course. Am I allowed to copy a letter I have sent to someone else, or will I be guilty of plagiarising myself?

How are you both? Our little boy Adam (six foot one, bigger than me, 19 yrs old) has gone off to South Africa to do a bit of gap year stuff. Every time we hear from him he is EITHER swimming all alone on a golden lagoon OR travelling in a mini-bus taxi with twelve black people, all of them debating in the native language which one should mug him first.

Right. I am taking part in a new competition. It's called "Let's see if you can get through the next fortnight without hearing any Tchaikovsky at all." I don't know if Stephen knows this, but I once wrote a play called "The Death of Tchaikovsky – A Sherlock Holmes Mystery". I also acted in it. There were two of us in it. Sometimes we played Holmes and Watson, sometimes Tchaikovsky and Madame von Meck. It went to the Edinburgh Fringe. It came back. In retrospect, I should just have written, not acted.

To MIKE WILLIAMS[1]
March 27, 2007

Dear Mike,

You silly impetuous boy, you. If you start sending drawings all over the place, you will have none left for your old age. That sounds like a prelude to me saying that I am going to send them back. Not on your nelly. I shall have them framed and have a princely outside toilet built to hang them in, probably named the Mike Williams Memorial Loo. There might be one or two measly Calmans in there as well, but they won't glow like yours. Thanks ever so much.

Somewhere – and I wish I knew where – I have a stash of *Punch* Lunch menu cards. Bill Hewison used to doodle on them during the after-lunch conversation, and leave them behind. "All right if I take it?" I'd say, and he would nod yes, like Leonardo da Vinci giving someone the first ever design of a helicopter (because he knew it couldn't fly) and eventually I amassed some eighty or so. When Hewison did his theatre or film drawings, he was rather static and arthritic, I always thought, even though his line was nice (hark at me), but when he doodled he relaxed, and these menu cards have some great flights of fancy on them. Am I trying to say that his doodles were better than his finished stuff? Of course I am. Build up the hearsay reputation now, sell them at a mighty profit later. But I have to find where I put them first . . .

The *Punch* days seem a long way away, like another marriage or a disused parallel universe. I occasionally hear from Jonathan Sale or bump into Alan Coren at an airport (when he's flying out to his house in France, and I have just popped into Terminal 2 to use the loo) and I sometimes swap emails with Pamela Todd – do you remember the lovely art secretary? – but that's about it. Actually, when I moved out of London in 1987, I left almost everyone behind me that I knew. Luckily, I have made a few friends since then who don't know my true age. That was a significant year for me. Leaving London, getting married again and having another child after a 20 year gap since the previous.

Don't want another year like that again. (Don't worry, says the doctor – you won't.)

I am going to drop Albert a line. I would like to get a copy of one of your prints for a friend of mine. I won't tell you which or you'll send it to me or something stupid.

I shall now come under a lot of pressure from Anita to write something on the next show, the *Alice in Sunderland*. I don't know Bryan Talbot's stuff. It looks very French in style, all that wild bandes dessinées stuff. Which I like, actually. But what do writers know?

———

To JOHN DANKWORTH
April 27, 2007

Dear John,

No, I am sorry – this letter does not contain lyrics, as you devoutly hope. The fact is that this week, Mon–Fri Apr 23–27, I have been stricken by some bug or virus or God knows what, and have been lethargically and quite painfully creeping on all fours from one daily chore to another. The doctor says, after some blood tests, that it looks like some kind of liver problem but she isn't quite sure yet, and has ordered some more, and fixed up for me to see a specialist.

Now, when I hear someone else complaining that they have hit a wall of inactivity, I always get impatient, tap my feet and wait for them to snap out of it. But when it happens to you, you sympathise with yourself a bit more, even if not everyone else does. So all I can say is that getting something to you and Cleo is number one on my shopping list, that I shall be working at it, and that if it's not there with you in the first half of next week, in proto form, then I am worse than I thought. It's not like me at all. I'm usually quite energetic. What are all these bloody siestas? Why can't we go for a walk? says the dog. I've tried explaining to him, but he's not very impressed either.

Good luck with the weekend.

yours

To JULIAN NANGLE[2]
May 19, 2007

Dear Julian,

I took special note of the fact that you were going to be at the Bath Book Fair and turned up on the second of the two days. Unfortunately, I got the two days wrong – I thought it was Saturday and Sunday – not Friday and Saturday – you can imagine how quiet it was when I popped along on Sunday. Just two people in the whole Assembly Rooms, and they had come to buy postcards. Still, as my wife said afterwards, "You may not have met your Mr Nangle, but at least you didn't buy any more books, thank God."

"He's not my Mr Nangle," I said stiffly.

"Then who's Mr Nangle is he, then?" she said.

And do you know, I didn't know.

Ever since then I have been in hospital with a strange blood or liver complaint that the doctors keep nearly identifying, but that's another story.

yours

To CATE OLSON and NASH ROBBINS[3]
May 19, 2007

Dear Olson and Robbins,

I bought a book by post from you a few months back, and I remember thinking at the time, when I looked you up on the Internet, how great your shop sounded, and how one day I would love to drop in on you, so I was amazed and delighted to read of your recent award. It doesn't get me any nearer to dropping in, but one day, one day . . .

Curiously enough, I am friends with one or two other people who run shops which were on the list a bit lower down (Mr B's Emporium in Bath and the bookshop in Chipping Norton) and I am just very glad that there still are such noble and quixotic people around. And I am very glad that you got the prize, because you must be really good to get it.

The other day I heard Ian Jack on Radio 3's *Night Waves* enthusing about Dawn Powell, an American comic writer I had never even heard of. Do you ever have any of her stuff floating through? (Don't answer.)

yours sincerely

———————

To CATE OLSON and NASH ROBBINS
May 22, 2007

Dear Olson and Robbins,

Gosh – what a thrill! To get not just a friendly answer but the start of my Dawn Powell collection. Mark you, I am always worried about booksellers who make presents of books to people – this is no way to make a fortune – but then, running an independent bookshop is no way to make a fortune either.

Only to have fun and meet people, I guess.

I have already made a start on *The Golden Spur*, and laughed out loud several times by page 7 which is a good sign.

There was a reference on page 6 to a funeral in New York, which reminded me of a story in Gardner Botsford's *A Life of Privilege, Mostly* (great title) about a genuine old lady who used to take an hour's constitutional in Manhattan every day but had to pause halfway round to spend a penny. She eventually found a friendly undertaker's where they would let her come in and use the lavatory. One day, as she was leaving, she was asked by a suited young man to "sign the book" and leave her address, which she did somewhat suspiciously. A week later she got a cheque for $10,000 through the post. It seemed that an old lady who was being buried there had decreed in her will that anyone who bothered to turn up to her funeral would get ten grand. Hence the request to sign. Hence the bequest.

What a very happy story.

See you one day.

To GILL COLERIDGE
July 20, 2007

Dear Gill,

As you know, I have been promising for some time to write to you with proposals for new books, and as you put it to me the other day: "I haven't heard from you yet."

Well, my recent visits to hospital and the discovery that I seem to have got a kind of cancer slightly change my view of the future. Not that I don't want to write books still, but the kind of book I try to write may be affected.

For instance, I know that a lucrative vein has been mined recently by people who had got cancer and determined, instead of being bowed down by it, to write brave and resilient books about their experiences. I haven't read any of these books, as I prefer to read stuff by people who have nothing to complain about, but I know they have made money and we can all respect that. If you think we ought to go down that path, let me know.

You would have been proud of me the other day. I had my first interview with an oncologist, and while he was patiently spelling out to me what kind of a future I might have, I was brave (and resilient) enough to ask him a professional question.

"How many stages will this break down into?" I said.

"Stages?" he said.

"Well, I really mean chapter headings," I said.

"Chapter headings?"

"I mean, if one were writing a book about one's experiences as a cancer patient, would it fall into obvious sections?"

He didn't answer my question directly, but I thought he looked at me with a new respect after that.

Incidentally, you will notice that I said "I seem to have got a kind of cancer . . ." I think this was because, although I know I have got a form of cancer, I haven't really had time to pass from the stage of not knowing to the stage of being sure. There should be an intermediary stage when the surgeon dangles the possibility in front of you, and then, when he thinks you are ready, confirms it.

Which, come to think of it, is exactly what my surgeon did. Perhaps I am going into slight denial about details already.

Do you think there is any juice in the idea of a book written by a cancer sufferer in denial? "A Year in Denial", perhaps. Of course, if he were in denial he wouldn't write it, would he?

As you can see, I am still a bit confused about the whole thing. But if I write to you again about it, I can probably start to clear it up in my own mind.

love

—————

To GILL COLERIDGE
July 21, 2007

Dear Gill,

I haven't had an answer to my first letter from you yet, probably because I only sent it today, but I had another curious encounter with the oncologist at the hospital yesterday afternoon. After we had run through a few things (attitude and diet, mostly; they are the key to cancer survival, he said; with the right attitude and the right diet you can keep going for years) he suddenly said: "So you're going to be writing a book about cancer, are you?"

"I had thought about it," I said cautiously.

"I don't want to be discouraging," he said, "but it takes years of research and experience to get anywhere near having the authority to write a book on some aspect of cancer. I am not entirely sure you will have enough years left to you to master the subject."

He has a tiresome way of coming back to my life expectancy. "Heavens above," I said, "I am not going to write a text book! Or a medical book! Or anything like that! It's going to be more like a diary, probably."

"A diary?"

"A daily content of my ups and downs as a cancer patient. How hope ebbs and flows. The daily annoyances, the little triumphs, the funny moments . . ."

"And who do you hope will buy this? I can't see it appealing to the profession."

"I should hope not!" I said. "It is supposed to appeal to the patients, people who are as scared and confused as I am now but who gradually get it all straightened out. I hope they will turn to my book as a plain person's guide."

"It seems a very good idea to me," said the specialist, looking happier.

A thought suddenly occurred to me.

"Are you writing a book on cancer?" I said.

"Yes," he said. "I have been for twenty years."

"I understand your reservations now."

"It's just that . . . well, I am glad we are not in competition. And it's a very novel idea."

"Not that novel, I'm afraid," I said. "There has already built up quite a sub-genre of cancer diaries. There have been lots by now, but the first one was by John Walsh, I think."

"Not a name I know," he said.

Which was quite understandable, I thought later, as I wasn't thinking of John Walsh at all, but John Diamond, Nigella Lawson's quondam husband, who gave us his final year of cancer in book form and on television. The oncologist had clearly heard of neither of them.

(Mark you, Gill, John Walsh would be the ideal person to do it. He has already written his life story in different versions. Once as a film-lover, once as growing up Irish in London and once as something else I can't remember. Brilliant. I just hope he doesn't fall ill of anything round about now. It would be quite hard competing with a twinkling Irish boy's account of cancer.)

Email to CAROLINE KINGTON
July 26, 2007

My dearest wife – this is a formal apology for going off the deep end and being violent about drops of water on our family road atlas of France.

The fact is that it brought back unpleasant family memories.

My mother, who had left her native Ireland under a cloud, after a string of abortions, miscarriages, potato-stealing and rent arrears, was stricken by guilt in later years at the memory, and whenever she came across a map of Ireland in the atlas, would weep uncontrollable tears. Often this would lead to terrible blotches on the page, which made it impossible to map read. In order to spare my mother's feelings, my father would refer to these messes as The Lakes of Repentance, and say: "We'll have to do a detour soon, to get round the Lake of Repentance", by which he simply meant that he would be trying to keep to such of the map as was left.

So you can see why for a moment I stopped being the loving husband and became more like Professor Henry Higgins.

It will never happen again.

As I always say.

    love

To ADAM KINGTON

August, 2007

Here is a very similar letter written by your father, but with better production values.

Dear Adam,

    Welcome back.

    Hope you had a good evening.

    What time do you want to be woken in the morning.

    Here is a brief list of my charges.

    TO BE WOKEN IN THE MORNING £1

    TO BE WOKEN WITH A CUP OF TEA IN THE MORNING £1.50

    TO BE WOKEN WITH A CUP OF COFFEE IN THE MORNING £1.75

    TO BE WOKEN WITH A CHOICE OF HOT BEVERAGE AND

A BRIEF SUMMARY OF THE DAY'S NEWS IN THE
MORNING £3

When you have chosen your option, simply enter our bedroom
and wake me up and tell me which one it is.

That will cost you a further £5.

Email to DEBBY HOLT
September 7, 2007

Debby – the other day I fell into bed crushed by the weight of your
gift, *The Assassin's Cloak*, which I use for weight-lifting and calis-
thenics from time to time, and for once I thought I might read it, so
I had a good go at it, and although you are meant to dip into it,
really, I took a good run at it and read a lot, and made some interesting discoveries.

1. The editors are overly fond of wartime diary extracts. Or perhaps that just means that I quickly got a bit tired of bravery under
shortage. I think wartime suffering palls quicker than most things.

2. Some of the famous diary writers, like the man "Chips"
Channon, depend a lot on how many famous people they know, not
on the quality of the stuff.

3. The editors keep coming back to one or two diarists who they
KNOW are good value, and after a while you start longing to read
more of those particular writers. In my case, it was often Noël
Coward who provided really good observation and really good
knowledge of human nature, so eventually you start thinking
to yourself: "Hmm – must search out a volume of Coward's
diaries . . ."

That's it, really.

Another of my dipping-into books at the moment is Martha
Gellhorn's letters. Do you know about her? Gutsy American writer
– war correspondent, novelist, woman of action. Married to that
dreadful man Ernest Hemingway. But divorced from him as well.
Yesterday I read a letter from her in the 1960s to her hopeless

adopted son, Sandy, who was joining the Flower People. Oh, for God's sake, says Martha, how could you adopt a hopeless case like Timothy O'Leary as a guru? All he utters is second-hand Indian philosophy and drugs. If you want to go down that path, at least go to India and talk to the real gurus. They have devoted years of poverty and thought and sacrifice to their position. All O'Leary has ever done is pop LSD. What YOU need, my boy, is a bit of character. You have plenty of personality already. Now develop your own character . . . Blimey – if I got a letter from my mother like that, I'd gasp.

love

———————

To RICHARD INGRAMS
September 12, 2007

Dear Richard,

I haven't had an invitation to your party on Thursday, so this is not a reply. On the other hand, Meg said I was sent one, so this is a reply after all, and yes, Caroline and I would like very much to come. Much to my surprise and pleasure, Rosie Boycott has asked us to stay the night in London, so we won't have to rush away after the first drink to catch a romantic train back to Bath.

This gives me the chance to say one or two other things which I wanted to say to you sooner or later. One is that after being in and out of hospital over the summer, I have pretty definitely been diagnosed with cancer, and not even a nice kind of cancer, but the kind that did for Luciano Pavarotti, so although I am not going to fade away overnight, they are not going to give me lots of years either. Bit of a bugger, as they say. I now intend to make a list of all the things I want to do before I die, take a pin and choose one of them at random. "Go to Richard's 70th birthday party." Well, could be worse.

I also wanted to say that I recently read your book on Paul Foot and found it very touching. Very well written, too. I wouldn't mind having something like that after my death. I won't, of course, unless

I do it myself, so I have now decided to write the first frivolous book about staring cancer in the face. The tentative title is "A Year in Denial". This is serious, incidentally. There have been far too many brave books about cancer. We need a change of tone.

Also, and en passant, or perhaps en terminant, I was always a little disappointed that *The Oldie* never reviewed the book I had out last year called *Someone Like Me*, which was an extremely funny pseudo-autobiography. Perhaps I should have been less the shrinking violet, and been a bit more pushy. Well, it's not long ago out in paperback, so it's never too late.

I hope you get this before we meet tomorrow. You can shake me firmly by the hand, say gruffly that you think I am being pretty brave and add softly: "And you can go whistle for a book review, mon vieux. We are incorruptible here at *The Oldie*."

yrs

To KEN PEARSON
September 21, 2007

Dear Ken Pearson,

It isn't often you get a letter like that, and perhaps it is just as well, as if you did, you would get a bad case of big-headedness, with galloping smugness.

Between you and me, I think *Someone Like Me* is a very funny book, too, perhaps the best I ever did, although my publishers never seemed to think so. They could never quite bring themselves to market it as a funny book, insisting that it was a branch of autobiography. "How can it be?" I used to ask them. "It's all made up!" "Yes, maybe," they would answer nervously, "but we shouldn't go around telling people that . . ." I used to go into bookshops and find copies of the book in all the biography shelves, and spent hours shifting them to Humour. I am amazed I never got arrested for shoplifting.

I see that you have gone through the same process as I did, of venerating various comic masters. (I also went through stages of venerating SJ Perelman, Woody Allen, DB Wyndham Lewis aka Timothy Shy, AJ Liebling, HL Mencken and other oddballs.) The sadness now is that sometimes I pick up my old idols and find them not quite as radiant as I remember. I had a go at *The Best of Myles* yesterday (being Myles na Gopaleen, the Irish genius) and some of the old magic had worn off. Alas, alas.

If I come across any more of my bound work, sitting dustily in the bike shed, I might feel moved to pass you a copy or two. Would that be all right?

———————

Email to MARK SMALLEY
September 27, 2007

Dear Mark,

I have left phone messages on all your various unanswered phones, apologising for being too up to my ears to give you a résumé of my ideas on two half-hour programmes on the fallacious art of Autobiography.

("Your Money or My Life" – possible title)

It's probably too late already, and I am about to hop off on a fortnight's hols, so what I am going to do now is jot down a few thoughts anyway to let you see how my mind is working.

FIRST PROG

Never trust an autobiog.

People's lives do not reside in their memoirs.

I remember being in the *Punch* office one day when Frank Muir came in and sat down with a big sigh. "What's up, Frank?"

"I've had a frightful day."

"How so?"

"I started writing my autobiography after breakfast this morning. And I'd finished it by lunchtime. I COULDN'T REMEMBER A SINGLE THING THAT HAD HAPPENED TO ME."

It was the same with Jeffrey Bernard. He wrote a letter to the readers of the *Spectator*, saying that he had been invited to write the history of his last thirty years, so if anyone out there had any idea what he had been doing, could they get in touch.

(He later said he regretted doing this, as it led to the discovery of an illegitimate daughter in Canada he didn't know about.)

People really can't remember things straight, even when they say they can.

Barry Took once reviewed both volumes of David Niven's memoirs for *Punch*, the *Balloon* one and the *Horses* one. He said that in both books Niven says he remembers exactly where he was when World War II broke out. But in both cases IT WAS IN A COMPLETELY DIFFERENT PLACE AND A COMPLETELY DIFFERENT COUNTRY.

Lord Lichfield once said to me. when we were talking about public speaking: "Have you ever bored anyone to death?"

"Not wittingly," I said.

"I have," he said. And he told a very funny story about giving a lecture on the QEII on photography, during which one old man pegged out. Which led to the problem of where you put a corpse on a big liner.

"In the kitchen fridges, it turns out," he said. "When someone dies, they clear a fridge of something they don't really need. And that night at dinner the waiter duly said to me, 'Caviar's on the house tonight, my lord.'"

Much later I met a doctor who had worked on the QEII who told me that there could be no truth in the story. There was a huge morgue.

Which leads to the puzzle: is it better to have a GOOD story or a TRUE story?

All writers would say, a GOOD story. I would go so far as to say that a GOOD story, if it is good enough, becomes TRUE.

The Auberon Waugh story.

Waugh claimed that he was once offered a free trip to Nigeria in return for doing a talk on "Breast Feeding". He knew nothing about breast feeding but badly wanted to go to West Africa, so he did some research on breast feeding and went and did the lecture. It was received very warmly. Afterwards, the organiser congratulated him and then said: "Of course, we were actually expecting you to do a talk on Press Freedom, but it doesn't matter . . ."

True? I doubt it. A good reason not to tell the story? Never!

It's a great story. I would never try to check its veracity, any more than I should really have checked Lichfield's story with the doc.

I myself have experiences of being believed when stories were patently false. As a humorist, I make up mad tales, which are often believed. I once did a piece about General Galtieri in *The Times* which led to the *Times* man in Buenos Aires getting death threats. You'd think that a humorist, of all people, would be treated with suspicion. Far from it. People lap it up.

A year ago I published a completely fictional memoir called *Someone Like Me*. To stress how fake it was, I wrote a dust jacket c.v. which was clearly made up. "Miles Kington ran away from home at an early age to join a library. Luckily, it was the University of Hull Library, where he worked with Philip Larkin, whom he helped to get the poetry section sorted out. 'It was a complete mess when I got there,' remembers Kington, 'because Larkin would only admit poets he approved of, so no Ted Hughes, no Plath, no foreign stuff. We had to keep that under the counter with all the dirty books. Which all belonged to Larkin, incidentally . . .'"

The first bit of publicity I did for that book was a *Yorkshire Post* lunch, along with Prunella Scales and Bernard Ingham. The chairman got up to introduce me. "And now Mr Kington, who I didn't realise till today was a close colleague of Philip Larkin, and I am sure he is going to tell us lots of fascinating stories about Mr Larkin today . . ."

You see? People will believe a story if it is a good story. The fact that it smells is irrelevant. My first half hour would be full of anecdotes like that, meaning DON'T TRUST ANYONE.

My second would be a look at people who had really written their life stories and could not be trusted (Lord Berners on downwards) and at people who ARE allowed by publishers to write their own memoirs, e.g.

- People who are famous now but won't be in a year's time
- Politicians who once had an affair with Edwina Currie
- Members of the Royal Family who have nothing else to do
  (I have a very good story about a bird book penned by
  Prince Philip forty years ago, called *Birds of the Britannia*)

– Showbiz people who were famous forty years ago and are about to peg out
– etc etc

Both half hours would be heavily anecdotal and humorous.

But the underlying theme, that stories evolve towards their natural artistic shape, and abandon truthfulness in the search for perfection, would be deadly serious.

(This can be seen in the average marriage, where the man always tried to tell a story in its best form, and the wife constantly interrupts to correct him. "No, darling, it was Singapore, not Hong Kong . . .")

Well, that's not bad for a starter.

I hope it will be of use to you, if not now, then next time round. I would say the sooner the better, as I am not as young or as well as I was, and I'd love to have it done, and bring glory to both of us.

yours

––––––––––

To TREVOR and POLLY HERBERT
October 31, 2007

Dear Trevor and Polly,

I am very touched that you should write such a nice letter to a lost soul like me. Of course, I don't really feel lost at all, and I am not perplexed at all by your Christianity. I came through a quite rigorous Christian upbringing, at least on the school side, and I am often regretful that I lost my faith at about the age of eighteen, which coincided almost exactly with my being confirmed. There is a part of me which still wishes I accepted it all unquestioningly, but it is not as big as the part of me which thinks that we are all part of a huge unpredictable kaleidoscope. The chaplain at my Oxford college used to say to me, "Ah, but if you reject Christ and his teaching, where do you think your belief in goodness and personal morality comes from?" "From knowing people like the Herberts," I would have said. But I didn't know you then. And even if I had, he would have said,

"And where do you think they got it from?" "Well," I would have said, "they think they get it from the Bible, but of course it really comes from the sense of social welfare and community that people build up historically if their species is to survive," and then we would have been off on one of those arguments which in those days occupied far too much time in college days. Do young people still talk about the meaning of life at that age? I have no idea.

Yes, I have indeed been diagnosed with cancer, pancreatic cancer to boot, which is not one of the nice ones, but at least it seems not to be one of those which involves lots of pain. Good thing. I am not very good at pain. They have no idea how long it will take. A year? Five years? "Can you at least promise me I won't have to live through the London Olympics?" I pleaded with one oncologist. He wasn't used to being asked questions like that and referred me to another colleague immediately.

After the initial shock, which was horrific, I have started to live with the knowledge, which is the only way to do it.

Indeed, I have started to ignore it on some levels, which is not a bad way of doing it either, although I have also started work on a book about the experience, which I aim to make a funny book about having cancer. Not many of those around. It's a bit of a puzzle, though. It would be nice to live long enough to finish the book. But will my agent then turn round and say, "Look, we can't really market a book about cancer if you're still looking so hale and hearty . . . ?"

"What are you hinting at?" I will say. "Do you want me to die to hasten sales of the book?"

"Well," she will say, "it's a point worth bearing in min . . ."

And then we will be off on one of those arguments which occupy far too much time in publishing days.

To SALLY and GEOFFREY WHEATCROFT[4]
January 3, 2008

Dear Sally and Geoffrey,

Many thanks for a long, leisurely and lazy lunchtime on Tuesday – just what the aromatherapist ordered. I am glad you put me between those two sharp-minded artists – talking to Maggie Drummond and Anna Teasdale was just what I needed to keep my mind from going rusty in the New Year. There was one very odd moment when, after I confessed to Anna that I was not a good person to talk to art about, she challenged me to name some recent artist I liked, and quite out of the blue I said Edward Burra, at which she promptly drew a big book of his paintings from her bag(!) and started lecturing me on him (very astutely, I may say), at which point Maggie said she had never heard of Edward Burra and didn't his stuff look wonderful, so whereas a moment before we had all been complete strangers – indeed, a moment before, I had been sitting on a sofa next door NOT watching horse-racing with Geoffrey – we were suddenly engaged in the kind of conversation which artists are supposed to have with each other, and which I never do, because I am not an artist. I hope Anna remembers to send us an invite for her Victoria Gallery launch. I have always wanted to go to a private view where I actually knew the artist, but I think Sally Muir is the only painter I have ever achieved this with. At this rate I shall be in the swim, if only in Bath.

God, what a rambling letter, even by my pointless standards. I have just been reading a huge swatch of Evelyn Waugh's letters, which makes me realise that I still have some way to go before I become a decent correspondent, but actually it is often quite hard work following his train of thought, because he refers to everyone by their nicknames and by that time I have forgotten who all these people are, Prod and Honks and Pig and so on, and even when he refers to people clearly such as Quennell and Duff Cooper, and refers to them sneerily, I can't remember whether he really likes them or not, or is just showing off to Nancy Mitford. He is also scarily honest sometimes, as when he replies to an invitation from Penelope Betjeman to come and stay by saying he can't, as he a) isn't sure whether John Betjeman actually likes him b) dislikes the Betjeman children c) needs more wine than he is ever offered at the Betjeman household. Even if it is a series of jokes, it's treading on thin ice. But rest assured that Caroline and I enjoyed lunch with you (have you noticed that every day has felt like Sunday for the past week?) and thanks a lot for so much meat and so many grand puddings . . .

love

———————

To JACKIE and ERIC NEWBEGIN[5]
January 4, 2008

Dear Jackie and Eric,

Someone once said to me that the longer you leave writing a thank you letter, the more you have to write to make up for it. Well, crikey, if I believed that I would spend most of my life penning end-less letters of gratitude for things that happened in the twentieth century, so I am rushing to the post now anyway to say how much we enjoyed our evening chez Newbigin last year – and indeed how much my gang of carol singers enjoyed our stop off in your house before Christmas, when you were so hospitable and made it so dif-ficult to get them moving again out into the cold and frosty. And if you can think of any times in the past when we came and enjoyed life at Orchard House, and I didn't write to say thank you, per-haps we can draw a veil over it now. I suppose I should also say thanks for asking my two sons, Tom and Adam, round to your house for pool and billiards and things, but the dum dums never seem to have availed themselves of the invitation, so bad luck to them.

And now the New Year stretches ahead of us, like a bleak land-scape full of mud and puddles. Look, father, what are all those half broken objects littering the land? Why, my son, they are New Year resolutions which are already broken down and abandoned all over the place. What is a New Year resolution, father? Why, my son, it is so long since I handled one that I cannot rightly remember how they work, but I think they have something to do with making your quality of life seem better, like the effect you get from writing thank you letters after Christmas. What is a thank you letter, father? Get out of here, you ungrateful wretch, and let me not see you again until you have written servilely to all your uncles and aunts, for otherwise they will not send you a present next year!

Thanks again from me and Caroline.

————————

To TISH FEILDEN
January 16, 2008

Dear Tish,

Thanks for small oasis of rest and tranquility last night in your lovely house. (I quote Caroline there. "What a lovely house." Her exact words. "What a lovely person Tish is", she said too, later. She ran out of compliments after that. "What's wrong with her cooking, then?" I said, witheringly. "Lovely cooking too," she said. "Too late," I said. "I've just said that." So you see, we have our bitter arguments too . . .)

Funny how we use words like "oasis" as I did just then, although most of us have never seen a real oasis in our lives, and probably never will. But that's what it felt like, dropping into your soft upstairs/downstairs room for a few hours. Now it's back to grey chilliness again. Mr Godwin from the farm delivered some logs to our yard half an hour ago, which means I have now got to go out there and do some stacking – or does it mean that I slip Adam a bit of cash to do some hard work?

Yes, I think that's the thing to do. Of course, everyone from the farm is called Mr Godwin, unless they are called Mrs Godwin – and there is even a Master Godwin who is only fourteen or so and in love with farming and apparently can't wait to grow up and take over the place.

And now we are off to Bradford tomorrow morning for a dose of acupuncture. Gosh, what an exciting life I lead.

Acupuncture is one of those things I thought I would never experience, being a grumpy anti-alternative bloke, yet I now think it might be quite plausible. Mark you, in the same little building in Church Street there is a homeopath whom I once consulted over some ailment or other, and I do remember realising halfway through the consultation that I thought it was a load of baloney, or more accurately that I didn't really trust any medical man who kept consulting a book written by a Swiss doctor in 1840, which homeopaths still thought was the latest word on the subject. I know that Christians think that the New Testament is still the latest news on Christianity, but that worries me too. Occasionally when I am waiting to see my acupuncturist this bloke comes down the stairs from his upstairs eyrie and our eyes cross and I wonder if he's thinking: "That's the bloke who rejected my life's work out of hand – I wonder what he's doing here . . . ? Perhaps I should set the bouncers on him . . ." But luckily they don't have bouncers in health centres. Just rather wan-looking homeopaths.

I started writing this on Tuesday. It is now Wednesday and the post goes in one minute. I go now.

Love from both.

Notes

Part One: *Punch*

1 Miles first met André Previn when he came to England in 1968 to work with the London Symphony Orchestra, and interviewed him for *The Times*.

2 A *Punch* correspondent.

3 News and sports reporter who contributed to *Punch*.

4 An American contributor to *Punch* who wrote an irritable note to Olivia Grogono, a literary assistant, about two typos that appeared in his piece. Miles's reply not only mollified him, but he declared it to be one of the most brilliant letters he'd ever received.

5 Author of *The Secret Orchard of Roger Ackerley*.

6 Quentin Oates was the pseudonym used for a regular column in the *Bookseller* which rounded up and commented upon the previous week's literary reviews.

7 Early sixteenth-century churchman, historian and controversialist.

8 Successful writer and cartoonist who had a weekly page-length cartoon strip in *Punch*.

9 Writer, publisher and founder of Robson Press in 1974.

10 McKay's editorship of *Punch* was brief (1996–7). He was followed by four other editors in quick succession and the magazine finally folded in 2002.

11 In 1997 Sue Bradbury commissioned Miles to put together *The Pick of Punch* for the Folio Society.

Part Two: Columnist

1 Editor of *The Times*.

2 Editor of *The Times*.

3   Editor of the *Daily Express*, was keen to enlist Miles as a columnist and tried to poach him from *The Times*.

4   An article Miles had written for *The Times*.

5   Journalist and Policy Editor of the *Independent* approached Miles when the newspaper was being set up.

6   Journalist who worked in management on *The Times*, going on to become its managing editor. He was Miles's immediate boss.

7   Senior management at *The Times* were slow to accept that Miles wanted to jump ship which led to this exasperation on his part.

8   The novelist was responsible for persuading Miles to join the *Independent*.

9   The Features Editor at the *Independent*. Miles cared passionately about how his column looked – the shape of it, the position on the page. When his photograph was introduced, it heralded the beginning of a long, unsuccessful campaign by him to have it removed.

10 Jan Morris fired off a fax because she thought Miles was mocking Welsh culture in general and the National Eisteddford in particular, when he suggested few Welsh would understand it.

11 A producer at the *Dateline* NBC television show. Miles loved it when his jokes and fantasies were taken literally. It happened quite regularly.

12 A sub-editor at the *Independent*. Miles worked from home, very rarely going to the newspaper offices. His chief working relationship, therefore, was with the subs, whom he seldom, if ever, met.

Part Three: Music

1   Assistant to Michael Kustow, associate director of the National Theatre.

2   On the English Tourist Board.

3   A schoolboy correspondent, studying O-level Music, who wanted to know why Miles chose to play the double bass.

4   Maggie Thatcher's private secretary. Michael Palin refused to believe that Miles had given the PM an Instant Sunshine album so Miles sent him a copy of Miss Stephens's letter and his reply.

5   Violinist, violist, teacher, lecturer, broadcaster, writer (1919–85). A prominent and influential figure in the UK's musical life. Miles had an intense and impassioned correspondence with him, which Keller brought to an abrupt halt because it was taking up so much time.

6   At Ronnie Scott's jazz club.

7   Flamboyant TV cook who wanted to book Instant Sunshine for a whole evening of entertainment.

8   Director of the Bath International Music Festival.

9   Poet and critic, and one of Philip Larkin's literary executors.

Part Four: Broadcasting

1   Director and cameraman, *Three Miles High* – a film made in 1980 for BBC's *Great Railway Journeys: Crossing the Andes*. It was Miles's first documentary feature; he loved it and the whole experience had a profound effect on him.

2   Miles had bought a toy llama which he carried around tucked under his arm as it was too big for his luggage.

3   Controller of BBC Radio 4.

4   Miles co-presented *In the Archives* on Radio 4, which was the precursor to *Archive on 4*. Elmes was the producer.

5   A programme researcher.

6   Director of Spokesmen, an agency for the media, who approached Miles after seeing him on television to suggest that she should represent him.

7   Head of BBC Network Features and a friend from University.

8   See note 4.

9   Controller of BBC 2.

10 BBC Radio Manchester.

11 In 1986/7 Miles went to Burma/Myanmar and to China following the route of the Burma Road for a documentary series, *Great Journeys of the World*.

12 Controller of BBC Radio 4.

13 Jazz musician, poet and friend.

14 Producer at BBC. Miles presented *Fine Families*, a series of TV programmes about Welsh families.

15 Germaine Greer, a highly respected writer, prominent intellectual and significant voice in the feminist movement. In the late nineties, Miles presented a regular chat show, *Double Vision*, which revolved around a theme, featured well-known guests and an outrageous Dame Edna-type figure in the form of Lady Margaret.

16 Another controller of BBC Radio 4.

17 Writer, war veteran and co-writer of the TV-series *Tenko*.

Part Five: Books

1   At the publisher Chatto & Windus.

2   Cartoonist, known as Thelwell, who depicted plump little girls astride

plump little ponies. He contributed to *Punch* from 1952 and produced many books featuring his cartoons. He turned Miles's offer down; *Nature Made Ridiculously Simple* was published in 1983.

3   Head of publicity at Penguin. The 'Franglais' columns from *Punch* became a great success, selling over 250,000 copies.

4   Travel writer and founder of Bradt Travel Guides.

5   Publisher of Prion Books.

6   Of Libanus Press.

7   Bookseller and friend.

8   Poet.

9   Publicity Director at Headline.

10 After much pressure, Miles settled down to write his autobiography, *Someone Like Me*. Except it wasn't. It was completely fictitious.

Part Six: Agent

1   In the contracts department of RCW.

Part Seven: On Writing

1   Assistant editor of *Punch* at this time; writer, poet, author of crime fiction and children's novels, for which he twice won the Carnegie Medal.

2   Journalist, and an author of "Londoner's Diary" in the *Evening Standard*.

3   One of a group of young writers who sent in regular contributions to *Punch*. Miles thought highly of Watson and encouraged his work.

4   Co-founder of Knockabout Comics.

Part Eight: Correspondence with Readers

1   Writer and journalist, known for his controversial opinions. Oex is Forbes's address in Switzerland.

2   At Trinity College.

3   Humorous columnist at the *Irish Times*.

4   In the Public Affairs department of Heinz.

5   An Albanian proverb: Knowledge is knowing a tomato is a fruit. Wisdom is not putting it in a fruit salad. Miles created over 500 of these meaningless, but quite poetic, proverbs.

Part Nine: Words

1   Journalist and manager at Reuters, News International, and fluent in French and German.

2 At HM Prison Wormwood Scrubs.

3 Well-known Scottish TV personality, actor and impressionist.

4 Managing Director of Boosey & Hawkes.

5 The new *Independent* offices in Canary Wharf.

Part Ten: Friends

1 Davies wrote a weekly article about the daily life of a harried dad for *Punch*.

2 Wife of Alan Maryon-Davis of Instant Sunshine.

3 Megan Jones (Lloyd George), a young friend, taken very much by surprise to receive this letter.

4 The cartoonist, Smilby; friend and fellow jazz addict.

5 c/o *Time Out* magazine.

6 Prominent contributors to the worlds of cinema and theatre, Bryan Forbes as a director and producer, Nanette Newman as an actress. They both wrote. Nanette appeared frequently on television.

7 Poet, jazz pianist.

8 A great and lifelong friend; historian, writer, performer, member of Monty Python.

9 Bath Boules began around 1990, in Queen Square, Bath, as a contest between local restaurants and between local businesses. Its primary purpose was to have lots of fun, eat and drink to excess, and to raise large sums for charity. All of which it still does.

10 Scriptwriter.

11 A long-time friend of Miles, moved from Penguin to found Colman Getty, a highly successful PR company that focuses on the arts and literary events, as well as the promotion of a number of prominent authors.

12 Cartoonist.

Part Eleven: Yes, No, Thanks

1 At the publisher, Transworld.

2 Miles did, a typed-over word before "personally".

3 The correspondent wanted to write a version of the Franglais books in German.

4 President of the Cambridge Union Society.

5 Miles received frequent requests to participate in a University debate. This was such a proposal at the London School of Economics.

6 Pan published a paperback version of Miles's Alphonse Allais translations as *A Wolf in Frog's Clothing*.

7 Stringfellow threw a party at his club every year for Larry Adler, the harmonica player.

8 Assistant Features Editor, *Daily Mail*. Genevieve Fox approached Miles to write a feature about his mother for a "mothers and sons" series.

9 At Eton College.

10 The signatory on a junk mail circular.

11 Administrator, Natural Theatre Company, a successful street theatre company based in Bath, and Ralph Oswick, its larger-than-life Creative Director. His alter ego, Lady Margaret, featured regularly on *Double Vision*.

12 Neighbours and friends.

13 Miles's Scottish cousins and close friends. When Miles was reviewing for *The Times*, he and Laurence spent a great deal of time together in the jazz venues of London.

14 Daughters (aged eleven and nine, respectively) of good friends.

15 Producer, broadcaster, writer and networker. Miles met Carole Stone when she was producer of Radio 4's *Any Questions*. The club was to be called Stones.

16 Director of Radio and Music at the BBC.

17 Richard Tyson was a judge and Catriona ran a vast costume-hire company that supplied costumes to television and the theatre.

Part Twelve: Fun

1 Of the *Sunday Times* and the *Observer*. Miles was commissioned to write for a feature for *Cosmopolitan* about losing his virginity and felt he'd pulled his punches.

2 Miles's elder son, now a journalist for *The Times*, based in Rome.

3 Director, University of Chicago Press.

4 To Caroline, just before their wedding.

Part Thirteen: Last Years

1 Popular cartoonist who sold his first cartoon to *Punch*. He sent Miles a number of his cartoons.

2 A bookseller.

3 Owners of Much Ado Books in Alfriston.

4 Artist and writer, respectively.

5 Friends and neighbours.

Acknowledgements

I would like to thank:

Michael Palin and Stephanie Cole for their help in launching the project with Jo Lumley, who has been remarkable in her unfailing response to everything I've asked of her.

Jonathan Sale and Hilary Macaskill for advice on *Punch* related matters.

Arnie Roth for allowing me to make free use of his cartoon.

The various writers who gave me permission to use their letters.

Wendy Hoile for her advice and friendship, and my family and friends for their enthusiasm and encouragement.

The friends who shared with me letters they had received from Miles, some of which appear in this collection.

Scott Pack for his infinite patience and good humour, and the rest of the Unbound team.

And most particularly, those who, by making their pledges of support, have helped to make this book possible.

Index

Unbound is the world's first crowdfunding publisher, established in 2011.

We believe that wonderful things can happen when you clear a path for people who share a passion. That's why we've built a platform that brings together readers and authors to crowdfund books they believe in – and give fresh ideas that don't fit the traditional mould the chance they deserve.

This book is in your hands because readers made it possible. Everyone who pledged their support is listed below. Join them by visiting unbound.com and supporting a book today.

Advent the318
Dudi Appleton
Peter Arnold
Dr Alan Bailey
Colin Bartlett
Angela Benbow Pullen
Steve Best and Mandy Majendie
Terence Blacker
Laurence Blair Oliphant
Iain Bonehill
Liz Booty
Nic Bottomley
Nick Bradshaw
Kathryn Braithwaite
Sally Breeden
Paul Brennan
Emma Brining

Tony Brock
Stephen Brough
Robert Bruce
Phil Bruce-Moore
David Bryan
Rhiannon Carey-Evans
David Chalker
Chris
Guy Clapham
René Closuit
Trevor Cook
David A P Cooke
Simon Coombe
Mark Cooper
Rosie Corlett
Andrew Cotterill
Michael Crees

William Cress
Alastair Cunningham
Emma Dain
Matthew Darlison
Darren
Sara Davies
Alice Davis
Gitte and Stephen Dawson
Kathy Day
John Dexter
Angela Dickson
Sheila Dunn
M. Patricia Dyson
Stephen Eeley
Alex Elmer
Alice Fairbrother
Tish Feilden
Frances
Averil & Martin Freeth
Belinda and Keith Froggett
Tom Galloway
David Gardner
Amro Gebreel
Hugh Gee
Gary Gibbon
Dan Gledhill
David Gledhill
David Gordon
Ian Gourlay
Christopher Griffiths
Eleanor Griffiths
Valerie Grove
Vanessa Hamshere
J Haynes
Paul Hensby
Trevor Herbert
David Hicks

Robert Hill
Robert Hills
Ian Hislop
Anthony Holden
Debby Holt
Tim Hornsby
Bob Howell
Sally Humpston
Steve Hunt
Brigitte Hyde
Ian Irvine
Dotti Irving
Polly Jaffé
Janette James
Jane Jarvis
Tim and Joyce Jeal
Kaci Johnston
Sophie Jones
Virginia Jones
Adrian & Suzanne Kennedy
Dan Kieran
Caroline Kington
Richard Knight
Jasmine Kok
Pierre L'Allier
Ian Lamont
Valerie Langfield
Stephanie Laslett
Andrew Lawrence
Jimmy Leach
Nicola Leader
John Leonard
Judith Liddell-King
Tamasin Little
Victoria Lloyd-Hughes
Wink Lorch
Arthur Lucas

Janusz Lukasiak

Mike Lynd

Hilary Macaskill

Jo Macdonald

Seonaid Mackenzie

Stephen Mair

Roger Mant

Alan Maryon-Davis

Andrew Maynard

Calvin Mcphaul

Alec Meadows

Lena Megyeri

Clive Mitchell

John Mitchinson

Tom Moody-Stuart (Elder)

Tom Moody-Stuart (Younger)

Bel Mooney

Sally Muir

Judy Murphy

Juliet Murray

Carlo Navato

Peter Newman

Christopher Nugent

Simon O'Hagan

Ralph Oswick

Scott Pack

Rachel Panter

Matthew Parfitt

Lev Parikian

Steph Parker

Nicky Parkinson

Geoff Patterson

James Pembroke

Hugo Perks

Justin Pollard

Jean Power

Neil Pretty

Ian Pye

Colette Reap

Simon Reap

Gillian Reynolds

Sheila Rhodes

Alasdair Riley

Wyn Roberts

Arnold Roth

Chris Schuler

Clementine Sellick

Pam Sewell

Frank Smith

Libby Smith

Rod Smith

Mary Snow

Richard Soundy

Ralph Sperring

Leigh Stewart

Jonathan Stoppi

Richard Storey

Peter Stott

Elaine Taylor

Steve Taylor

Jillian Tees

Ben Thacker

Adam Tinworth

Pamela Todd

Graham Tomlinson

Christopher Trent

Mark Vent

Patricia Volk

Sir Harold Walker

Steve Walker

David Wallace

Lucy Ward

Atlanta Wardell-Yerburgh

Laura Watts

Richard Watts

Colin Webb

Gordon Wemyss

Anne Wheelhouse

Adam White

Graham White

Richard White

Debbie Williams

Sean Williams

Clare Willison

Emily Woolf Vallier

Alan Wright

Robert Wringham

David Young